P9-CJJ-861

DATE DUE

DE 2 0 00			
NO 3 0 00			

DEMCO 38-296

Veils and Words

Contemporary Issues in the Middle East

R

Veils and Words

The Emerging Voices of Iranian Women Writers

FARZANEH MILANI

SYRACUSE UNIVERSITY PRESS

Riverside Community College
·96·
Library
MCT 4800 Magnolia Avenue
Riverside, CA 92506

PK 6413.5 .W65 M5 1992

Milani, Farzaneh.

Veils and words

Copyright © 1992 by Syracuse University Press
Syracuse, New York 13244-5160

ALL RIGHTS RESERVED

First Edition 1992
92 93 94 95 96 97 98 99   6 5 4 3 2 1

The paper used in this publication meets the minimum requirements of American National Standard for Information Sciences—Permanence of Paper for Printed Library Materials, ANSI Z39.48-1984. ∞™

Library of Congress Cataloging-in-Publication Data
Milani, Farzaneh.
    Veils and words : the emerging voices of Iranian women writers /
Farzaneh Milani. — 1st ed.
        p.   cm. — (Contemporary issues in the Middle East)
    Includes bibliographical references and index.
    ISBN 0-8156-2557-X (alk. paper). — ISBN 0-8156-0266-9 (pbk. :
alk. paper)
        1. Persian literature—Women authors—History and criticism.
    2. Persian literature—20th century—History and criticism.
    3. Women authors, Iranian—20th century.   4. Feminism and
literature—Iran.   I. Title.   II. Series.
    PK6413.5.W65M5   1992
    891'.55099287—dc20   91-28640

Manufactured in the United States of America

For Faridoun

Farzaneh Milani is an Assistant Professor of Persian at the University of Virginia. Herself a poet, she holds a Ph.D. in comparative literature from the University of California, Los Angeles.

To stay alive you must slay silence.
—Simin Behbahani

A Note on Transliteration

Persian words are transliterated as pronounced in Persian. I have used the Library of Congress list for consonants. The short vowels are represented by (˗) *a*, (˗) *e*, and (˗) *o*. The three long vowels are (ﺍ) *a*, (ﺱ) *i*, and (ﻭ) *u*. To avoid diacritical marks *a* represents both the Persian short vowel (˗) and long vowel (ﺍ). The two diphthongs are represented by (*ey*) and (*ow*). All transcriptions of Persian words are based on this system, except for cases in which a different system was used in a quoted text.

My translations are an attempt to bring the Persian across to English as intact as possible. Clearly, in the process, I have lost much of the beauty and linguistic complexity of the original. If no English translation is listed in the endnotes, the translation is my own.

Contents

PART FOUR
Voices Through the Veil

Preface

*T*here are no walls around the houses here," I wrote in my diary, in an entry dated December 24, 1967. This was a few days after my arrival in America. It took me years to realize that in America other kinds of walls, mainly invisible, existed. I had to learn about their presence, respect their sovereignty, abide by their rules. I could not neglect them, trespass them. I could not disregard them. This meant not only learning the English language but also mastering the metalanguage, the verbal and nonverbal codes of interactions, the different systems and styles of communication.

Many times, unaware of these "walls," I asked the wrong question, volunteered the inappropriate answer, looked too closely when I was supposed not to "see," listened too intently when I was assumed not to "hear." Heaven knows how often I talked when I should have kept silent and how frequently I should have talked but remained mute, producing nothing but silence—long, embarrassing silence. Heaven knows how often, with eyes wide open, I stumbled over those walls, mile by glorious mile of invisible walls.

I had thought if you don't want people to hear, you whisper; if you don't want them to see, you cover. To protect your privacy, I had thought, you erect easily perceptible walls around the private object or subject; you cover it from view; you conceal it with silence. My acclimatization to American society, however, taught me that privacy can take different shapes and can be protected in more ways than one. Life taught me that silence can speak eloquently and that words can veil profusely.

A product of two cultures, I felt outside the circle of both, out of place, dislodged, dislocated. I was immersed in discontinuities; engulfed in geographical, cultural, and temporal exile. Neither the daughter of my mother nor the mother of my daughter, I felt suspended between the twentieth century A.D. and fourteenth century Hegira. The gap between my mother and my daughter, products of different cultural experiences, values, systems of signs, dreams, and nightmares, had caused a disturbing disruption in the matrilineal chain of my identity. I lived surrounded by a past that was breaking up around me with violent rapidity. Uprooted and transplanted, with an unpronounceable name and coming from a country that was first not quite known and then known for all the wrong reasons, I looked every which way for a sense of familiarity, of belonging and reunion. I wanted something solid to hold on to. Perhaps my choice of "veiling"—this portable wall—as the topic of my research was above all a symptom of a boundary crisis. Perhaps by reconstructing, piece by piece, my understanding of this aspect of Iranian culture, I wanted to find a lost or hidden part of myself.

A poem I wrote years ago best epitomizes my frantic search for bearings, for familiar boundaries. It portrays my internal turmoil at this point, as if I were running in two directions at once. One, nostalgically backwards, for familiar walls and veils, for certainties lost, perhaps certainties that I never had and that I now needed to find in a veiled grandmother. The other, frantically running sideways and forwards to master the vertigo of open spaces, to master how to negotiate the new, unfamiliar, invisible walls. Memories of Jasmine and Grandmother allowed me, in this poem, to cut through the thickening distance. Although my grandmother's world was small and bounded, and I clearly yearned for a larger and less confining space, still some elements of her more sharply circumscribed universe—bounded like her prayer rug—attracted me.

Jasmine, too, derived from the Persian word *Yasaman,* seems locked forever, like Grandmother, with my childhood memories. There is something about jasmine that captures with special intensity the incandescence and luminosity, the simplicity and innocence of childhood. Is it its starlike whiteness? Is it the trembling delicacy of its blossom hovering over its stem and leaves almost like a dream? Is it its ephemeral beauty, its long-lasting sweet fragrance, its generous yielding of flowers every single day of summer? Whatever it is, there's something about the jasmine that takes me to places where I have to leave words behind, to the places where I have left my childhood, places that continue to invade my dreams—in the setting of my earliest memories. In my past.

There, there is jasmine; plenty of it; in abundance; in profusion. I grew up with it. The hot summer sun. Dust in the air. And suddenly, the jasmine. Like fresh snow; like a mind untainted by questions. Like certainty.

> She always smelled of jasmine
> and wore black shoes that shined
> crowned with a ribbon on top.
> It is Grandmother I'm talking about,
> with her jasmine scent
> and her world marked and bounded,
> as clearly as her prayer rug.
> And as she prayed
> her arms would rise from the prayer rug
> like pillars soaring into the sky
> above sadness
> above storms
> to the height of creativity
> to the pinnacle of heaven,
> then again to the depths of submission.
> She always smelled of jasmine
> and never harbored any doubts
> as to her choice of perfume.
> It is Grandmother I'm talking about.
> She knew with astounding confidence
> that her life-story was but her destiny
> that she held in her own hand
> the key to eternity,
> she even knew that if she wanted
> she could summon the prophet Khezr
> to demand of him whatever she desired.
> And how generous he was,
> Grandmother's green-clothed phantasm,
> magnanimous, bearer of plenty,
> without anger, without guile,
> beyond needs, beyond expectations
> with his blessings and gifts
> flowing free like the waters
> of an endless stream.
> She always smelled of jasmine
> and wore black shoes that shined
> crowned with a ribbon on top.
> I'm telling you about my grandmother.[1]

After the loss of a jasminelike certainty and years of disorientation, I finally found a surrogate home in Iranian literature, a place to return to and to embark from. I put down roots in it and found myself especially drawn to women's writings. I saw reflected in this literature a persistent effort—now overt, now covert—to negotiate the aesthetics of silence, to free women's public voice, to come to terms with the symbols and institution of the veil. In the writings of Iranian women I found the exquisite eloquence of my mother tongue. Through their voices, their richness and diversity, I discovered my own voice. I began to rediscover, not without pride, Iranian women such as I knew them rather than as I read about them in male-authored texts.

Iranian women writers gave eloquent voice to my feelings of marginality, of not belonging, of homelessness. They, too, were exiles, even though in their own homeland. They, too, were marginalized from women's conventional spheres of identity as daughters, wives, mothers. They, too, had to explore new territory; construct new plots, create their own style and literary personas with little help from tradition.

In this literature, I could see and hear women loud and clear, dancing, laughing, crying, loving, going mad, dying, attempting suicide, seeking refuge, giving shelter but always communicating, reflecting, interpreting, creating art out of life. Theirs was the dance of the once immobile, the song of the once mute. These were the women who had escaped the censoring of their culture and transcended the limits on their bodies and voices. Their fervor was contagious; their survival, reassuring; their art, an affirmation of power, continuity, and creativity.

I started studying Iranian women writers in a serious way in the mid-seventies out of a sense of enthusiasm for and fascination by a contemporary woman poet, Forugh Farrokhzad (1935–1967). Although my reading of her poetry has radically changed over the years, then as now, I found in her an exile who refused to vanish into the quasi absence of exile. An unyielding rebel, an adventurer of both body and mind, she relentlessly explored new domains, refused silence or exclusion. She ceaselessly outgrew herself, transgressed her designated limits. She refused to submerge her voice or vision in aesthetic or ideological trends or fashion alien to her sense of self as artist and woman. She trespassed, time and again, social and literary boundaries. She resisted assimilation.

Although Farrokhzad's poetry delighted, comforted, and encouraged me, I was amazed, not to say disturbed, to find no deep and detailed treatment of the critical issues raised by her writing or by that of other Iranian women writers. One of the exceptionally few critical books I could find that was devoted in its entirety to a woman writer had as its central thesis the affirmation that the poet, Parvin E'tessami (1907–1941), had been wrongly "accused" of being a poet. It argued that a woman, especially a "timid" and "cross-eyed one," could not possibly have produced such a masterpiece as the collection of poems published under E'tessami's signature.[2]

No full-length study of women's literary tradition in contemporary Iran was undertaken despite the popular attention women writers had elicited. Major studies of literature dealt almost exclusively with the works of men. The enormous gap between the time, space, and quality of critical attention devoted to male writers and that devoted to women writers was profoundly troubling. Soon, I came to realize that women's veiling can be practiced on many levels. Literary criticism was one such arena. In conventional approaches to literature, I saw a failure to chronicle and capture women's unveiled voices and the many internal and external hardships women faced in their efforts to counter exclusion—spatially or verbally.

Perhaps the subject of veiling, its paradoxes and ambiguities, its multi-layered symbolic significance, would not have preoccupied me so long and so intensely had it not been for the many connections that I gradually came to see between veiling, women's literature, and literary criticism. My exploration of the visible and invisible topology of the veil, its symptoms and consequences, became a journey of discovery and self-discovery.

> One window is all I need
> One window to the moment of awareness,
> Of seeing and silence.
> By now, the sapling walnut tree
> has grown tall enough
> to explain the wall to its young leaves.[3]

Perhaps transparency is an illusion that refuses to be called what it is. Perhaps there is always yet another layer of walls and veils to rend.

Charlottesville, Virginia   Farzaneh Milani
September 1991

Acknowledgments

*J*t took me well over a decade to write this book and much of the exhilaration of writing it came from the collaborative efforts of family, friends, and colleagues. My father and my beloved mother, a lost poet, sacrificed much for my education. For that, and much else, they have my love and gratitude. My brothers, Hossein, Hassan, and Mohsen Milani helped me develop and clarify my arguments. 'Abbas Milani, a soul mate ever since my childhood, closely read the whole manuscript and with characteristic insightfulness shaped my revisions. Unfailingly, my brothers have been a source of intellectual growth, emotional support, and sheer delight in my life.

A chapter of this book originated, in part, in the doctoral dissertation I completed at the University of California, Los Angeles, in 1979. I remain grateful to the readers of that dissertation and especially to my teacher, Amin Banani, who continues to listen, encourage, and inspire. I have benefited from years of discussions with Iranian writers, some of whom form the substance and focus of this book. Mahshid Amirshahi, Simin Behbahani, Sadeq Chuback, Simin Daneshvar, Nader Naderpur, Partow Nuri-'Ala, Shahrnush Parsipur, and the late Ghollam-Hossein Sa'edi have helped me better understand the Iranian literary scene as well as their own works.

Several colleagues, generous with their time and counsel, have offered wisdom, invaluable suggestions, and judicious comments. Ehsan Yarshater, Ruhi Ramazani, 'Abdulaziz Sachedina, John Roberts, and Ann Lane have been a cherished source of intellectual support and challenge. Janet Beizer, in the midst of exigent demands of teaching and writing, found the time to read the whole manuscript and to offer illuminating perspectives. Mary

McKinley gave much of the manuscript a most careful and informed reading. The whole book, especially the introduction, has been improved thanks to her perceptive comments. I thank Mahnaz Afkhami, Dan Kinney, Nancy Ghalligher, Bahiyeh Nakhjavani, and Suzanne Gallick for their generosity in reading and criticizing parts of this book. Faramarz Naeim's faith in and enthusiasm for this project from its beginning to its conclusion deserve special thanks. Although a hematologist by profession, he read through the entire manuscript in its various permutations and never ceased to offer a critical ear. Much appreciation is due to Elizabeth Fernea and Afsaneh Najmabadi, readers of the manuscript, for their meticulous reading, considered commentary, and invaluable suggestions. I owe a special debt to Kaveh Safa. For twelve years, we have discussed the ideas presented in this book. Frankly, at times, it is hard to say where my ideas end and his begin. For his poetic sensibility, his critical insights, his incisive comments on various drafts of this book, but above all, for his friendship, I am especially grateful to him.

Thanks are also due to Afsar 'Adl, Sol Altman, Heideh Akbarzadeh, Homa Bahrami, Sharon Davie, Shahla Haeri, Anne Kinney, Feelie Lee, Nahid Massali, Parviz Mafi, Jila Malekzad, Fa'eqeh Mofidi, Esther Naeim, Fatemeh Shahidi, Vida Samiian, Homa Sarshar, and Parvaneh Tahmassebi (Oskoui), who have helped me in many vital ways. For their inspirational and enduring support, I am most appreciative.

The enthusiastic support of Cynthia Maude-Gembler of the Syracuse University Press and her gracious and calm efficiency in seeing the book through its various stages of completion have made the process of publication a most pleasant and gratifying experience. My special thanks to Cynthia.

The University of Virginia's several summer grants and a year of leave gave me time to work on this book. For these gifts of time, I am much indebted. I also wish to express my appreciation to Gail More, who gave me technical assistance in preparing the manuscript.

My family deserves heartfelt thanks for support beyond all calls of conventional expectations. To my husband, Faridoun, my son, Faramarz, and my daughter, Farnaz, and their all-enabling love, I owe more than words can express.

Versions of some chapters of this book have been previously published. Grateful acknowledgment is made to the following: the University of Texas Press, the Center for Middle Eastern Studies of Harvard University by Harvard University Press, the Center for Middle Eastern Studies at the University of Texas at Austin, and the Society for Iranian Studies.

I am also grateful for permission to quote from the following books: *A Nightingale's Lament,* Parvin E'tessami, translated by Heshmat Moayyad and A. Margaret Madelung (Lexington, Ky.: Mazda, 1985); *Bride of Acacias,* Forugh Farrokhzad, translated by Amin Banani and Jascha Kessler (New York: Caravan, 1982); and *Red Umbrella,* Tahereh Saffarzadeh (Iowa City, Iowa: Windhover Press, 1969). I want to acknowledge the original publishers of the following editions: *Selected Poems of Emily Dickinson,* edited by James Reeves (London: William Heinemann, 1959); and *From Darkness into Light,* Badr ol-Moluk Bamdad, translated by F. R. D. Bagley (Hicksville, N.Y.: Exposition-University, 1977).

Veils and Words

1

A Walled Society

Literature in Iran has long possessed a predominantly masculine character. Conspicuously absent from it has been the presence of women as writers or critics, as makers of literary tradition. Until recently, little has been heard of women writers, painters, musicians, architects, actors, potters, calligraphers. The achievements of those women who, against all odds, managed to nurture their creative talents, have remained for the most part unrecognized, invisible. This invisibility extends beyond women as makers of art to women as objects of representations.[1] The palace reliefs of Persepolis are telling manifestations of Iranian women's invisibility—pictorial or otherwise: "Among the many figures in Persepolis women are completely absent. The hidden force in history is particularly hidden in this first Iranian Empire. Even the animals carried as gifts for the king by various delegations are, with one exception, male. And the presence of the only female creature, a lioness, brought by the Elamites, can easily be explained by the age of the two cubs she accompanies: they still need suckling."[2]

For centuries, the written literary potential of Iranian women has been repressed, muffled.[3] Easy access to the power, privilege, and arena of the written word was for long denied them.[4] The long silence of women in more than a thousand years of a rich written literary tradition needs to be studied and elaborated upon. Why are women writers almost absent from our classical literary scene? How could anyone or anything have been so successful in silencing such a large number of people for so long? Why does the beginning of women's literary tradition in Iran coincide with their attempt to unveil? What is the

1

relationship between physical and verbal self-expression, especially, as it concerns experiences and constructs of gender?

If Iranian women writers, or their many mute foremothers, are to be understood and appreciated more fully, if the true impact of their writing is to be felt, then the conditions out of which their literary tradition was born have to be understood. In a society concerned obsessively with keeping the worlds of men and women apart, with an ideal of feminine as silent, immobile, and invisible, women writers have not found it easy to flourish. They had to subvert the system that had for centuries confined their bodies and their voices, exiled, and excluded them. Even if they were lucky enough to be allowed some education and the opportunity to cultivate their creativity, their effort to build an identity as writers has often entailed a conscious rebellion against stereotypes of women's place in both society and literature, against their culture's idealization of woman as *Sangin o Samet,* "solemn and silent."

Although there are many ways of approaching the writing of women in Iran, I emphasize just one point of view: the relationship between women's literature and the social practice of veiling. The veil has an amazingly rich range and vocabulary for expression. God "has seventy thousand veils of light and darkness,"[5] and *Mokashefeh* [spiritual illumination] is to intuit some of the secrets behind this many-folded veil. Historically, kings, God's shadows on earth, also practiced veiling. "Khosrow Anosiravan (r. 531–79) came into the audience hall to receive Zuyazan of Yaman covered, and only when he was seated on the throne under the hanging crown was his veil removed. Khosrow Parviz's head was veiled when he was brought to the house where he was to be confined during his last days."[6] The title *Pardeh dar, Hajeb* [veil or curtain holder], which came to mean the intermediary between the king and his people, could have its etymological basis in this tradition.

In pre-Islamic Iran, according to some sources, women of the court and high aristocracy also practiced veiling. "At least as early as Achaemenid times Persian queens were hidden from the people. Plutarch, discussing the reign of Artaxerxes (r. 404–359), writes that Queen Stateira was beloved by the common folk because the curtains of her carriage were always up, and thus the women . . . were permitted to see and greet her."[7]

The veil, from the perspective of this book, refers to any form of extra covering a woman has to wear on top of her dress when in public or in the presence of forbidden men, that is, all the men who could marry her, those who are free of incest taboos. This definition includes the different shapes, sizes, and forms of the veil: from the all-encompassing cloak that covers the whole body but leaves the face bare, to the kind that covers the face as well, to the head scarf worn by rural and tribal women who can ill afford to wear the full veil.[8]

In Iran, the veil has been so much a part of common thinking and belief, so much honored as an integral part of a woman's appearance in public, that like the blue sky, it was considered normal, indispensable. Only in the mid-nineteenth century was veiling publicly challenged for the first time. An Iranian woman, a poet named Tahereh Qorratol'Ayn (1817–1852), unveiled herself in 1848. Years later, in 1923, in another part of the Middle East, Huda Shaarawi and Saiza Nabarawi, upon their return from an international feminist meeting in Rome, appeared unveiled at the Cairo railway station.[9] Four years later, Ambara Salaam (whose brother, Saeeb Salaam, later became prime minister of Lebanon) appeared without her veil to speak at the Women's Renaissance Society in Beirut. She maintained that wearing the veil when speaking in public "hampered her and blocked her thoughts."[10] Yet, in spite of over 150 years of struggle for the choice not to wear the veil, in spite of the compulsory unveiling act of 1936, unveiling remains a controversial, religious, social, political, and cultural issue to this day.

Normatively oriented discussions of veiling have often maintained that seclusion of women symbolizes female powerlessness.[11] Yet, it seems to me that issues of power and authority are much more complex. Dependence does not necessarily mean passivity, just as subordination is not synonymous with powerlessness. It would be grossly oversimplifying to consign Iranian women to all-powerlessness or to what is loosely termed "negative powers," that is, powers acquired by default within the domestic sphere: to withhold favors, to gossip, to humiliate, to manipulate husbands, and to instill loyalties in sons.[12]

Power and control have not been solely the prerogatives of Iranian men. It is true that women had long been systematically barred from the arena of formal political and economic power. But there are other forms of power, and women have exercised them. Women were sources of constancy while empires rose and fell. They had survival power. They controlled everyday activities of life such as childbearing and child rearing. They fought epidemics and droughts. They forged alliances of affines, kinship, and friendship. They claimed and were believed to possess special powers of intuition, foreknowledge.

Furthermore, socially and politically marginalized, women become central symbolically, an important feature of the imaginary repertoires of the dominant culture.[13] Excluded from the public domain, they come to rule the symbolic order. Absented in one arena, they become an overwhelming presence in the other. From their veiled seclusion, they come to dominate the psychic order, inverting hierarchical norms of gender, position, and rank. They embody their nation's dreams and nightmares. They become an idiom of political and religious expression, an emblem of national identity. Forcefully unveiled, they personify the modernization of the nation. Compulsorily veiled, they embody the reinstitution of the Islamic order. They invade the imagination, elicit the most powerful desires. They derive magical power from the hold they have on their sons. *Be jun-e madaram* [on my mother's head] turns into one of the more common and serious oaths taken by a man. By the same token, curses involving the sexuality of a man's mother or sister become the most serious assaults. In the proper behavior of a wife, daughter, mother, sister lies a man's social honor. Unseen behind their portable wall but seeing, unheard but hearing, mute but pregnant with mystery, women challenge the imagination, reject containment, refuse absence. Pushed out of the door, they return through the window and cracks and crevices in the wall.

Discussions of the veil have more often than not been oversimplified by polemic or reductionism. A major problem in such discussions has been the tendency to take extreme, all-or-nothing positions. Those who support and positively valorize the institution have seen it as a religious ordinance that symbolizes and assures women's respect, pride, and virtue. Those who refute it view it as oppressive and abusive of women and blame its practice on the clergy. Both groups seem to neglect the all-encompassing cultural significance of the veil. They consider its meaning, practice, or importance entirely from the single vantage point of religion, which, however illuminating, undervalues the overdetermined significance of the veil. Both factions, it seems, turn a woman's issue into a solely spiritual matter seemingly unrelated to such mundane matters as power, domination, and exclusion.

The veil is such a pervasive cultural issue that unveiled/veiled could be added in the case of Iran (and Islamic Middle Eastern countries) to the rather universal dichotomization of masculine and feminine in terms of such polarities as culture/nature, reason/passion, self/other, subject/object, law/chaos, day/night, rational/emotional. Although the adequacy of these polarized categories has been challenged and redefined, although feminists and deconstructionists have questioned the terms and the logic through which these claims have been made, although the privileging of the "masculine" side of such polarities has been seriously debated, and although most men and women stand, in fact, outside this rigidly constructed binary opposition, these gendered polarities continue to inform and deeply affect everyday experience of life for both men and women.

The values expressed by veiling, I believe, are not only related to woman's concealment or even to moral, sexual, political, economic, and aesthetic considerations concerning her. The cultural significance and corollary of the veil are many and varied. They relate to notions of masculinity, privacy, and taboo. In a veiled society, walls surround houses. Religious *Taqiyeh* [deliberate dissimulation] protects faith. *Ta'arof* [ritualistic mode of discourse] disguises some thoughts and emotions and plunges both parties, the addressee and the addresser, into a kind of factual suspense. Houses become compartmentalized with their *Daruni* [inner] and *Biruni* [outer] areas. Feelings become disjointed in *Zaheri* [external] and *Bateni* [internal] spheres. Abstractions supplant concreteness. Autobiographies become a rare commodity in the literary arena. Generalities replace the specific. Indirection becomes a common practice. Concealing, keeping what is considered private private — veiling — is not just a woman's problem. It is a relative constant, everyone's preoccupation.

The veil, in its traditional sense, not only polarizes but delineates boundaries. It consigns "power," "control," "visibility," and "mobility" to one social category at the expense of the other. It not only separates the world of men and women not related to each other by marriage or blood but also creates hierarchies across this divide. The indoors, the domestic, the "private," the "personal," the world of women is trivialized. And the out-of-doors, the "public," the world of masculine politics and money is affirmed, elevated.

Until recently, female seclusion in Iran affected woman's control of and access to the public domain in several ways. Politically, she was excluded from certain crucial activities. Economically, though Islamic law accorded her legal rights, she confronted difficulties in fully exercising them. Occupationally, she was prevented from pursuing a variety of careers in the public sector. Educationally, she was denied easy access to public educational institutions. Artistically, she could not fully develop her talent and potential in public forms of art.

For centuries, veiling not only curtailed women's bodily expression but also inhibited their verbal self-expression. Their public silence was long legitimized, spiritualized, fetishized, and idealized. Coerced into silence though they were, they were given numerous rewards and motivations for accepting it. Their social self-effacement, their public inertia and passivity, their *Sharm* [charm, shame], were considered, among other things, key criteria of their beauty. Like the "dumb blond" in the West, the traditional Iranian beauty appears to be made more alluring by not saying anything. Silence was one of her hallmarks.

It is not surprising that, given the religious, social, and aesthetic constraints on women's self-expression in public, exceptionally few women could or perhaps even wanted to break this ancestral silence. Women writers had to transgress feminine proprieties that shut them out of the public domain. They had to expose their voices because literature transmits and translates the human voice to the printed page. Writing, with its potential for public communication, for entering into the world of others, could be considered no less a transgression than unveiling. In both, a woman expresses/exposes herself publicly. Through both, an absence becomes a presence. Both are means of expression and communication: one gives her voice a body, the other gives her body a voice. Writing, like unveiling, makes a woman publicly visible and mobile. Naturally, it could not be included in the repertoire of proper behavior for women. Instead, it was closely defined as a filial activity passed down from fathers to sons.

Although there is no simple cause-effect relationship between national literary traditions and the specific social and cultural context in which they develop and flourish, it is difficult to ignore a possible relationship between the conspicuous lack of women writers in Iran and the institution of veiling. And although veiling cannot be considered the only obstacle to women's efforts to become writers, it has been a major one for centuries.

Iranian male authors, too, have repeatedly complained of the agonies of veiling and have openly expressed the desire to unveil. The celebrated fourteenth-century poet, Hafez, said: "Happy the moment when from my face I cast off the veil."[14] The great mystical poet, Jalal ed-Din Rumi (d. 1273), said: "This is love: to fly heavenward / To rend, every instant, a hundred veils."[15] Their wish, interpreted by many as a mystical metaphor, can also be viewed as a more universal problem in literary creation. Is publishing an act of unveiling or, on the contrary, an act of veiling to hide behind? Do we reveal or conceal the truth of ourselves in the poems we craft, in the stories we spin? Perhaps writers unveil only by spinning veils of another form. Perhaps the veil moves from the physical to other dimensions. Perhaps words are not only means of expression but also invisible walls we erect to contain the otherwise uncontainable.

Still, shouldn't we ask ourselves why the greatest of Iran's poets, like Hafez and Rumi, represent their own literary anxiety, their struggles with love and words, in terms of the woman's unveiling? Is the search for truth and love an act of dis-covering, un-masking, dis-closing, unveiling? Perhaps the anxieties attached to the confrontation of love and reality are displaced onto a woman's body and its nakedness. Perhaps the veil, because of its symbolic potency, becomes a vessel in which to place both the anxieties and the exhilarations of love and creativity.

Although I believe there is no state of full veiledness nor of absolute unveiledness, full transparency, it is important to recognize the distinction between mystical, metaphorical veiling and the compulsory physical veiling of women. Hafez and Rumi's desire to unveil is quite different from the desire expressed by many women who live under the constraints of compulsory veiling in their daily lives. This difference is one of degree and of kind; a difference with far-reaching implications; a difference that makes all the difference. Women experience their confinement not only metaphorically and mystically but also spatially, physically, and verbally in their social segregation, cultural confinement, and forced silence.

Significantly, the movement to unveil in Iran is associated with women's attempt to break into print as writers. Pioneering women writers unveiled both their bodies and their voices. Despite the obstacles presented by a culture that idealized women's silence, despite the anxieties of exposure and authorship, despite accusations of shamelessness and charmlessness, many women chose to write. They lifted the veil of secrecy to show the many faces underneath. Soon, however, their unveiling became a sign of contamination; expression of an unleashed sexuality; proof of religious, sexual, and literary transgression. Women paid for their literal and literary unveiling dearly with loss of reputation, with allegations of immorality, promiscuity, lunacy, even heresy.

The veil, one might argue then, was a major barrier to a woman's struggle for autonomy and authorship. It immobilized her body, muted her voice. It sanctioned the submissive voices of domesticity. It curtailed her access to the public domain in more ways than one. It cemented her to the private domain of the house and left few options outside marriage for her.

Why, then, we should ask ourselves, has veiling been practiced for so long? Or yet more importantly, why are so many educated women voluntarily donning the veil? For, I should hasten to add, throughout the long history of veiling, not only men but also many women have fully supported the institution. It is likely that these women never considered veiling a source or symbol of their oppression or dependency. More likely, to them it was a source of pride. It was honorable, convenient, and virtuous. These women sought the veil, opposed its banishment, and perpetuated its practice. They valued it, respected it, and derived gratification from it.

On the level of everyday life, Iranian society provided women with numerous incentives and rewards for accepting their seclusion and their domestic roles. The veil gave them moral as well as aesthetic appeal. Veiled women were not only virtuous and proper but also ideal. The veil also protected women. It blocked the masculine gaze, subverted man's role as the surveyor, and removed women from the category of object-to-be-seen.[16] Instead, women became the seers, the surveyors who gained power, agency, and control. The veil protected women's bodies, sources of fascination and terror for all patriarchal societies. Now idealized now demonized, now reviled now desired, a woman's body has long embodied dreams and nightmares, fears and fantasies, nurturance and destruction. Mysterious and mystified, it has been handled with unrestrained imagination. Revealed and concealed, mutilated and objectified, its significance has been both physical/sexual and symbolic—a construction of the low Other. Thousands upon thousands of women had their feet mutilated and bound over several centuries in China.[17] Large numbers of women were burned as widows in India and as witches in Europe and America;[18] countless numbers were subjected to various forms of clitoridectomy, a practice predating Islam, in Africa and parts of the Middle East;[19] their necks were elongated, their lips flattened, in Africa. Numerous women were treated harshly socially, psychologically, and clinically as hysterics in Europe.[20] Untold numbers of girls, in an internalized version of such mutilation, suffer from anorexia nervosa and bulimia in the West.[21] Paradoxically, the body of the Iranian woman has not undergone any such maiming. Iran has no known history of the above mutilations nor of officially sanctioned burying of female children upon birth, of chastity belts, steel pins, corsets, iron body locks, or gang rapes.[22]

Has the veil protected Iranian women, or on the contrary, has it been so restrictive that women never became enough of a threat to call for such large-scale punishments and radical countermeasures? Maybe muteness has been their mutilation, not a physical amputation but a verbal one. Perhaps the postrevolutionary large-scale attempt by the government to reveil women is a reaction to gains in power by a previously submissive group, a realization that many women have taken off their veils and many more might. As Fatima Mernissi, the Moroccan sociologist, remarks, the call for the veil has to be "looked at in the light of the painful but necessary and prodigious reshuffling of identity that Muslims are going through in these often confusing but always fascinating times."[23]

In recent years, a major shift has occurred in the meaning of the veil, which no longer signifies women's segregation but, on the contrary, facilitates their access to the public arena, a means to renegotiate boundaries. The traditional equation of veiled/unvoiced/absent is not as clear or as immutable as it once was. Now a woman can be veiled and also have a public voice and presence.

A real revolution is, in fact, shaking the foundations of Iranian society, a revolution with women at its very center. Veiled or unveiled, Iranian women are reappraising traditional spaces, boundaries, and limits. They are renegotiating old sanctions and sanctuaries. They are challenging male allocations of power, space, and resources. Exercising increasing control over how reality is defined, they are redefining their own status. It is in this context of the negotiation of boundaries that the veil is now worn by some women, not to segregate, but to desegregate.

The genealogy of this revolution can be traced back more than a century. Women writers, at the forefront of this movement, have consistently spoken the previously unspoken, articulated the once unarticulated. Their voices can be heard loud and clear in their literature. And the formerly silent, the supposedly invisible have discovered surprising resources in their reappropriated voices and presences and sheer dynamism of their mobility. In the words of one poet, Forugh Farrokhzad:

> Why should I stop, why?
> The birds have gone off to find water ways
> the horizon is vertical and moving is rocketing.
> Shining planets spin
> at the edge of sight
> why should I stop, why?[24]

This book covers 150 years of an exhilarating dynamism. Through literature, which in the words of Edward Said is "singularly avoided" in the "social science attention to the Orient,"[25] it delineates the atmosphere of the time, the literary boundaries allowed women, and their struggle to free their bodies and their public voices.

My approach is unabashedly gender oriented. Yet, Iranian literary women, if they have ever addressed the issue, have frequently asserted their independence in their works from gender consideration. The prominent novelist Mahshid Amirshahi (b. 1937) finds it even "silly" to classify literary works on the basis of the writer's gender. In an introduction to a collection of short stories by Iranian women writers, she writes:

> The truth is, that I find no difference between the creative works of men and women, and what is more I am not even after finding any. The sex of the author definitely does not figure among my criteria for choosing a book. Therefore the division of literature on the basis of the writer's gender appears to me extremely arbitrary, and to be frank quite silly, as silly as trying to classify literary works into "originally hand-written" and "typed," or produced by "ambidextrous" and "left-handed" authors. These divisions and subdivisions, which can go on eternally, do not interest me in the least.[26]

Even those women writers who have not refuted the importance of gender as a category of analysis and a determining factor in the creation of literary texts have requested, in no unequivocal terms, to be judged solely as authors. When Farrokhzad was asked in an interview to address the issue of femininity in her poetry, she found it "quite natural that a woman, due to her physical, psychological, and emotional characteristics, might perceive things differently than a man. She might have a feminine vision that is different from a man." Having said that, however, she was quick to express resentment at being measured against a feminine rather than a more universal literary standard: "If my poetry, as you mentioned, has a certain air of femininity, it is obviously due to my being a woman. Fortunately, I am a woman. But if artistic standards are being evaluated, I think sex should no longer be a consideration. It is inappropriate to even raise such an issue."[27]

The poet Simin Behbahani (b. 1927) is no less opposed to considering women writers as a separate category. In an interview with the literary journal, *Doniya-ye Sokhan,* she said: "I suffer from this curtain that is drawn between men and women writers. If a poet is truly a poet why should the issue of sex turn into a privilege? The arena of poetry is no wrestling ring in which sex and weight are criteria for categorization."[28]

Another poet, one of the only two women ever admitted to the Iranian Cultural Academy, Tahereh Saffarzadeh (b. 1939), goes even further and involves world imperialism in conspiratorial plans to classify her with other women poets when she says that "one of the vulgar tricks of the mercenaries of Imperialism was their propping up, every now and then, a certain literary woman beside me. I am sure, however, that historians and scholars of 'independent' art, even if it is after we're gone, will consider my resistance through poetry superior to the men who claim all contemporary art as their province."[29]

A most telling element of the above statements lies in the absent words, the implied concern that placing women in a gender-marked category automatically downgrades their works to a subsection created especially for them. Isolating women from the mainstream of Persian literature, understood to belong to men, is feared to be damaging, at best condescending, to women.

It is as writers, and, for that matter, as some of the foremost writers of Persian literature, that many of these women deserve literary acclaim and ought to be remembered and studied. Their works are too intricate to be viewed from the single vantage point of their femaleness. Like any complex literary work, they defy rigid categorization and elicit multiple readings. Still, these writers were women writing in a society consumed by masculine values and worldviews. And when they chose deliberately to challenge, reject, and transcend mores characterizing femininity, they were avoided, patronized, or abused by an unresponsive, often bewildered, sometimes hostile, predominantly masculine literary establishment.

It is important to approach the works of women with the awareness that many of their attitudes and preoccupations reflect and respond to these cultural and social realities. In fact, I would argue that to avoid or deny, at this juncture in time, the issue of gender is to ignore an essential part of this literature's context as well as its content. Aware of the problems in female literary creativity, the novelist Shahrnush Parsipur (b. 1946) places herself squarely within an all-woman tradition. In this genealogy, suited to her needs and aspirations, she names not a single man. She makes for herself a female pedigree and draws nourishment and energy from it. "I write," she says, "because I have a limited ancestry—Rabe'e 'Adaviyee [the eighth-century Muslim saint], a few mystics, half-famed, half-crazed, Tahereh Qorratol'Ayn, Parvin E'tessami, Forugh Farrokhzad, Simin Daneshvar, Simin Behbahani, and those of my own generation: Mahshid Amirshahi, Goli Tarraqi, Ghazaleh 'Alizadeh, Mihan Bahrami, and possibly a few others constitute the whole repertoire of my written or attempted literary tradition."[30]

Recognizing gender, at this point in Iranian literary history, is a necessary critical perspective. Looking at the works of women writers as written by women is an act of compensation, a search for neglected features, an examination of misconceptions, omissions, sexually biased assumptions. It should not be construed as an attempt either to segregate women or to place them in a lower category. The refutation of double standards does not negate the consideration of gender in evaluating art. Furthermore, women, exactly because of their sex, have been systematically denied recognition for their various social initiatives. For too long, for instance, it has been assumed that the stimulus behind the movement for unveiling and the liberation of woman's literary voice in Iran has been either masculine or culturally exogenous (i.e., Western). As if notions of autonomy, equality, and development are solely the prerogative of Westerners or of men; as if Iranian women neither desired nor struggled for them. Both the movement for veiling and the movement for unveiling are viewed as governmental decrees, as if their patterns of implementation, their pace, their timing, and all else were determined by men. Portrayed as cosmetic reform or Islamic fundamentalism, as an obsession with modernity or tradition and advocated in order to include or exclude women in the labor force, they are considered to be reforms from above. This book isolates some of the indigenous feminine forces that, against all odds, championed and achieved basic and fundamental changes in women's lives by taking initiatives voluntarily to veil or unveil themselves — physically or verbally.

This book, like my life, has a double orientation. It is a hybrid, an eclectic borrowing from Iranian and non-Iranian sources. It is also doubly marginal. I speak as a foreigner in a foreign language about a group of writers not only marginalized in their own country but also by and large excluded from the mainstream of Anglo-American attention to world literature. I write as an exile about exiles. I concentrate on problems of authorship specific to women in a sexually segregated society. While I discuss Iranian women writers, I also draw from Western feminist literary criticism. Although veiling is a culture-specific issue with which Western feminists have not been overly concerned politically or theoretically, many of their works have contributed to the development of my ideas.

The erosion of my assumptions and presuppositions about conventional literary criticism received a major stimulus from reading Virginia Woolf's essays and fiction. She intensified my perception of how the development and flourishing of women's writing depends on conditions such as financial independence and easy access to education and privacy. Simone de Beauvoir's pioneering analysis of the politics of culture clarified for me some of the processes through which women are transformed into men's Other. Kate Millett's writings on sexual politics proved to me the importance of cultural and social context not only in understanding heterosexual relationships but also in the production and interpretation of literary works. Patricia Meyer Spacks, Elaine Showalter, Cheryl Brown, Karen Olsen, Ellen Moers, Sandra Gilbert, and Susan Gubar believed in and convinced me of a distinctively female literary tradition that can be studied as a separate category, a subculture. Julia Kristeva, Luce Irigaray, and Hélène Cixous elaborated for me a sense of the interconnectedness of body, voice, and writing, and showed me how mutilating and censoring one censors and mutilates the other. Many others, too many to list them all here, impressed me with their argument that the critical enterprise cannot be disengaged from the poetics and politics of sexuality. They helped me rethink the relationships between women's literature and women's bodies. I have benefited from theories of the fetishism, objectification, and mutilation of women's bodies, the silencing of women's voices.

Elaine Showalter claims that feminist criticism does not derive "its literary principles from a single authority figure or from a body of sacred texts."[31] This has certainly been true in my case. My critical perspective has evolved partly through reading theoretical works but also in significant part from reading the lives and works of Iranian women writers. My mother, whose many beautiful poems were never published, made me aware of the many subtle ways through which women are excluded and exiled from what is considered literature. Tahereh Qorratol'Ayn showed me how dangerous and yet exhilarating it was for a woman to move into the forbidden field of intellectual self-assertion and to challenge a system that for centuries had claimed a monopoly on truth and was endowed with the institutional power to defend its privileged position. Parvin E'tessami proved that women can be poets and good ones at that. Simin Daneshvar showed me the costs and benefits of aesthetic commitment and the difficulties of enlarging the circle of fiction writers to include conventionally excluded members—women. Forugh Farrokhzad made me more aware of the poetic potentialities of using the language of intimacy and also of the costs that a woman writer may have to pay for transgressing aesthetic and sexual conventions. Tahereh Saffarzadeh proved to me the richness and ambiguities of the current meanings and functions of the veil, that a woman can voluntarily choose to veil herself and still have a literary voice and presence. And from the poetry of Simin Behbahani, I learned the possibility of overcoming and reconciling, transcending, seemingly primordial cultural dichotomies.

The writers I am writing about represent diverse genres, from lyric poetry and short stories to novels, from didactic and religious poetry to autobiographies. I make a special attempt to view this tradition as a continuing process, as a moving picture rather than as a series of still frames, isolated shots. Each chapter, even those that focus on a single writer, depends on the others for significance.

Part 1 explores the literal and metaphorical significance of the veil and how it has affected women's literary expression. Part 2, titled "From Tahereh to Tahereh," delves into poetry. Starting with the revolutionary and symbolically significant unveiling of Tahereh Qorratol'Ayn, it ends with a revolutionary and charged reveiling, after 150 years, of another woman, also a poet and also named Tahereh. Exploring this body of poetry not only uncovers some highly imaginative poems but also makes possible a more accurate map of female social, psychic, and emotional reality. It establishes how for over fifteen decades women have been actively involved in shaping their own identities and destinies. For various reasons, many women, far more than is commonly recognized, turned to poetry to exercise literary capacities otherwise frustrated by social and cultural restrictions. No document charts more accurately the difficult road to liberation of the Iranian woman than her poetry. It is a rich, virtually unexplored record of the development of her consciousness and identity, experienced within, but not limited by, traditional Iranian culture.

Part 3 examines one of the ironies of Iranian literary history: although women have always been recognized as storytellers, their emergence as fiction writers is a rather recent phenomenon. The first major collection of women's short stories was published in 1947, and it was two decades later before the first novel written by a woman was published. I discuss the emergence of women's narrative prose and masculine monopolization of the written word, noting that writing about women's lives from a woman's perspective as novel or autobiography has become a preferred medium of women's literary expression.

In my conclusion, I briefly review women's postrevolutionary writing and especially the emergence of Simin Behbahani as a major literary figure. Her last two poetry collections herald a new beginning: a graceful reconciliation of the old and the new, the personal and the universal. In this poetry we witness the coming together of the modern spirit of voiced mobility and traditional poetic form and figures. She integrates aspects of an exclusively male tradition with her distinctively feminine vision. In her neoclassical poetry, she finds her unique voice.

I pursue an argument rather than provide a comprehensive survey of women writers in Iran. Some of Iran's important women writers are inevitably omitted. No attempt to present such a rich tradition can hope to be exhaustive or comprehensive. I write mainly about those writers whose works I consider to have marked important new beginnings concerning notions of veiling/unveiling. At best, I am scratching the surface, hoping that this effort will present a step toward a fuller and more nuanced view of women writers in Iran and will bring into sharper focus a rich field for appreciation and study at home and abroad.

The tradition of women writers in contemporary Iran is a record of the development of a consciousness and of an identity, within and transcending the limits of traditional culture.[32] It is here in her literature that the Iranian woman finally speaks for herself and provides a fresh perspective on her life. No longer sealed in secrecy or hidden in anonymity, she celebrates in her literature a double victory: a hard-won dominion over her body and her voice.

> I'll come, I'll come, I'll come
> with my hair — fragrances from beneath the earth —
> with my eyes — darkness, intensely felt —
> with shrubs I've pulled from those woods beyond the wall.
> I'll come, I'll come, I'll come
> and the gate will be filled with love
> and at the gate I'll greet once again
> those who love
> and the girl waiting there, at the gate
> I'll greet them all once more.[33]

PART ONE

Tradition

Wearing the Veil

2

The Concept of Veiling

To veil or not to veil? For well over a century Iranians have debated this question and, through it, alternative models of female identity. Governmental decrees have required and forbidden the veil, merchants have refused to do business with veiled or unveiled women, and public transportation officials have declined to serve women based on whether or not they wear the veil. Many have fervently spoken for or against the veil with an implacable inflexibility. In fact, veiling has functioned more like a code that allowed anyone and everyone to vent their private aspirations, fears, dreams, and nightmares. An emblem now of progress, then of backwardness, a badge now of nationalism, then of domination, a symbol of purity, then of corruption, the veil has accommodated itself to a puzzling diversity of personal and political ideologies.

An older woman in Iran today has been veiled by tradition in her youth, forcefully unveiled by government edict in 1936, and obligatorily reveiled in 1983. In other words, the actual wearing of the veil has been imposed, withdrawn, and reimposed within a single lifetime. It is hard to imagine a more heavily charged symbol than the veil in the modern history of Iran.

The veil takes its meaning from situation, time, and place, and therefore has no single fixed importance. To cite one extreme example, among the North African Tuareg tribe, men veil themselves. Their veiling, however, is an expression of men's status and power. In the West, the veil is usually associated with the face veil that

was worn by the Goddess, particularly in her Crone aspect, which represented future fate. Her Celtic name of Caillech meant a Veiled One.

19

The ancients believed that a peek behind the veil often meant a view of one's own death, which is why the Goddess's hidden face was dreaded and thought deadly, like the face Athene-Gorgo, or Medusa. According to the Goddess's inscription on the temple at Sais, "No man has ever lifted the veil that covers me." Much as people earnestly desired a look into the future, they also feared what it might reveal. . . . Veils were formerly worn by widows in expression of their Crone character. Then it was said the veil was to protect the woman from attack from the ghost world, whence her spouse had gone. Then brides were veiled, because at a transitory stage in life they were thought especially vulnerable to evil influences. Nuns . . . were veiled to conceal their sexuality.[1]

Chador, the form of veiling prevalent in Iran, is an all-enveloping piece of cloth that covers a woman from head to toe. The word itself means tent, perhaps in reference to the earlier, pre-Islamic practice of moving women around in covered sedan chairs. The *Chador* is kept in place by clutching it under the chin by one hand. The face is usually left uncovered or is covered, if at all, by a separate face veil.

Much debate and disagreement surround the origins of veiling. Part of this confusion can be attributed to the treatment of women in Iranian history. Aptly called "masculine," Iranian history has not allocated much attention and space to women's lives in general, let alone to their veiling.[2] Yet, despite this paucity of historical evidence, many have argued with unfounded conviction and passion about the origin of veiling.[3] Some assign it to an aristocratic Zoroastrian habit, while others think that Islam first imposed and then perpetuated the practice. These conjectural arguments, interesting as they might be, shed little light on the present practice of veiling. For the fact remains that veiling, whether or not it originated in Iran, accompanied the Islamic faith, or came earlier, still holds an extraordinary appeal for many Iranians.

Although it may not be certain when veiling became common practice, there is little doubt about a tradition of female seclusion in pre-Islamic Iran and about the institutionalization of veiling through the *Shari'a* [canonical law of Islam], which asks women to cover themselves modestly. Furthermore, although from the beginning Iranians rejected some elements of the invading Islamic culture, veiling and the beliefs associated with it seemed not to have provoked much—if any—cultural resistance.

Muslim women, according to the Qor'an, should cover themselves modestly: "And say to the believing women that they should cast down their eyes, and guard their private parts, and reveal not their adornment save such as is outward; and let them cast their veils over their bosoms, and not reveal their adornment."[4] The Qor'an itself discusses veiling in general terms and does not establish the limits and details of women's covering. The assumption that a woman's garment should cover all but her face and hands and be loose fitting enough to conceal her figure is only an interpretation of this verse—albeit confirmed by the consensus of many Islamic authorities. Some also argue that this interpretation is based on the authority of the Prophet Mohammad and especially the *Hadith* [authoritative narrative] in which he is reported to have said: "If the woman reaches the age of puberty, no part of her body should be seen but this—and he pointed to his face and hands."[5]

The ambiguity of meaning built into the Qor'anic verse allows different readings with far-reaching implications. The great disparities of religiously acceptable clothing in the Islamic world at large best prove the viability and possibility of such varying interpretations. Furthermore, Iranians have insisted upon the concept of *Ejtehad* [the formulation of new solutions to new problems facing the Islamic community]. This concept allows ample space for reorientation, adaptation, and even innovation. Indeed, the dominant Shi'ite clerical figures and judicial authorities in Iran have taken full advantage of this enlightened principle and have selectively formulated changes that were deemed necessary. Significantly, however, with regard to a woman's code of modest dressing, no such modification has been sanctified.

The details of veiling may be a point of contention among theologians of different sects, but the function of the veil is beyond any dispute. It is to hide the woman from the view of forbidden men. It is a deliberate, obsessive attempt to keep that which symbolizes the private realm—that is, woman and anything associated with her—hidden. In fact, the veil can readily be compared to a portable wall, a strategic mobile segregation.

Although the Qor'an does not specify any penalty for women who unveil, still the ideal state for both men and women is a covered one. From the point of view of Islam, the function of clothing is not to display the body, but to conceal it and to reduce sexual enticement. Even in the Islamic paradisiacal order, men and women are covered. The Qor'anic story of the Fall from the Garden of Eden best exemplifies this point. Adam and Eve [Hava] in the Garden of Eden were properly covered. Sura 20:115 of the Qor'an reads: "He brought your parents out of the Garden, stripping them of their garments to show them their shameful parts." Again, in Sura 7:27: "Children of Adam! let not Satan tempt you as he brought your parents out of the Garden stripping them of their garments to show them their shameful parts." Nakedness was a punishment for the fallen Adam and Eve, as it continues to be for their Muslim sons and daughters today. In the Judeo-Christian version of this story, Adam and Eve are naked in the garden and must cover themselves on expulsion. Although the conclusion is the same for both versions — covering is necessary in a fallen world — the ideal state for the Judeo-Christian seems to be uncovered, and for the Muslim, covered. Accordingly, the Persian word *Pushesh* [clothing] is derived from the verb *Pushidan,* which means to cover up, to conceal from view; whereas the English term *dress* means, among other things, to decorate, to adorn.

Celestial ideals correspond closely to terrestrial patterns, and exposure can cause all sorts of ailments for the Muslim children of Adam and Eve. Varied and manifold afflictions such as sudden death, sickness, unexpected calamities, and failures of all sorts can be brought about by exposure and are attributed to the evil eye [*Cheshm-e bad*]. Although this quasi-magical power assigned to the eye might be an attempt to explain the unforeseen and unwelcome occurrences that happen to someone, it also reflects the underlying fear of exposure. Although the eye of anyone has the potential power voluntarily or involuntarily to cause harm, there is no attempt at retribution against the person responsible for casting the evil eye. Ultimately and invariably, it is one's own responsibility to avoid *Cheshm-e bad* and to take precautionary measures to prevent its detrimental effects. Talisman and amulet can be worn to avert it, seeds of wild rue [*Esfand*] can be burned to stop it. But these and many others are anticipatory and counteractive. The safest method of course is preventive: to keep out of sight, concealed, and covered.

Veiling is thus much more than a matter of taste in clothing or a religious ordinance affecting women alone. It is a cultural trait. Its multiple means and meanings do not merely regulate interactions between man and woman or dictate the control of one over the other. They also indicate modes of being and behavior that are shaped or misshaped by varying degrees and types of protection and censorship, both external and internal.

With a history clouded by the neglect of historians, with sanctions defined more by the people than by any single religion, with magical fears of being exposed, it comes as no surprise that the institution of veiling resists any clear definition. Only the broadest attempts at definition suggest its cultural and social parameters. Veiling is perhaps one of the most symbolically significant structures of a complex cultural heritage that expresses, among other things, Iran's prevailing attitude toward the self and the other. It indicates ways in which people relate to or interact with each other and, ultimately, with themselves. It is a ritualistic expression of culturally defined boundaries. Like walls that enclose houses and separate inner and outer spaces, the veil makes a clear statement about the disjunction between the private and the public. Like *Parde-ye Bekarat* [the hymen or, more literally, the virginity curtain] that stands for and becomes an instrument for regulation of women's sexuality, the veil reasserts men's control over the gateway to women's bodies. Like regulated and coded communication that leads to a ritualistic mode of discourse, veiling sanctifies a system of censorship and self-censorship. It sustains a system of silencing the concrete, the specific, and the personal. In short, veiling is not only the expression par excellence of a sexually segregated, male-dominated society, it is also an indication of the strong forces of deindividualization, protection, and secrecy.

Sexual segregation strives to minimize or circumvent the frequency of male/female interactions. In other words, what can be revealed about a woman is carefully separated from what must remain concealed. Generally speaking, a woman's personal life has been, historically, a privatized experience. Just as a wall of fabric surrounds her body, so a wall of silence encloses the details of her life. She is the personal, the private. She is the secret. Accordingly, the term *Mahram*, besides referring to one freed from male/female interactional constraints, also signifies a confidant.[6] A *Mahram* can see beyond the veil and can be trusted with secrets. By the same token, the verb *Kashf Kardan* can be used for both disclosing a secret or unveiling a woman: *Kashf-e Raz* is divulging a secret, and *Kashf-e Hejab* is a woman's unveiling.

A veiled society is like a garden invaded by snow. Just as trees, flowers, weeds, and every little space in the garden get covered by the mantle of snow, so, too, every corner of the society is pervaded by the veil. Nothing can evade its all-encompassing presence. A society that veils its women is a veiled society. In other words, women are not the only ones veiled. Men are veiled, too.

Veiled men? Well, yes. Even though according to popular belief a physically veiled man is degraded to the level of a woman, hence denied his privileged, manly position, men, too, can be metaphorically veiled. For example, the escape from Iran of Mr. Bani-Sadr, Iran's first president, and of Mr. Rajavi, the Mojahhedin-e Khalq's leader, both men allegedly covered by veils, has been used time and again to show not only their cowardice but above all their effeminate nature.

Escaping a physical veil, Iranian men carry a mental veil. They are indeed prisoners in jails of their own making. To begin with, although women are the secluded ones, the degree of man/woman access remains curtailed for both sexes. The restriction is thus not on women alone; it is against heterosexual interactions in general. Furthermore, patterns in men's everyday activities and behavior, concepts of inner/outer and of identity, betray men's constant preoccupation with veiling in a metaphorical sense. For if women need to be covered and protected, men must incessantly cover and protect them. If women are confined by the veil, men are restricted by stringent codes of *Mardanegi* [masculinity] and *Gheyrat* [honor]. If women are to veil their bodies, men are to veil their eyes. In fact, Sura Nur in the Qor'an first addresses men: "Say to the believing men that they should lower their gaze and guard their modesty." Conforming to their understanding of this Qor'anic injunction, many Muslim men have refused to look at women, especially the unveiled ones. An unveiled woman, like Medusa, should not be gazed at. At least one did not leave home after the mass unveiling of 1936 so that he would not risk seeing an unveiled woman. Writes Gh. Hadad Adel, "In 1967 I myself visited an old respectable clergyman at his home in Shiraz who had not ever left his house since 1935 [1936], i.e., the same year the veil was abolished. He finally died at his house without ever going outdoors during all those years because, since Reza Khan had compelled women to be unveiled, he regarded it as forbidden to cast his eyes upon unveiled women."[7]

In a veiled society, seeing, far from being considered a mere physiological process, takes on a socially determined, potentially dangerous, and highly charged meaning. Considered much more than windows to the soul safely concealed, eyes become subject to the strictest regulations for both men and women. Men's eyes attain phallic power. According to Ghazali (1050–1111), the famous Muslim philosopher, "the look is fornication of the eye."[8] And Sheykh Mahalati, the twentieth-century Iranian religious scholar, emphatically states:

> The seduction of lustful men and even of scholars often occurs through looking at the faces of beautiful women. Many tales and accounts from Adam's time until now confirm this claim. . . . The [forbidden] glance brings about love and lust, distracts and enamors youngsters, makes them wander in coffee houses and movie theaters. The glance demolishes houses and destroys he who looks. It excites, delights, seduces, and murders. It breaks hearts, brings tears to eyes, and ruins families. It is the glance that demoralizes, increases envy, and dements young people. Looking is the key to fornication, and fornication causes syphilis, and syphilis discontinues procreation, and this is the onslaught of disaster of human society.[9]

Men's forbidden act of seeing thus becomes a violation, a sin, a visual rape. In order to be controlled, it must relinquish its neutrality or freedom of movement.[10] In the words of President Rafsanjani: "A cleric could not walk through the university with those scenes on the grass, in classes, in streets. We could not go to government offices. If you stood in front of a desk, you would commit a sin, because there was a nude statue [an unveiled woman] behind the desk."[11]

A man's sinful gaze becomes no less problematic than a woman's unveiled body, his desegregation no less unsettling than hers. The experience of Badr ol-Moluk Bamdad, one of the first twelve women admitted to Tehran University in 1938, is quite revealing:

> While the girls had deliberately and prudently prepared themselves for entry, the boys were completely disconcerted. For most of them, mixing with girls was something quite unforeseen. They therefore avoided talking to the girls or even answering them, and if there was no escape they blushed from ear to ear and stuttered. At the lectures, wherever a girl sat, the bench on each side of her stayed empty.
> Certain elderly professors were just as nervous as the boy students about speaking to the girls and looking them in the face. One girl, then in her second year at the university, asked a professor who had shut his

eyes when replying to a question from her, "Don't you trust your eyes, professor?" He was puzzled and asked, "What do you mean?" "I mean why won't you look at girls?"

As for the librarian, the sight of the girls side by side with the boys disturbed him so much that he marked off a special corner like a harem [women's quarter in the family home] where the girls might safely sit.[12]

Thus, veiling restrains and constrains relations, creating a sense of confinement not exclusive to women. In the absence of the veil, men who are used to it become uncomfortable, their personal interactions with women problematized. Previously delineated boundaries blur. "Masculine" territory becomes indistinct in outline or shape as women invade forbidden physical and mental spaces. Order turns into chaos; confusion creates more confusion; and in this foggy atmosphere where everything seems to be out of its normal and proper place, an explosive force gathers momentum until it becomes powerful enough to explode at the slightest provocation or at the first available opportunity. Bamdad recalls an almost surrealistic episode that reminds one of an aborted witch-burning scene in the West:

> Two or three years after the admission of girls to the university, some boy and girl students clubbed together in the days before Nowruz (the Iranian New Year on 21 March) and worked long and hard to organize a convivial celebration with the traditional bonfire on Chaharshanbe-ye Suri (the Wednesday before Nowruz). (The bonfire symbolizes the end of dark days and the burning away of past evils.) It was arranged that the bonfire should be lit in a certain large courtyard, and that the girl students, whose number had now risen, should form a ring round the fire and the boys should stand behind them and all should sing a Nowruz song. Probably at the suggestion of an agitator outside the university some boy students acting in concert stationed themselves just behind the girls and joined hands and all at once pushed, with the intention of driving the girls so close to the fire that they would get scorched or burned. This odious design was spotted by other students just as it was being put into operation and was stopped in time; but the uproar and commotion took all the expected fun and joy out of the party.[13]

Boundaries and enclosed spaces have a lingering hidden dimension. Even if circumstances or economic conditions necessitate physical closeness and mingling of the sexes, the psychological segregation may remain. To this day, for example, most Iranian parties, inside and even outside the country, inevitably divide into two groups; invisible walls separate men from women. The treatment of women in leftist and Islamic political groups with unavoidable closeness and mingling of the sexes illustrates another method of keeping women at a distance. In order to be detached from sexual allure, all militant women are called "comrade" *[Rafiq]* or "sister" *[Khahar]* by their male compatriots, who are instructed never to get sexually involved with them. The imaginary walls of the private world can be stretched endlessly. Women outside incest taboos can miraculously turn into "sisters" and "comrades" and thus become sexually forbidden. Imaginary boundaries replace the real ones. Old sanctions remain almost untouched, just transformed into new shapes.

Considering the privileged position the veil held in Iran, it is no wonder that early advocates of its abolition confronted hostile, and at times fatal, resistance. The first men who supported unveiling were harshly criticized, ostracized, or sent into exile. Yet, theirs was not as harsh a fate as that meted out to Tahereh Qorratol'Ayn, the first woman known actually to unveil herself publicly in nineteenth-century Iran. She was later executed by strangulation. Before Tahereh unveiled herself, no documented history of women's protest against veiling exists in Iran.

The few isolated instances of unveiling seem less to be acts of protest against the institution than challenges to men's masculinity or bold ways of pleading a case. For example, "upon the death in 922 A.D. of the famed Mansur Hallaj, his sister appeared in public unveiled, and to shocked criticism responded, 'Yesterday there was at least half a man in the world, today there is no man; for whom should I veil?'"[14] Unveiling was such a potently symbolic act that it immediately attracted attention, and women used it as a readily available platform from which to speak:

On the death of Mahmud Shah, Abu Sa'id appointed Sheikh Hussein Ibn Chuban to the governorship of Fars, a lucrative and much-coveted post. Sheikh Hussein took the precaution of ordering the three sons of Mahmud Shah to be seized and imprisoned; but while they were passing through the streets of Shiraz in the hands of their captors, their mother who accompanied them, lifted her veil and made a touching appeal to the people, calling upon them to remember the benefits they had received from their late ruler. Her words took instant effect; the inhabitants rose, released her and her sons, and drove Sheikh Hussein into exile.[15]

Women also unveiled themselves in groups to make a political statement. According to W. Morgan Shuster, the first U.S. financial adviser
in Iran, three hundred women marched to the *Majles* [House of Rep-
resentatives] at the turn of the century:

> Many held pistols under their skirts or in the folds of their sleeves. . . .
> In his [the president's] reception-hall they confronted him, and lest he
> and his colleagues should doubt their meaning, these cloistered Persian
> mothers, wives and daughters exhibited threateningly their revolvers, tore
> aside their veils, and confessed their decision to kill their own husbands
> and sons, and leave behind their own dead bodies, if the deputies wavered
> in their duty to uphold the liberty and dignity of the Persian people
> and nation.[16]

There are also those women who had to unveil themselves in order
to participate in battles. The story of Zeinab, among many others, who
disguised herself in male attire and showed amazing courage and resil-
iency, is noteworthy: "Donning a tunic and wearing a headdress like
those of her men companions, she cut off her locks, girt on a sword,
and seizing a musket and a shield, introduced herself into their ranks.
No one suspected her of being a maid when she leaped forward to take
her place behind the barricade. . . . Her enemies pronounced her the
curse which an angry Providence had hurled upon them."[17] In recognition of her prowess and bravery, Zeinab was called "Rostam-'Ali." This
curious nickname for a woman combines the names of two men: the
pre-Islamic mythic male figure, Rostam, and the highly revered First
Imam of Shi'ites, Hazrat-e 'Ali, the cousin and son-in-law of the prophet
Mohammad.

Other than such rare and uncommon instances, the veil was part of
common thinking and belief, honored as an integral part of a woman's
appearance in public. Even in the mid-nineteenth century, Tahereh's unveiling was an isolated, singular event. The atmosphere of the time was
not receptive to such arguments or acts, and public pressure made the
practice of veiling an imperative. Not until the turn of the century did
opposition to the veil become widespread, included within the larger
movements of modernization, Westernization, and women's rights.[18]
By this time, the early advocates of unveiling, although condemned,

labeled, and harassed, were not to be silenced again. Their mutinous demands for reforms grew louder and clearer. Slowly but surely, the issue of women's emancipation gathered momentum and commanded increasing attention.

Many of the ideologues and writers of the constitutional revolutionary period (1905–1911) felt compelled to challenge inequalities on all levels, including the sexual. The "women's issue" held a privileged position in their writings. A challenge to traditionalism on political, social, and literary levels, the constitutional revolution opposed autocracy. The literature of this period, closely involved with sociopolitical events of the day, had new concerns, new characters, new demands, and ultimately, new readership. The promotion of revolutionary causes, the championing of individual rights, nationalism, and the emancipation of women were its main thematic concerns. Dehkhoda, Malcolm Khan, Mirza Aqa Khan Kermani, Akhundzadeh, Lahuti, 'Eshqi, and Iraj Mirza, among others, argued repeatedly for women's equality. They attributed Iran's "backwardness," to use the prevalent term of the day, to women's condition and especially to their "imprisonment" in veils. Calling the veil a "shroud," a "sack," or a "jail," and a veiled woman a "walking bundle," a "black crow," or an "ink pot," they maintained that the veil had prevented women from developing to their fullest potential. They saw in women's oppressive condition a cause of larger social evil and insisted that women's abilities and ideals had atrophied or died an early death, leaving scars on the whole society. 'Eshqi (1894–1924) railed against "burying" women in veils. He called for action:

> What are these unbecoming cloaks and veils?
> They are shrouds for the dead, not for those alive
> I say: "Death to those who bury women alive"
> If a few poets add their voices to mine
> A murmur of discontent will start
> With it women will unveil
> They'll throw off their cloak of shame, be proud
> Joy will return to lives
> Otherwise, as long as women are in shrouds
> Half the nation is not alive.[19]

This general condemnation of veiling on aesthetic, functional, and social grounds by constitutional revolutionary intellectuals reduced the issue to an artificial, often static, abstraction. It pieced together a distorted picture of veiling and denied it its dynamic dimension. It focused attention on the merely physical existence and uses of the veil. It ignored or denied its cultural, social, and psychological complexity, its power to express and organize male/female relationships. Religious clerics, it argued, were solely responsible for perpetuating the veil. Therefore, they alone became the target of anger. The following poem, entitled "Image of a Woman," by the celebrated contemporary poet, Iraj Mirza (1874–1925), illustrates this attitude:

> On the door of a traveler's inn
> A woman's face was drawn in ink
>
> From a reliable source of news
> The turban-wearers heard the news
>
> "Woe to our faith," they said
> "People saw a woman's face unveiled"
>
> From inside the mosque in haste
> To the front of the guesthouse they raced
>
> Faith and order at the speed of light
> Were disappearing when the believers arrived
>
> One brought water, another dirt
> With a veil of mud they covered the face
>
> Honor, scarce gone with the wind
> With a few fistfuls of mud was saved
>
> Religious laws thus saved from danger
> They returned to their homes to rest
>
> With a careless mistake, the savage crowd
> Like a roaring lion was jumping about

With her face unveiled, completely bare
Her chastity they tore apart

Her beautiful, alluring lips
Like a sugar candy they sucked and sucked

All of them, the men in town
To the sea of sin were drawn

The doors of paradise stood shut
The whole lot was hellward bound

The day of Judgement was at hand
Even the horn was blown at once

Birds from their nests, beasts from their lairs,
Even the stars in the sky went wild

Thus, before creator and created
The religious scholars remained exonerated

With saviors such as this bunch
Why are people still so cynical?[20]

For an increasing number of women, too, the veil became an emblem of social deprivation and oppression. Anger and revolt against it turned into a galvanizing force. Women came out of mansions and ghettos to fight for equal rights and the abolition of the veil. "A group of women were seen in broad daylight marching in the most crowded streets of Tehran and taking off their veils while shouting, 'Long live the Constitution. Long live freedom.'"[21]

In this same period, women poets, though not as a group, were also taking off their veils and struggling for what they perceived to be freedom. Shams Kasma'i (1883–1961), a pioneer of modernistic Persian poetry, unveiled herself in the city of Tabriz and was forced to endure much pain and agony as a result.[22] Jaleh Qa'em Maqam (1884–1946), Zand-Dokht Shirazi (1911–1952), and others used their writings to express their condemnation of the practice.[23] In fact, poetry became a forum for demands for equal rights by a wide spectrum of women.

Until the turn of the century, women's published literature was basically confined to poetry; and with few exceptions, the authors were educated women of the court and high aristocracy. But in the early decades of the twentieth century, a large and diverse group of women poets appeared on the Persian literary scene, creating a literature of their own and enjoying a fame that has been shared by few women in the history of classical literature. Although the works of these pioneering women have remained for the most part unexplored, they constitute a phenomenon of great significance in the development of the women's movement in Iran. Displaying unusual courage in articulating women's experience from women's perspectives, these women were dedicated to changing what they perceived to be the forces victimizing them. In their largely topical poetry, the veil became a target of rage, and unveiling became an expression of revolt elevated to the level of a panacea for all the ills of Iranian society. The vast majority of these poets attacked veiling whenever the occasion presented itself. Qa'em Maqam spoke reproachfully against the imprisonment of women behind "tar-colored" veils.

> His laughter is a dagger
> In my anguished body and soul
>
> Ah! Who am I? Just a "Weakling"
> Labeled with mockery and ridicule
>
> Alas! In this oppressive land
> A woman has no refuge, no justice
>
> Her life is a disgrace
> Because she is wrapped in a tar-colored veil.[24]

Eyewitness accounts, memoirs, political pamphlets, and newspaper clippings of the constitutional revolutionary period all prove that women were ardently involved in the revolution. Yet, in spite of their active role, the revolution, once won, failed to realize its goals for them. Although as early as 1911 an appeal for women's suffrage had been made in the House of Representatives, women remained disenfranchised—along with criminals, minors, and beggars—until 1963. In spite of the fact that compulsory education for girls was written into the constitution (article 19 of the Supplementary Fundamental Law of 1907), public schools for girls were not founded until 1918. As for veiling, public pressure made it a necessity, and those who stopped wearing a veil or advocated its banishment were still harshly punished. As late as 1928, "the Queen mother visited the shrine at [the city of] Qom wearing only a light *Chador* instead of the traditional black one; for her temerity, she was chided by one of the 'olama [religious scholars]. When he heard of the incident, an enraged Reza Shah went at top speed to Qom, strode into the shrine without removing his boots, and beat the offender with his riding crop."[25]

Finally, more than eight decades after women's attempts to unveil, Reza Shah Pahlavi (r. 1921–1941) ordered the mass unveiling of 1936. The issue of women's emancipation as symbolically represented by their unveiling was part of a major campaign against what came to be called the "obscurantism" and the "black reactionary nature" of the mosque. The state fully supported emancipation and saw women's backward status and especially their veiling as a major obstacle in its drive toward modernization. According to his daughter, Reza Shah

> decided to abolish the "chador," the traditional veil. Here again was an example of the paradox that was my father. Though I never felt he was willing to relax his strict control over us at home, he did make the historic decision to present the Queen, my sister Shams, and me, unveiled, to the population of Tehran. To Reza Shah, as to any Persian man, anything concerning his wife and family was a private matter. You could sooner ask him how much money he earned or how much his house cost before you could ask questions about his wife or daughters. At home my father was very much a man of an earlier generation (I remember he ordered me to change my clothes "at once" because I had appeared at lunch in a sleeveless dress). But as the King, he was prepared to put aside his strong personal feelings in the interest of bringing progress to his country.[26]

First, the Ministry of Education was instructed to take steps and prepare the ground for unveiling. Women inspectors were sent to girls' schools to encourage unveiling. In 1934, women teachers and students were encouraged to appear in schools unveiled. Another "innovation occurred in June 1935; the Prime Minister Foroughi gave a tea at the Iran Club for cabinet ministers and their under-secretaries and they were instructed to bring their wives along. Other mixed teas soon followed."[27]

But in its haste in this direction, the government attempted to eradicate the cultural institution of veiling through legislation. Eventually, in 1936, all women, regardless of age, personal and religious inclinations, or circumstances, were ordered out of their veils. The message was clear and nonnegotiable: no veiled woman was allowed on the streets of Tehran or of any provincial city. The female members of the royal family appeared unveiled in public. Civil servants were compelled to bring their unveiled wives to official ceremonies, "old friends and even kinsfolk then met each other's wives and daughters for the first time."[28]

Unveiling was to be fully implemented. Law enforcement agencies were directed to tear women's veils from their bodies. "Women wearing the *chador* were not allowed in cinema houses or in public baths, and taxi and bus drivers were liable to fines if they accepted veiled women as passengers."[29]

January 7, 1936, when unveiling became a royal decree, was considered such an important day that thereafter it was celebrated as Women's Day, that is, the day of "liberation" for women. (After the institution of the Islamic Republic, the same day was labeled "the day of shame," the day in which allegedly corrupt Western values and norms were imposed forcefully and brutally upon Muslim women.)[30] On this day Iran became the first Muslim country to outlaw the veiling of women. In the words of Bamdad:

> The scene of this great occasion was the (men's) Teacher Training College (now the Faculty of Education of Tehran University on Roosevelt Avenue). At the expressed command of the Shahanshah [King of Kings], it had been decided that all the women teachers in the capital should attend without veils. They duly made their way to the college.
>
> The authoress well remembers the looks of astonished disbelief on the faces of the men in the streets and the crowd lining the royal route when they saw some schoolmistresses walking by, unveiled. . . .
>
> On reaching the college, the schoolmistresses were shown to the places in its auditorium which had been allotted to them. Then, into this great hall, came the royal ladies. . . . Then, amid the applause of the assembled teachers, the wives of the ministers and generals entered and took their seats. Some of the elderly ladies among them, however, were visibly so upset by the loss of facial cover that they stood almost the whole time, looking at the wall and perspiring with embarrassment. Then, accompanied by the ministers and generals, came the king of the coun-

try, Reza Shah Pahlavi. The Shahanshah began his historic speech, which the women who were present still carry inscribed on their hearts, with the words "My mothers! My sisters!" and he ended by saying "Ladies, know that this is a great day, and use the opportunities which are now yours to help the country advance."[31]

This forced unveiling inflicted pain and terror upon those women who were not willing or ready to unveil.[32] To them, the veil was a source of respect, virtue, protection, and pride. It was a symbol of passage from childhood into adulthood. It was convenient, feminine, honorable. By wearing it, they conformed to a recognizable and cherished set of beliefs and sanctions. These women valued and respected the veil. They sought to undermine its banishment with all the ingenuity they could muster. Some refused to go out at all. Others, incapable of leaving home unveiled, in cases of emergency, such as a visit to the public bath, made their sons, husbands, or brothers carry them on their shoulders hidden in sacks. Some encouraged their husbands to get a temporary wife who would accompany them to official ceremonies;[33] others preferred divorce to appearing unveiled in public; according to Ayatollah Khomeini, many angered or terrified pregnant women miscarried their children.[34] Still other women, with their families, left Iran and sought asylum elsewhere.[35]

Many men were also deeply disturbed by the mass unveiling, and they were no less harshly treated. In her autobiography, *Faces in the Mirror,* Princess Ashraf Pahlavi writes: "When one mullah [religious cleric] publicly condemned the Shah for allowing the women of his family to show their faces, one of my father's generals responded with an equally public gesture: he pulled the turban (the symbol of his religious office) from the clergyman's head and then shaved his beard."[36]

In spite of the harsh methods adopted by the government to eradicate the veil, the institution of veiling proved to be stronger than the government. Soon the veil reappeared, perhaps less all-encompassing, but still a veil. Numerous women disregarded the government pronouncements and veiled themselves publicly. Finally, the ban was rescinded after Reza Shah's abdication in 1941. During its five years of enforcement the ban had caused repeated objections and even unrest. A book published in Iran in 1982, *Qiyam-e Gohar Shad* [Gohar Shad Uprising], claims that "more than two thousand (and up to five thousand) people were killed and fifteen hundred taken captive" in the shrine city of Mashhad alone due to the unveiling act.[37]

Although compulsory unveiling was forced and unwelcome exposure for some, for many others it was a cherished change. Women were finally able, and in fact encouraged, to participate in the public sector. Literacy greatly increased for women. For the first time women were admitted to Tehran University. They entered governmental and professional employment, where their numbers rose astronomically. "In 1976, of some 1,500,000 women in employment, about one-third had jobs in industry. . . . There has been a significant increase too in the number of women working in the service-based occupations."[38] The establishment of universal suffrage in 1963 allowed women to vote. The same year, six women were elected to the House of Representatives and two to the Senate. In 1976, Mahnaz Afkhami, head of the Women's Organization of Iran, became a member of the cabinet as minister of the newly established Ministry for Women's Affairs.[39] In short, women in large numbers left their traditional territory, the house, and entered the public, male, domain. No longer in their secluded houses, walled gardens, segregated spaces, no longer invisible behind their veils — voiceless and faceless — they altered the underlying structure of the society in which they lived.

Many people, however, could neither absorb, nor readily accept, nor quite ignore these profound changes. Return to Islam proved to be both a logical development and a reaction against the rising culture. Regarded as a fundamental threat to Islamic principles, veillessness became a focus of attention and wrath. Many argued that veiling should be reinforced to stop further dissolution of the Iranian identity and culture. The large numbers of fashionable women who wore veils during mammoth demonstrations before and after the revolution were making, among other things, a personal statement. Taking up of the veil was not only a sign of hostility to the shah or a rejection of Western domination, it also testified to the disturbing psychological dilemmas and cultural dislocations experienced by many.[40]

Thus, in the late sixties and seventies, Iran experienced a renewed interest in the veil. Not only did traditional women who had never relinquished the practice continue to veil themselves but many educated, hitherto unveiled women, voluntarily took up the veil. Newly veiled women became a novel feature of the Iranian cultural scene.[41] They could be seen in workplaces, in universities, even in the royal palace. Princess

Shahnaz, the daughter of Mohammad Reza Shah Pahlavi, covered her hair assiduously. One of the Queen's maids "had become very religious. 'She went from wearing a miniskirt to the veil,' said the Queen later."[42]

It is in such an atmosphere that the compulsory veiling took shape. I believe its implementation would have been impossible had it not been for the attraction the veil held for many as well as for the apathy and equivocal conduct of the educated elite. Many, it seems, were oblivious to fourteen decades of struggle to unveil and the high price already paid for the option. A veilless woman became the personification of cultural imperialism. Not only did many refuse to take a firm stand against forced veiling in the early stages of its implementation; on the contrary, they reprimanded and condemned those who openly objected to it. In the name of national independence, rejection of corrupt royalists, and in view of supposedly more important and pressing issues, they advocated and, in fact, practiced silence and conformity.

Most if not all of the political parties and groups believed like the Mojahedin-e Khalq that "to propose questions, which in the present circumstances are not part of the main problems of our society and movement is to cause deviation and the waste of forces and energies. It will provide opportunities and pretexts for plotting and agitation by the counter-revolution. Such is the debate aroused today by the question of *Hejab* [the veil]."[43]

The compulsory veiling thus became a reality and was imposed through different phases. Within a month after the revolution, on March 7, 1979, Ayatollah Khomeini proclaimed that working women should wear the Islamic form of modest dress. This led to the first massive wave of demonstrations. The regime retreated. Mr. Bazargan, then prime minister, announced that the left-wing troublemakers, corrupt royalists, and counterrevolutionary elements had distorted the ayatollah's statement. He emphatically assured women that there would be no compulsory veiling and that, in fact, the ayatollah believed in guiding rather than forcing women. Several other officials also argued that, in the spirit of Islam, veiling would only be encouraged and promoted rather than imposed by coercion or force.

Yet with the political consolidation of clerical rule, slowly but surely the veil became institutionalized again. First, it was made mandatory in all government and public offices in the summer of 1980. This move evoked only dispersed reactions and disorganized demonstrations, in contrast to the antiveiling demonstrations of 1979. The regime was encouraged, and three years later, in April 1983, veiling was made compulsory for all women, including non-Muslims, foreigners, and tourists.

The sociocultural implications of the veil, however, seem to have failed to maintain their traditional hold. The conventional equation: veiled/silent/absent proved to be no longer operative. Some veiled women are both publicly articulate and visible. In this shifting meaning of the veil, women are neither eliminated from communal life nor relegated to the domain of the private. They are voiced and ever so present in the public scene.

The veil has thus developed new connotations quite different from the traditional notions. It is argued, for instance, that the veil frees the country of alien ideologies and establishes women's independence from Western domination or styles.[44] Moreover, those who support the veil use every occasion to justify and glorify its use not only in religious or nationalistic terms but also in terms of interests serving women's own welfare. The veil, it is maintained, does not imprison women or limit their social mobility. On the contrary, it facilitates their access to social institutions without objectifying their sexuality. For, as Ayatollah Khomeini said, "What we don't want and what Islam does not want, is to make a woman an object, a puppet in the hands of men."[45] In this view, veiling protects woman. It is a rejection of all relations and beliefs that reduce her to the level of a naked yet sexy doll, an exploited yet presumably liberated commodity. It covers a woman like an oyster embraces a pearl. It saves her from man's uncontainable lust and unwelcome attention so that she can fully develop her potential.[46]

The veil, it is claimed, neither demands extravagance in clothing nor conveys gradation of wealth (although at different historical periods the quality of the fabric used and its color have indicated wealth and status). It can be worn over any dress. It also emphasizes femininity, makes the woman more alluring, and by its very nature allows the mystified imagination of men free play. And in this modernized argument for veiling, some of the bases for its practice are altered. Far from eliminating or attenuating the sexual appeal of women, the veil allegedly intensifies it. "Is a house with curtains better and more interesting or a house that lacks curtains and covering?"[47] asks 'Abdul Karim Biazar Shirazi. And the Western-educated, secular philosopher Dariush Shayegan believes that "when a veiled woman gracefully walks, she not only covers herself up but also makes her movements doubly-attractive. Indeed, her concealment both repels and attracts."[48] And in his much acclaimed and highly popular book, *Mas'ale-ye Hejab* [The Issue of Veiling], Ayatollah Mottahari quotes Alfred Hitchcock as having said in some unnamed "woman's journal":

> I believe a woman should be full of excitement and intrigue like a film. In other words, she should conceal her nature and make men rely on their imagination in order to discover her.
> Until a few years ago, Eastern women, because of the veil, were of and by themselves very alluring and this very allurement gave them incredible attraction. But gradually with their attempt to emulate Western women they unveiled themselves and decreased their sexual appeal.[49]

Yet, it is also argued with astounding certainty that the same seductive veil is an antiseductive device. It protects man from the potentially dangerous and highly vigorous sexual power of woman. Much time and energy are spent to establish woman's special aptness for lust. Arguments range from the allegedly scientific claim made by the first president of Iran, Abol-Hassan Bani-Sadr, that some sort of rays exude from her hair and excite men to lose control, to the more traditional argument that women have overwhelming sexual power and unquenchable sexual needs and desires.[50] Their whole body and especially their hair send out rays like radar in search of vulnerable men. The whole Muslim community should be protected from their active sexuality.[51] To focus attention on the inherent danger of women's sexual allure for men, the West is used as a handy example. Its alleged widespread fornication and adultery, which have presumably caused chaos, corruption, and all sorts of catastrophes, are seen as a direct result of women's veillessness.

It is really not clear who should be protected from whom. There is a paradox at the center of all of these arguments: does the veil protect or entice? On the one hand, man is represented as a creature with gargantuan sexual appetites, unable to control himself, a potential threat to any woman who through displaying her body might provoke or arouse him. The woman needs to be veiled in order to prevent him from succumbing to his own sexuality. Yet it is the veil itself that entices one to imagine what it hides. It teases and torments some men and protects others from what they cannot see.

Yet, far from being solely a matter between men and women, the veil is, in fact, an issue among men themselves. It is like a privacy screen, a demarcation of space where outsiders trespass at their own peril. Lack of trust between men seems to be an important factor even though it is barely, if ever, referred to in discussions of the origin and use of the veil. In the rare instances when reference is made to this underlying fear, the argument is camouflaged in political terms. Reza Barahani, for instance, maintains that men built high walls and pushed women behind the veil in order to protect them from "the Big Father, the Shah." "The possessive power of men," he writes, "built those walls around women and at the same time shrouded them in veils."[52]

In any event, the veil, it is argued, restricts erotic relations to legal partners. Ironically, though women are allegedly possessed by an uncontrollable sexual passion, men are offered numerous sanctified ways of indulging their sexual desires. Through polygyny (up to four wives at a time), serial unions (unilateral repudiation rights), and temporary marriages, men have a multiplicity of sexual relations at their disposal. Female sexuality, however, is only recognized, even encouraged, within the sanctified boundary of marriage. Celibacy is not approved of for women. Unlike the brides of Christ, who dedicate their lives to God and remain celibate, or the Buddhist nuns, Muslim women are not encouraged to remain virgins. However much valued and cherished, virginity is not an eternal ideal state for Muslim women. Although it is the most essential prerequisite of the ideal unmarried woman because it establishes her purity before marriage, it should not negate or deny her active sexuality after marriage. Even *Houris* [fairies] in paradise are not expected to abstain from sex. Promised in the Qor'an to faithful men, they are blessed with renewable virginity. No wonder there is no counterpart for the Virgin Mary in Islamic heritage.

Perhaps this accepting attitude toward sexuality in both sexes makes the veil useful in defining boundaries. The veil not only functions as one visible boundary between the sexes, presumably keeping "fire" and "cotton" (i.e., men and women) separate, it also maintains the social, or rather the natural, order. Refusing to view gender differences as culturally and ideologically determined, advocates of veiling see gender-constructed (social) roles as based on physiological differences.

This biologically oriented argument assumes a divine legitimacy. Men and women, it is argued, are created different for some specific reason.

To overlook this divine wisdom is morally wrong and socially disruptive. Westerners' concepts of equality between men and women are considered corrupt at best, impractical at worst. Western women might have attained some similarity of rights with men but certainly no equality. After all, the law of nature has made the two different on biological, psychological, and intellectual levels. The argument continues that women are weaker, have smaller brains, weaker nerves and senses, and are inherently emotional rather than rational. Similarity of rights denies the obvious. In a just Islamic society, accordingly, there is equality but no similarity of rights. According to a 1984 editorial of the women's journal *Zan-e Ruz* [Today's Woman]: today, the Muslim woman accepts the natural and hence the legal, social, and political differences between man and woman. She does not, however, accept any privileges between them except those acquired through doctrinal virtues.[53]

The separate-but-equal dogma accentuates the natural differences between the sexes and subtly blurs the possibility of important and major differences among women themselves. Like the veil, this line of argument denies a woman her individuality, categorizes her, and assigns to her one major role: motherhood. Woman's sense of devotion as a mother and her singleness of commitment to the domestic sphere remain her most valued role and value. This is best expressed in the image of the ideal woman created by the Islamic Republic. Textbooks, especially at the elementary level, have been changed in order to train the future Islamic citizen. In such textbooks, women occupy the traditional roles of wives and mothers at home. If they have a profession, it is one of the jobs deemed appropriate for a woman: teacher, nurse, secretary, or office worker.

The ideal role models presented by the Islamic Republic for Iranian women to emulate are Hazrat-e Fatemeh, the daughter of the Prophet Mohammad, and Hazrat-e Zeinab, his granddaughter. Hazrat-e Fatemeh is admired mainly for her female virtues as daughter, wife, and mother. Hazrat-e Zeinab is remembered for her militancy and active participation in what she thought to be a just struggle undertaken by her brother, Imam Hossein, to challenge the despotism of the caliph who had usurped power. Upon the martyrdom of her brother in A.D. 680, Hazrat-e Zeinab showed amazing courage, resilience, and eloquence in defending and pursuing his cause. In the words of the Iranian women's delegate to the United Nations Decade for Women Conference, "the Zeinabic way is to bear the message, to speak out against oppression and injustice."[54]

These two role models betray a fascinating contradiction in the ideal role of women within the Islamic Republic. On the one hand, the stress is on motherhood and singleness of commitment to family. On the other hand, there is the demand that women serve the state. Awakened to women's revolutionary potential, the Islamic Republic has had to change its stance and reinterpret religion according to those values and standards that are consonant with and serve to fulfill its present interests.

For instance, in the early sixties, many clerics, including Ayatollah Khomeini, objected to women's enfranchisement as un-Islamic. In postrevolutionary Iran, however, women's right to vote and be voted for are not only encouraged but religiously sanctified. Whereas before the revolution many religious figures objected to women's military training, by 1986 the Women's Defense Committee offered six months of intensive military training for interested students at universities and teacher-training institutes. Whereas birth control was banned in the early days of the revolution, it is in favor now because of Iran's amazingly high birth rate. Whereas discussion about woman's equality with man was once considered un-Islamic, now many praise Islam for "empowering women" and "putting them next and equal to men." Referring to women's active participation in society in the early years of Islam, Ayatollah Khomeini argued that women's access to public/social life deteriorated progressively:

> People say that for instance in Islam women have to go inside the house and lock themselves in. This is a false accusation. In the early years of Islam women were in the army, they even went to battlefields. Islam is not opposed to universities. It opposes corruption in the universities; it opposes backwardness in the universities; it opposes colonial universities. Islam has nothing against universities. . . . Islam empowers women. It puts them next to men. They are equals.[55]

The image of women fully veiled but carrying guns on their shoulders or participating in conventionally male arenas contrasts sharply with any traditional or simple definition of womanhood.[56] And herein lies the paradoxical nature of this neotraditionalism regarding women: veiled, but not excluded from the traditionally male domain, silent and obedient, yet at the same time outspoken and articulate like Hazrat-e Zeinab in the city of Kuffeh.

Thus the popular prediction that the Islamic Republic would strive to eliminate women from social and productive life and limit them to the four walls of the patriarchal household has not materialized. Intentions and causes aside, women have played an active, militant role in postrevolutionary Iran. Visible in the public arena, they have been negotiating boundaries. For example, traditionally, only men have interpreted the sources on which the practice of Islam is based. They have used the Qor'an, *Fegh* [jurisprudence], and especially the *Hadith* literature [the words and deeds attributed to the Prophet Mohammad and other imams] to define the status of women and to legitimize a male-dominated, male-centered social and political system portrayed as divinely instituted. Unarmed with masculinity and its concomitants (authority, money, legality, and especially the power of the written word), women have rarely been given a chance to challenge publicly the androcentric "Muslim" ideology that pervades Islamic institutions. Neither have they had the power to emphasize the Qor'anic passages that would support their struggle for the equal treatment of men and women.

This state of affairs seems to be changing in significant ways. Women are increasingly exercising control over how reality is defined by redefining their status from the theological to the political. Religiously oriented women discuss issues from within the Islamic tradition itself. For instance, the veil has never before been so thoroughly debated by women themselves and from such widely varying perspectives. Not only secular women but also religious women now debate the institution of veiling or methods of its implementation. Zahra Rahnavard, a prolific writer married to the Islamic Republic's fifth prime minister, Hossein Mussavi, questions the validity of imposing a dress code and restrictions of behavior on women only and wants the roots of the problem to be tackled:

> Unfortunately, after the Imam's message about purification of the workplaces and the country in general from the remnants of the imperial regime, a number of administrators, instead of tackling the roots of the problem, have emphasized one aspect out of proportion and have left other aspects in abeyance. The over-emphasized aspect is women's clothing and the imposition of *hejab* [Islamic modest dress] on them.

But we should remember that in Islam men are also required to observe modest dress and behavior.[57]

As for secular women, many have used all their ingenuity to circumvent the veiling ordinance. Some have left the country. Others, although jailed, publicly humiliated, and even flogged for their improper Islamic garments, continue to resist—in whatever way they find it possible—the veiling act. For those who write, especially women outside the country, opposition to the veil has emerged as a central theme. For them, the veil symbolizes social deprivation and oppression; it is an anachronism antithetical to progress. With anger, they oppose it and view all previous steps taken toward liberation as being eclipsed by this forced return to the Dark Ages, with which in their mind the veil is associated. Paralyzing inertia, they argue, inevitably results from being engulfed by this wall shrunk to a portable size. Sousan Azadi, after her escape from Iran, explains the sensation of being forcibly veiled in her autobiography, *Out of Iran:* "As I pulled the *chador* over me, I felt a heaviness descending over me. I was hidden and in hiding. There was nothing visible left of Sousan Azadi. I felt like an animal of light suddenly trapped in a cave. I was just another faceless Moslem woman carrying a whole inner world hidden inside the *chador*."[58]

For the overwhelming majority of women writing in exile, the veil is a mobile prison, a terrifying form of solitary confinement. Defiance of convention, flouting of masculine authority, or any challenge to patriarchal gender relations seems to start with opposition to the veil. Liberation becomes inseparable from unveiling. "Modern" becomes synonymous with "unveiled" and almost equivalent to "civilized." Calling the veil a symbol of subjugation and ignorance, Shusha Guppy, the author of the highly acclaimed *The Blindfold Horse,* equates discarding the "yards of black cloth" with dropping the chains. According to her, a "virus" had attacked the collective psyche of a nation when "in 1978, the black veil reappeared: there they were, women in their tens of thousands, wrapped in black, shaking their fists and shouting slogans, like an army of malignant crows in a nightmarish sequence of science-fiction film, presaging doom and destruction."[59]

If forced veiling is seen as the religious zealots' patriarchal response to women's improved status in the public domain, then women's resistance to it proves their continued struggle for freedom and emancipation. As A. Rahmani describes the situation in her short story entitled "A Short Hike":

> You must be a woman to understand how much of the efforts of this massive body of turpitude is directed toward the creation of devices to make women believe that they are contemptible. And if you, as the object of these attempts, fall into their trap, then you have accepted their values and will naturally fall apart. You have to interpret each rock and each shout of "Death to unveiled women!" as the sign of their desperate reaction to your resistance. As insignificant as it may seem to you, your struggle to hold up your chin and your endeavor to convince yourself that you exist, is an expression of our freedom—despite those vultures' attempt to reduce our existence to those of slaves whose only recognized right is to breathe. They want me to believe that I do not exist.[60]

In short, the forced veiling of 1983, like the compulsory unveiling of 1936, has not been entirely successful. True, authorities in both cases managed to coerce women to unveil or veil themselves in public, but they failed to suddenly revolutionize women's beliefs or to alter the underlying social structure according to their intentions. The veil might indeed be proclaimed as illegal or obligatory by the stroke of a pen whose edicts are supported by force or political and religious power; but the gestures, behaviors, and worldviews attached to years of wearing or not wearing the veil cannot be transformed so easily and overnight. Women might be, as they have been, veiled or unveiled by force; but they will remain enfolded and covered by physical and psychological traces of their modes of acceptance or rejection of the veil.

3

The Perils of Writing

*O*ranian women, for centuries, were suppressed physically and verbally by the conventions of the veil and public silence. The norms and values that regulated women's physical concealment applied equally to their literary expression. Theirs was a private world, where self-expression, either bodily or verbally, was confined within the accepted family circle. Exceptions aside, in Iranian society, a virtuous woman maintained a closed-in individuality that did not intrude into or merge with the outside world. Traditional propriety, *Hojb-o-Haya,* or *Sharm,* demanded that a woman's body be covered, her voice go unheard, her portrait never be painted, and her life story remain untold.[1] Public disclosure of any of these aspects of a woman's life was considered an abuse of privacy and a violation of societal taboos. Thus, a woman's physical invisibility was completed by her silence, her public nonexistence.

But if women were required to cover themselves, men were required to see that they remained covered. These conventions were upheld century after century, and punishments for disregarding them were many and varied. Paradigmatically, Majnun, the hero of the popular romantic epic, *Layla o Majnun* [Layla and Majnun], broke this rule by openly expressing love for an individualized, distinctive woman.[2] His verbal unveiling of Layla cost him dearly—he lost her and his sanity. Not that Majnun should not have sung love poetry. Persian literature abounds in this literary genre. But love poetry had to be ambiguous enough so that almost anything could be read into it. As a matter of fact, almost everything has been, from the real but anonymous woman to the symbolic woman who functioned as a source of inspiration for masculine spiritual realization and artistic expression. The aura of secrecy and ambiguity drawn around woman made her real character disappear, leaving in its place an abstraction. Indeed, because her characterization was unindividualized and even linguistically genderless (Persian language is not gender marked), it is practically impossible to guess not only the individuality but also the sex of the beloved in a large segment of Persian literature.

This cloak of secrecy that physically and verbally veils women is not confined to any one genre or era. It infuses the writings of men and women alike. It can be detected in famous and obscure, conventional and radical authors. It is not limited to a specific period or a particular genre. It pervades the imagination and finds its way to unpredictable spots. In Roy Mottahedeh's delightful fictional history of Iranian culture, *The Mantle of the Prophet,* published as recently as 1985, women are literally erased from the text. Not even marginalized, they are absent. In his explanation of this conspicuous nonappearance, Mottahedeh writes that "the reader may also notice how little is told of the adult family life of the figures prominent in the personal narrative. My Iranian friends were reluctant to speak about such matters, and I have respected their reticence. Ali Hashemi's [the protagonist] silences reflect his character as much as does his own narrative of his life."[3]

The public opacity of woman has even extended to her name. Traditionally, the mention of her proper name was considered inappropriate in public. Even among the twelve women alluded to in the Qor'an, none, other than Mary, mother of Jesus, is referred to by name. In the same tradition, men preferred not to mention their women's names in front of strangers. They devised a creative system of oblique reference when her name could not be avoided. *Manzel* [House], *Khaneh* [home], *'Ayal* [wife], or the name of her eldest son, among others, were used when a wife was to be addressed or spoken of in public.

This tradition lingers to this day. For instance, an avant-garde writer such as Jalal Al-e Ahmad, in his highly controversial and unconventional autobiography *Sangi bar Guri* [A Tombstone on a Tomb], published in 1980, is reluctant to refer directly to his wife, a respected and established writer in her own right, by her name.[4] The name Simin Daneshvar appears only once in the whole book, which seems to have been written under the watchful eye of some internal ancestral censor.

A Tombstone on a Tomb is the story of Al-e Ahmad's childlessness and an attempt to come to terms with what he sees as a failure of manhood—the failure to produce a child, preferably a son, who like a tombstone on a tomb will carry his name and his memory. It eloquently gives the personal and cultural context for understanding the dilemma of a son doomed ever to remain a son; a son who never discovers the power and pleasure of fatherhood. Although Daneshvar is present throughout the book as the other party to this ordeal, she is nonetheless repeatedly—more than forty times—referred to as "my wife." Interestingly enough, in her much shorter memoir, *Ghorub-e Jalal* [Jalal's Sunset], Daneshvar uses Al-e Ahmad's name more than one hundred times.[5]

Not surprisingly, and given the correspondence between physical and nonphysical repressions of her expression, a woman's voice was considered part of her *'Owrat* [pudenda] and subject to strict concealment. Her tongue, like her body, was surrounded by prohibitions and precautions. Exposure of either was considered a transgression, outside the bounds of allowable discourse. After all, both tongue and body can speak. Both have a language and a voice of their own. Both are powerful transmitters of messages. Both can be muted, mutilated, appropriated. No wonder both were exiled, for long years, to the realm of the private. "It is not permissible for a stranger [male] to hear the sound of a pestle being pounded by a woman he does not know," said the Islamic philosopher Ghazali. "If he [a man] knocks at the door, it is not proper for the woman to answer him softly and easily because men's hearts can be drawn to [women] for the most trifling [reason] and the greatest number of them. However, if the woman has to answer the knock, she should stick her finger in her mouth so that her voice sounds like the voice of an old woman."[6] Centuries later, another Islamic scholar, Ayatollah Khomeini, could maintain that "the conversation of a woman with a man in a provocative manner, the mellowing down of her expression, the softening of her talk, and the prettifying of her voice so that a heart-sick person is enticed is *Haram* [forbidden]."[7]

Although religious interdictions against women's public speech are invoked, defining it as sinful, there is no Qor'anic injunction demanding their silence. If biblical scripture ordered women to "keep silence in the churches. For they are not permitted to speak, but should be subordinate, as even the law says" (1 Corinthians 14:33–34), and if they were ordered to "learn in silence" (1 Tim. 2:11), no such edicts can be found in the Qor'an. And yet in Iran, the silence imposed upon women became an ordinance sanctioned by religion and extended to all domains of public life. Not by a small coincidence, Tahereh Qorratol'Ayn, who may be considered the founder of the tradition of women's literature in Iran, was strangled to death. The Persian term for strangulation, *Khafeh Kardan*, also means, or more commonly conveys, "suppressing, stifling, silencing."

It should be recognized that the expected silence of a woman is different from the silence of a man. His silence, when he chooses, may actually be the voice of authority or a means toward expressiveness. Jalal ed-Din Rumi, the thirteenth-century mystic who expressed and formulated an entire system of thought in monumental works of poetry, frequently refers to himself as *Khamush* [the silent one]. *Kalileh-o-Demneh* [Kalileh and Demneh], an ancient series of fables written to instruct and entertain, calls voluntary silence an invaluable jewel for a king. "Each word that jumps out of the prison of mouth will be as difficult to bring back as each arrow that is released from a bow. Silence is an invaluable jewel for a king."[8] This willed silence, for kings, poets, or commoners, is only maintained in specific places and at specific times. It is self-controlled and calculated, temporary, but most importantly, voluntary. In contrast, the silence imposed on women was sustained, demanded in all public places, sustained at all times, whether voluntary or not.

Actually, so important was a woman's silence, so cherished, that it became a key criterion of her beauty and desirability—the prerequisite of the ideal woman. The expression *Sangin o Samet* [solemn and silent], still in abundant use to this day, defines an ideal woman who is self-effacing rather than self-promoting, enclosed rather than exposed, mute rather than vocal. Persian literature abounds in eulogies about "gracefully silent" women. As the protagonist in Shahrnush Parsipur's *Zanan Bedun-e Mardan* [Women Without Men] describes his ideal mate, he echoes an age-old aesthetic model: "She is a girl, eighteen years of age, excessively beautiful, gracefully silent, bashful, timid, kind, industrious, diligent, modest, chaste, solemn, and neat. She wears her veil when in public and always casts her eyes down. She blushes all the time."[9]

The idealization of women's silence is by no means unique to one writer or another. Major and minor, traditional and modernist writers have paid their tribute, over and over again, to this ideal of feminine virtue and charm. Evidence that her silence continues to attract men may also be found in many contemporary works. Even a modernist novel such as *Buf-e Kur* [The Blind Owl] by Sadeq Hedayat equates woman's beauty with silence.[10] The ethereal girl, the only woman who excites the narrator's aesthetic admiration and desire and is his source of comfort and delight, is a perpetually silent woman. This nonthreatening, nonaggressive, irresponsive sleeping beauty is marked above all by her silence. Never throughout the whole novel does she talk. Her silence is complete and uninterrupted. It is her most distinctive and desirable attribute. Her demonical double, on the other hand, expresses herself profusely and earns herself the epithet *Lakateh,* the Bitch.

Interestingly enough, both the ethereal girl and her doll-like material counterpart, the storefront mannequin, two ideal woman protagonists in Hedayat's work, are contained and carried around in coffinlike suitcases. Mute, covered, and immobilized, they mesmerize. In a later short story entitled "The Doll Behind the Curtain," the narrator explains why the protagonist, Mehrdad, is so captivated by a statue rather than by a real woman: the statue was "always silent. She embodied all his ideals. She neither needed food nor clothing, neither nagged nor got sick; she had no expenses; she was always satisfied, always smiling, but above all she never talked; she never expressed an opinion."[11]

Not only did a woman's charm and allure depend to a large extent on her silence but the peace and happiness of the whole community also seemed to depend on her voicelessness. The prominent didactic thirteenth-century poet, Sa'di, is explicit about this feminine quality. In chapter 7 of *Bustan* [The Orchard], entitled "about education," and in chapter 8 of the best-known work of Persian prose, *Golestan* [The Rose Garden], called "manners of speaking," he writes: "Bid farewell to happiness in a house / From which a woman's voice can be heard out loud."[12]

Women are presumed to have no control over their tongues, which ceaselessly and compulsively move about and cause noise pollution. Others have to control their tongues for them. Women's public baths, where woman's loquacity runs riot, provide the evidence, the proof. These baths were meeting places for women where they spent long hours chatting, collecting and spreading news, finding new friends, expanding their networks of association. To compare a gathering to a woman's bath, *Mesl-e Hammam-e Zananeh* [like a woman's public bath], has come to mean loud babel, hubbub, chaos, commotion, uproar, meaningless noise.

No wonder a long-tongued woman *[Zan-e Zaban Deraz]* is the ultimate inverse of the ideal woman.

It is not surprising that given the social and symbolic constraints on women's self-expression, exceptionally few women could or perhaps even wanted to opt for breaking this ancestral silence. Our glorious classical heritage yields not numerous successful women writers. Even those few who, against all odds, managed to nurture their creativity were denied any readership. Layla, the cherished beloved of classical literature, was an accomplished poet. According to the twelfth-century poet Nezami Ganjavi, "now Layla was not only a picture of gracefulness, but also full of wisdom and well versed in poetry. She, herself, a pearl unpierced, pierced the pearls of words, threading them together in brilliant chains of poems." Yet, these brilliant chains of poems were delivered to the wind, which remained Layla's sole privileged audience. "Secretly she collected Majnun's songs . . . committed them to memory and then composed her answers on scraps of paper which she entrusted to the wind."[13] If Majnun's poems could be collected and committed to memory, no such destiny awaited Layla's poems. Neither Majnun nor anyone else for that matter ever saw the "body" of her writing. Composed and written on little scraps of paper, her poems reached no one. They became dust in the wind.

Deploring the imposed silence foisted upon her, Layla lamented the many restrictions placed upon her verbal expressiveness. "He is a man, I am a woman. . . . He can talk and cry and express the deepest feelings in his poems. But I? I am a prisoner. I have no one to whom I can talk, no one to whom I can open my heart: shame and dishonor would be my fate."[14] Centuries and many suppressed voices later, the contemporary poet Forugh Farrokhzad could reiterate the same grievance. "I wanted to be a 'woman,' that is to say a 'human being.' I wanted to say that I too have the right to breathe and to cry out. But others wanted to stifle and silence my screams on my lips and my breath in my lungs. They had chosen winning weapons, and I was unable to laugh anymore."[15] Or again, in a poem from the *Rebellion* collection, Farrokhzad writes:

> It was I who laughed at futile slurs,
> The one that was branded by shame

> I shall be what I'm called to be, I said
> But oh, the misery that "woman" is my name.[16]

Both the fictive character, Layla, and the poet, Farrokhzad, talk of *Sharm* as an obstacle to their public expressivity; they talk of the *Sharm* that accompanies their voice heard in public, the *Sharm* of transgressing feminine proprieties.

Deeply rooted in the Iranian culture, *Sharm,* or *Hojb-o-Haya,* is as difficult to define as it is pervasive. *Sharm* maintains distance, rules the social world, and stretches into the utmost reaches of the individual's psyche. It involves both an internal state and an external behavior. It accompanies feelings of embarrassment, shyness, or self-restraint and a woman's public self-erasure. Although "shame" or "charm" are wholly inadequate translations for it, they nonetheless cover the wide spectrum of meanings that the word conveys. *Sharm* not only perpetuates ideals as values in moral terms, it also strengthens the ideology of modesty by giving it aesthetic significance. As Salman Rushdie puts it, *Sharm* is a "short word, but one containing encyclopaedias of nuance. It was not only shame . . . but also embarrassment, discomfiture, decency, modesty, shyness, the sense of having an ordained place in the world, and other dialects of emotions for which English has no counterparts."[17]

Sharm in this environment is one of the main constellations of attributes that qualifies a woman as beautiful and desirable. Ferdowsi (d. ca. 1025), in his monumental epic, *Shah Nameh* [Book of Kings], enumerates the necessary qualifications for the ideal woman and gives foremost importance to her *Sharm.* It takes precedence over wealth, physical beauty, and fertility.

> Three qualities make a woman
> Fit for the throne of superiority
>
> The first is her *Sharm* and her wealth
> With which to adorn her husband's house
>
> The second is her procreation of auspicious sons
> Who will increase her husband's delight
>
> The third is her face and her figure
> Coupled with her covered hair.[18]

It is *Sharm*, this short, untranslatable word with encyclopedias of meanings and implications, that women writers had to overcome. If walls impeded their movement and silence concealed their voices, *Sharm*, combining both woman's silence and immobility, was a major barrier to women's prospect for becoming writers. *Sharm* enclosed them, engulfed them. It silenced them. It buried women's creativity in layers upon layers of silence and secrecy. As an ideal that combined such virtues as chastity, silence, seclusion, and obedience, it immobilized their bodies, muted their voices. It sanctioned the submissive silences of domesticity. One need only glance at the literary reception accorded to pioneering women to see that many talented women writers were paralyzed or plagued by potential and actual allegations of verbal promiscuity and shamelessness just because they wrote. Even to this day, Shahrnush Parsipur, a foremost novelist, is bitterly criticized by some for her lack of *Sharm*. It is hardly surprising that the most negative criticisms of her last popular novel, *Women Without Men*, revolve around the author's alleged unconcern for *Sharm*. "This book is written with total disregard for moral considerations and utter shamelessness *[Bisharmi]*" writes one critic.[19] "The only art of this writer is her guts to say things that others have shame in expressing," complains another.[20]

Many women writers have implicitly or explicitly rebelled against this feminine ideal that condemned them to *Sokut-o-Sokun* [silence and immobility]. Forugh Farrokhzad is perhaps the most vocal among them.

> Don't put the seal of silence on my lips
> I have untold tales to tell
> Take off the heavy chain from my foot
> I am disturbed by all of this.[21]

And again in the poem entitled "O Land Bejeweled" she openly ridicules the "angels" and their plans for immobility and silence.

> I know the art of "good writing"
> I have stepped on the field of existence
> Amid the creative masses
> Who own in place of bread
> A horizon vast and open
> A horizon, geographically bound

In the North by that lush and verdant Square
Called "The Rifleman's Square,"
In the south by the ancient "Hangman's Square,"
Extending to the thickly crowded "Canon Square."

And from sunrise to sunset
Beneath its safe and secure sky
Six hundred and seventy-eight huge plaster swans
Along with six hundred and seventy-eight angels
Angels made of earth and water
Proclaim their plans for stillness and silence.[22]

By exposing their bodies and their voices (oral or written), women writers transgressed feminine proprieties that shut them out of the public domain. The poet Owhad ed-Din Owhadi (b. about 1271) cannot forgive the presumptuousness of such a woman who intrusively crosses boundaries and enters male territory by writing. He goes so far as preferring that women die rather than gain access to writing:

The shroud her paper, the grave her inkpot
They should suffice if she insists on knowledge.

Keep away from the pen woman's obstinacy
You write, why should she?

She who has not produced Al-Hamd
Why expect her to write Vis-o-Ramin?[23]

For artistic talent to blossom, certain conditions are required. Iranian women lacked the two essential conditions for creativity that Virginia Woolf insisted on: a room of one's own and five hundred pounds a year.[24] Even though no legal restrictions are placed on an Iranian woman for buying and selling goods, for lending or borrowing money, for engaging in any transaction without her husband's or legal guardian's approval; and although Islam has granted her economic independence and the privilege to handle her own property, inheritance, and money; still, since she has been almost completely excluded from the public political arena and sources of public institutional power, her "theoretical" economic independence has not afforded her the independence, authority, and respected privacy that Woolf considered a prerequisite for a woman to become a writer.

Literary history alleges that, with a few exceptions, up to the modern era only the educated women of the court and the upper classes had a chance to develop their literary and public artistic potentials. With few other outlets to exercise their creative energies, such women resorted to poetry. Out of the 107 poets of *Az Rabe'e ta Parvin* [From Rabe'e to Parvin], an inclusive and reliable anthology of women poets in Iran, 43 are members of the court, and the rest belong almost entirely to the upper class.[25] (Amazingly, 15 of these poets were wives and daughters of one king, Fath 'Ali Shah of the Qajar dynasty. Perhaps he should be considered one of the earliest husbands in recorded Persian history to have encouraged his wives in their literary endeavors.)[26]

But even those exceptionally few women who had relative economic independence and perhaps even rooms of their own could not easily escape their culture's expectation of *Hojb-o-Haya*. This interdiction to any form of public self-exposure functioned on many fundamental levels. For instance, it kept many women away from education—not a minor requirement for a writer—because education for long was associated inversely with women's chastity. In fact, "women's literacy was such a social stigma," writes Eliz Sanassarian, "that many women tended to hide their literacy from others. Naser al-Din Shah (r. 1848–1896), for example, reportedly had eighty-five wives, some of whom could read and write; however, none would make their knowledge known to him. Some would read his memoirs (since he wrote them in their presence at night) and would serve as spies for other members of the court."[27]

As a general rule, women were barred from education until the turn of the twentieth century.[28] It was believed that education was useless for women as well as an agent of corruption. Presumably, it caused a loss of control over their minds and sexuality. It made them *Bisharm* [shameless, charmless]. Amazingly, this interdiction was legitimized through religion in spite of the fact that there is no Qor'anic injunction against women's education. As a matter of fact, the *Nabavi Hadith* [authoritative narrative attributed to the Prophet Mohammad] recommends the pursuit of knowledge by all Muslims regardless of their gender. "It is incumbent upon all Muslims—male and female—to seek knowledge throughout life, even if it should lead the seeker to China," said the Prophet Mohammad, rejecting women's illiteracy or seclusion. Yet today, Muslim women throughout the world have a very low literacy rate. Even with recent compulsory education in some countries, the gap between boys' and girls' enrollment remains alarmingly large.[29]

In Iran, where "the *madrassehs* made their definitive appearance (after a century of uncertainty and largely unsuccessful attempts to appear) in the late eleventh century, at least a hundred years before their Western counterparts, the European Universities,"[30] girls were not admitted even to elementary schools until the turn of the present century. In enlightened families, fathers and husbands took it upon themselves to educate their daughters or wives. Some hired private tutors. No institutions for women's education existed.

The first girls' school, the American Girls School, was established in Iran in 1874 by an American Presbyterian missionary group. It was attended at first by non-Muslims. Two Muslim girls entered the school in 1891, seventeen years after its establishment, for the first time. Some sixteen years later, the first Iranian school for girls, *Namus* [Honor], was founded by Tuba Azmudeh. Several pioneering women started other girls' schools throughout Iran. They all confronted enormous hardships, apathy, and antagonism. The experience of Mah-Soltan Amir-e Sehhi, the founder of one of the first girls' schools, was shared by many others:

> The first problem was the unwillingness of landlords to lease a house for the school, which they imagined would be a center of corruption. After a house had been found and the landlord had been reassured, certain people in the locality began to stir up opposition and cause trouble. They several times removed the school signboard or threw stones at it . . . neighbors used to get loiterers—very often psychopaths who then prowled the streets as there were no lunatic asylums—to walk into the school's premises and grin at the terrified girls, while they themselves would gather outside the gateway to enjoy the spectacle and jeer. In reply to complaints from the school's governors, they stated that the best way to avoid further trouble would be to close this "den of iniquity" and let no more girls through its gate.[31]

Girls' schools were considered "dens of iniquity," "centers of corruption," and a curious reverse relationship between female chastity and education was established more forcefully than ever before. "Defamatory songs in versified slang accusing the girls of unchastity were composed and spread about."[32] Soon, women's education became a symptom of sexual corruption and defilement. "The clergy accused these schools of being centers of prostitution and corruption. In many cases the schools were attacked and looted by angry mobs aroused by religious leaders."[33] And because women's chastity was and still is of crucial importance because of its associations with economic concerns (i.e., inheritance) as well as with norms for segregating and subordinating women, the devastating effects of such charges need no elaboration.

Women's chastity represented masculine power, wealth, and authority. As the property of fathers, brothers, and husbands, it was under strict surveillance and not negotiated lightly. Hence, we find the anxious efforts of the founders of these schools to justify female education without challenging the supreme value and importance of women's chastity. The selection of names for these schools is one proof of this attempt at ideological rationalization, compromise. The schools that followed *Namus* [Honor] had names no less revealing in their rhetoric: *'Effatiyeh* [House of Chastity], *'Esmatiyeh* [House of Purity], *Maktabkhaneh-ye Shari'at* [School of Holy Law], *Ehtejabi-ye* [Place of Seclusion], and *Nosratiyeh-ye Pardegian* [Nosratiyeh School for Veiled Girls].

The association of women's education with unchastity lingered on, however, and decades later, in December 1979, Mrs. Farrokhru Parsa, the first woman to serve in the Iranian cabinet as the minister of education from 1968 to 1974, was executed on the charge of "expansion of prostitution, corruption on earth, and warring against God."[34] She was the first prominent woman politician to be executed in Iran. The very extremeness of the response to what Mrs. Parsa stood for is illuminating because in its exaggerated form it reveals concealed and more subtle cultural apprehensions about women's education.

In such an environment, to become a writer was not an easy task. Denied easy access to education, cloistered indoors, hidden behind veils and walls of brick and silence, it was difficult for women to cultivate their creative potentials. Although they perfected the arts of cookery, weaving, story telling, and other domestic arts, they could not develop their talents in the public domain. Out of the various public art forms (music, painting, sculpture, photography, and cinematography), literature proved to be the most accessible to women. Their sporadic entrance into the literary arena can be explained partly by literature's being the most private of the public art forms. Rushdie elaborates on its relative freedom from external control: literature is "the art least subject to external control, because it is made in private. The act of making it requires only one person, one pen, one room, some paper. (Even the room is not absolutely essential.) Literature is the most low-technology of the art forms. It requires neither a stage nor a screen. It calls for no interpreters, no actors, producers, camera crews, costumiers, musicians."[35]

Poetry, out of all literary genres, proved to fit most closely women's circumstances and possibilities.[36] Not only is poetry thoroughly integrated in Persian daily life, it can also be produced and transmitted in the privacy of the home without venturing into the social, economic, and political public world barred to women. Perhaps poetry does not demand the uninterrupted time, concentration, and leisure required by other literary genres. Also, its highly stylized and formulaic nature makes it ideal for expressing the otherwise inexpressible. By no small coincidence has poetry been for so long the main vehicle for women's literary creativity—in fact, until recently, their only acknowledged contribution to Persian literature.[37]

Almost invisible up to a few decades ago in the mainstream of Persian literature, women have broken this spell of invisibility coincidentally with their attempts to unveil. Take, for example, the mid-nineteenth-century act of unveiling by Tahereh. Wanting to give body to her voice and voice to her body, Fatemeh Baraghani, better known as Tahereh Qorratol'Ayn, publicly unveiled herself, as she unveiled her voice in her poetry. Tahereh used her self as text and context, as a medium through which to break out of the absence and the silence that concealed her culturally. Her act of unveiling and her poetry were assertions of individuality and distinctiveness in an age that demanded conformity and anonymity from women.

But soon, women's unveiled voices and bodies became signs of contamination; expressions of unleashed sexuality; proofs of religious, sexual, and literary transgressions. Indeed, the exposure of the body of their writing, like exposure of their own bodies, proved to be a costly enterprise. Women paid for their literary unveiling with reputations of immorality, promiscuity, even heresy. Struggling in isolation, they were locked behind bars as lunatics, driven to suicide, forced into exile.

Fittingly, *Savushun,* the first novel written by a woman, brings this cost into focus in the shape of the tragic fate of Miss Fotuhi, its anti-heroine. Rejecting blind obedience, stubbornly claiming her freedom of choice, and irrepressible in her desire to express herself, Miss Fotuhi unveils herself publicly: she uncovers herself and writes. Her "deviant" behavior, however, soon comes to be perceived as a threat to the society at large, not to be tolerated.[38] Facing increasing hardship and apathy, she eventually ends in an asylum.

> When normal, Miss Fotuhi had a productive pen. She published articles for women's emancipation and against male oppression in local news-papers. She even managed a journal in which she invited girls to awaken. Miss Fotuhi should not be underestimated. She was the first woman to wear a colored veil and the first to discard the "black shroud," as she would call the veil. The mass unveiling was not proclaimed yet when she set aside even her colored veil. When she was feeling fine, Miss Fotuhi had confided to Zari that no one valued her, that men were not ready to accept a woman of her kind, that they first thought she was honey and when they wanted to stick their fingers in the honey and she told them she was off limits, they ridiculed her or ignored her. And sud-denly, she would scream: "They drove me crazy! They drove me crazy!"[39]

Had Miss Fotuhi not responded to the urge to remove her veil and to use her pen, had she controlled her tongue, had she silenced her voice, she could have probably avoided her tragic fate.[40] Like Zari, the heroine of *Savushun,* she could have lived a "normal" life. Although Miss Fotuhi may be thought to serve many different functions in the novel, a major one is to serve as a "double" for Zari.[41] She is a distorted mirror image of Zari's own repressed desires and propensities for independence. She is an unruly surrogate for Zari's docile self. She presents a warning as well as a model.

Although the author, Simin Daneshvar, does not idealize insanity or recommend withdrawal and confinement, she portrays Miss Fotuhi's insanity sympathetically. She presents her madness as a revolt against the constraints confining her life and her search for liberation as doomed. Miss Fotuhi's will broken, she is an unfulfilled woman, a suppressed writer. Confined to the asylum and isolated, she is forced to become another woman without a proper name, without a story. Labeled and filed away, her voice is erased from any public expression. Her body and voice locked behind bars, she is declared null, void. Trapped, with no exit, she is captured in a world of madness. Abandoned by others, she abandons herself; unrecognized by others, she becomes unrecognizable to herself. Literally and literarily, she gets buried alive.

But Daneshvar saves Miss Fotuhi and the women she represents from vanishing into oblivion. By telling her story, Daneshvar makes sure she leaves a trace behind. Miss Fotuhi might represent failure as a writer, but in her is voiced the subjectivity of her madness as an ultimate discursive defiance. And, indeed, a madness articulated by a woman was nonexistent in Persian literature before Daneshvar's story of Miss Fotuhi. Woman's madness was covered up like her body and her voice.

Although folk culture has it that women lack logic and are generically a bit on the crazy side, still this accepted feminine feature is not taken to the extreme of lunacy. *Zanha yek dandeh kam darand* [women lack a rib] is used as a clear, divinely ordained indication of women's lacks, including logic. Interestingly enough, in the Qor'an woman was neither an afterthought nor created out of man's crooked rib. Adam and Eve were created congruently. But the Judeo-Christian version of the creation story had such an appeal for the Iranian psyche that it was given credence over the Islamic version, and Eve was believed to have been created out of Adam's rib. Although the relation between ribs and logic is not quite clear to me, still if Eve was created out of Adam's rib, it is Adam who should be missing a rib. Yet, in an act of symbolic displacement, it is Eve and, by implication, all women who are viewed as lacking a rib and thereby, logic. In any event, although woman's irrationality is accepted as part and parcel of folk wisdom, her madness rarely became a subject of public discourse.

To return to Miss Fotuhi, she portrays the tragic fate of a woman who angrily rejects silence and being closed in. She reminds the reader, as the other women in the novel do not, that the price for self-expression is exorbitantly high for women. Miss Fotuhi is a tribute to all stifled women writers. She bears witness to the literal and literary suppression of women who, like her, have transgressed their allotted boundaries and have paid for that transgression with their lives and art, punished ultimately by outside or inside silences.

Persian literature is not filled with only the painful silences of women, however. In it can also be found the voices of women who refused to be crucified on the cross of ideal femininity constructed for them by Iranian society and culture—women who declined to remain selfless to the point of extinction from the literary arena and who by demanding formal and authorized access to public discourse, rebelled against the hegemonic figure of female selfhood; women who challenged patriarchal authorship and, through it, patriarchal authority; women whose works chronicle voices regained, but whose lives bear the scars of much suffering, conflict, and sorrow.

The price pioneering women writers paid for their transgression was very high. Tahereh, the precursor of Iranian women's literary tradition, was charged with heresy and executed at the height of her creativity when only thirty-six years of age. Parvin E'tessami, the first woman who published a poetry collection, died at the age of thirty-four of a mysterious typhoid fever. Taj-os Saltaneh, the first woman known to have written an autobiography, attempted suicide three times. The poet Zand-Dokht Shirazi died at the age of forty-three, an early death caused by overwork and mental depression.[42] Forugh Farrokhzad, a foremost poet who died in a car accident at the age of thirty-two, lived a life marked by bouts of severe depression, by nervous breakdowns, and by attempted suicide. She "ingested a container of Gordenol sleeping tablets. Her maid discovered her in time, and she was revived."[43] The novelist Mahshid Amirshahi slashed her wrist. She, too, was discovered in time and lived to write about her attempted suicide in the short story entitled "After the Last Day." In this autobiographical piece, Amirshahi talks for the first time about a woman's attempted suicide: "And even now I don't want to talk of that incident. It is still too soon. The stitches are not taken out yet and I feel pain and weakness. I might not talk about it later on either. Besides, what is there to talk about? Should I tell you how I tried to commit suicide but did not succeed? That's ridiculous. Suicide is a very heroic and beautiful act provided it is carried through. If one doesn't die it becomes ridiculous."[44]

Suicide for these women was ultimately an idiom of public defiance as well as an expression of individual despair. Other women writers in other parts of the world have also resorted to suicide. With her pockets full of rocks, Virginia Woolf drowned herself and her voice in a river. A few months later, in another part of the world, disillusioned and embittered, Maria Tsvetaeva hanged herself in the Russian countryside. In still some other corner, another poet, Sylvia Plath, fatigued and frustrated, stuck her head and her creative energies in an oven. Anne Sexton drove into her garage, closed the door, and left the motor running. And thus have many women writers committed their ultimate act of insurgency and authored their own deaths.

Perhaps one can consider pioneering women writers as social and cultural mutants and take cognizance of the fact that not all mutants survive. But even if women survived, their struggle for identity as writers entailed a life of continuous rebellion against stereotypes of women's place in both society and literature. Often, the woman who takes her creativity seriously is no longer the woman who renounces her art in favor of her family. Accounts of the lives of contemporary women writers in Iran, as well as their writing, attest to the feelings of sadness, anxiety, dislocation, loneliness, and guilt associated with this renunciation of traditional roles as wives and mothers.[45] Whatever else they are about, their literature portrays, with a terrifying consistency, the perils of writing.

Many writers have given expression to the special problems confronted by women artists in the friction between society's expectations, claims of love and family, and demands of creativity. Although ideally one would like to discard this apparent irreconcilability, in practice it seems impossible to do so. The very identity of women has been defined in terms of their dependencies and obligations within the institutions of family and marriage as daughter, sister, wife, or mother. Art chosen as a vocation could clearly conflict with these more traditional occupations.

In the West, full-length books have been dedicated to the dilemma of the woman artist and her attempts to combine woman's nurturing roles and woman's art. *Corinne* by Mme. de Staël, *Aurora Leigh* by Elizabeth Barrett Browning, *The Story of Avis* by Elizabeth Stuart Phelps, and *The Golden Notebook* by Doris Lessing, among others, have addressed this issue with eloquence, sensitivity, and urgency. They portray how women artists have been deprived of the opportunity to combine the joys and comforts of home and family and of fulfilling their talent and potential. The woman who wants to be a poet, writes Suzanne Juhasz, "is in a double-bind situation, because she is set up to lose, whatever she might do. The conflict between her two 'selves' is an excruciating and irreconcilable war, when both sides are in fact the same person. If she is a 'woman,' she must fail as a 'poet'; 'poet,' she must fail as 'woman.' Yet she is not two people. She is a woman poet whose art is a response to, results from, her life."[46]

And indeed, a bird's eye view of the life and work of most women writers — in the East or West — conveys the impression that, until recently, women have too often been deprived of the right of both creative achievement and the joys of families.

An overview of the lives of the better-known contemporary Iranian women writers indicates that the choice of literature as one's vocation is one that requires a drastic shifting of priorities and, ultimately, of one's entire way of life. So far, social conditions and expectations have made it difficult for women, especially women with family and children, fully to develop artistic gifts. Tahereh Qorratol'Ayn abandoned her husband and her three children. Parvin E'tessami remained married for only a few months. Taj-os Saltaneh "was unhappy in her married life, which soon ended in divorce. She then had to face many difficulties and anxieties. Her daughters were taken away from her to live with their father's next wife."[47] Simin Daneshvar didn't have a child. Mahshid Amirshahi, Goli Tarraqi, and Shahrnush Parsipur are divorced. Tahereh Saffarzadeh, now remarried, was divorced for many years. Farrokhzad, after a short married life, lost forever the custody of her only son.

The seeming irreconcilability of family life with the cultivation of artistic gifts is not confined to Iranian women.[48] The realities of women's literary history in the West have led Tillie Olsen to conclude that:

> In the last century, of the women whose achievements endure for us in one way or another, nearly all never married (Jane Austen, Emily Brontë, Christina Rossetti, Emily Dickinson, Louisa May Alcott, Sarah Orne Jewett) or married late in their thirties (George Eliot, Elizabeth Barrett Browning, Charlotte Brontë, Olive Schreiner). I can think of only four (George Sand, Harriet Beecher Stowe, Helen Hunt Jackson, and Elizabeth Gaskell) who married and had children as young women. All had servants.
>
> In our century, until very recently, it has not been so different. Most did not marry (Selma Lagerlof, Willa Cather, Ellen Glasgow, Gertrude Stein, Gabriela Mistral, Elizabeth Madox Roberts, Charlotte Mew, Eudora Welty, Marianne Moore) or, if married, have been childless (Edith Wharton, Virginia Woolf, Katherine Mansfield, Dorothy Richardson, H. H. Richardson, Elizabeth Bowen, Isak Dinesen, Katherine Anne

Porter, Lillian Hellman, Dorothy Parker). Colette had one child (when she was forty).[49]

Although the option not to get married has not been a socially viable alternative for Iranian women writers—every prominent Iranian woman writer has been married at some point—most of them have not remained married very long. And although many writers included in the few anthologies of Iranian women writers are married and have children, the overwhelming majority are either divorced or have no children to take care of. Is it mere coincidence, or is it symptomatic that a sustained commitment to creative art cannot be reconciled with a simultaneous commitment to family obligations?

The biographies of many writers seem to answer unequivocally that, for artistic talents to flourish, complete dedication is required. The poet Ferdowsi said that he suffered for thirty years in order to produce *Shah Nameh,* a masterpiece of Persian literature. The poet Hafez (d. 1390) talked about the forty years he fully dedicated to the writing of his *Divan,* another masterpiece. Indeed we can repeat with Tillie Olsen that "substantial creative work demands time, and with rare exceptions only full-time workers have achieved it. Full-timeness consists not in the actual number of hours at one's desk, but in that writing is one's profession, practiced habitually, in freed, protected, undistracted time as needed, when it is needed. Where the claims of creation cannot be primary, the results are atrophy, unfinished work, minor effort and accomplishments; silences."[50]

Persian literature abounds in such silences, atrophies, unfinished works, minor efforts and accomplishments of women who did not succeed in killing the "angel in the house."

Virginia Woolf confessed she had to kill the "angel in the house," that ideal Victorian Lady who was immensely "sympathetic," "charming," "unselfish," who "excelled in the difficult arts of family life," who "sacrificed herself daily." She had to kill her in self-defense and in order to save the writer within her, or else the "angel" would have killed her and "plucked the heart out of her writing."[51] Art demands constant toil, incessant work, and undistracted time. "Until you reach your liberated and free self, isolated from the constricting selves of others," said Farrokhzad, "you will not accomplish anything. . . . Art is the strongest love. It avails itself only to those who thoroughly surrender their whole existence to it."[52]

The lives and works of contemporary women writers in Iran depict the tension and frequent paralysis that result from confronting such conflicts. But nowhere in Persian literature is this conflict more fully explored than in the poetry of Farrokhzad. The agonizing dilemmas of the woman artist, the conflicts between a woman's creative urge and her femininity are dramatized in all five of her poetry collections.

In *Captive*, Farrokhzad explores the nature and the magnitude of the problems she faces as a woman and a poet. If she denies her poetic impulses, she is not living up to her own standards and ideals. If she pursues her poetic career, she is not living up to the traditional female roles. In many of the poems of this collection, Farrokhzad depicts this split within herself between the poet who defines herself in her vocation and the traditional woman who defines herself only through her relationships with others, especially her husband and her son.

> Every morning from behind the bars
> My child's eyes smile at me
> As I begin happily to sing,
> His kissing lips near mine.
>
> O God! If I need to fly out one day
> From behind these lonesome bars
> How will I answer this child's crying eyes?
> Let me be, a captive bird am I![53]

Slowly and painfully, the devoted artist triumphs. The poet resolves the duality of commitments and decides to pursue a poetic career. Neither doubts, nor fears, nor ingrained beliefs in, nor nostalgia for the comforts of dependent femininity stop her from making poetry her vocation. In one of the last poems of *Captive*, Farrokhzad explicitly acknowledges her determination fully to dedicate her life to poetry:

> I know happiness has been driven
> From that distant house
> I know a weeping child mourns
> His mother's loss.

> Yet, fatigued and despaired
> I set off on a road of hope,
> Poetry is my love, my lover
> I leave here to go to it.[54]

From this point onward, after her revolt against the roles and the rules she found stultifying, Farrokhzad presents her choice of a poetic career as a sacrifice to the *Elaheh-ye Khun Asham* [bloodthirsty goddess] of poetry, a submission to forces stronger than herself. The lack of options, mainly of an option that would allow her to reconcile home and family with a poetic career, causes much pain for the young poet. The poem entitled "Offering" is an eloquent expression of the sacrifices a poet has to make to tend her art:

> You seem quite oblivious of the sufferings
> You've inflicted upon your disciple
> You instilled your love in her
> And tore her apart from everything else.
> . . . .
> Other than these two tearful eyes,
> What have you left me? Tell me!
> O poetry—bloodthirsty Goddess—
> Stop. Enough sacrifices.[55]

The high price she has paid to tend her poetic impulses occupies the foreground of Farrokhzad's poetry and agonizes her to her last days. The poem "Green Delusion" is undoubtedly one of the most eloquent statements of the sacrifices she had to make for her art. It is an intense and agitated poem, an excruciating evocation of a woman who knows only too well that the price she has paid for her success has been her most valuable emotional bond. It is the tormented cry of a woman who, despite passionate involvement with her profession and despite the recognition accorded her writing, is still left with a barren feeling. It is the embodiment of a yearning for the life of all "simple whole women" whose singleness of commitment saves them from the agony of ambivalence, guilt, or loneliness. It is the agonized expression of failed femininity, linked to home and mothering. The poem is striking enough to warrant quoting in full.

I wept all day to my mirror
Spring had given my window away
to the green delusion of trees
how cramped I was in my cocoon alone
my crown of paper mildewed
and polluting the air of that sunless realm

I couldnt anymore, I couldnt
Street sounds, birdsong
tennis balls bounding away
flurry of children fleeing
balloons bobbing, climbing
like soap bubbles
to the tips of their branches of string
and through ancient clefts in my fortress of silence
whose walls securely hemmed me in
the wind called my heart by its name
panting as though sunk in love's deepest, darkest moment

All day my gaze
lay locked in my life's gaze
those two anxious, fearful eyes
avoiding my unflinching gaze
like liars hiding
behind the safe solitude of their lids
What peak, and what heights?
Dont all these winding paths
converge and close
in that sucking, frozen mouth?
What, oh you seductive words, what have you given me
and you, oh renunciation of bodies and desire?
If I'd fixed a flower in my hair
wouldnt it have been more charming than this fraud,
this paper crown already moldering on my head?
But I was led away by the desert spirit
drawn from the flock's faith by the magic of the moon
In my halfgrown heart the void grew
and no other half was joined to this half
So I stood, and so I saw
the ground vanishing beneath my own two feet

and no warmth from my body's mate
pierced the wan vigil of my body

What peak, and what heights?
Give me sanctuary, O anxious lamps
and O you bright, doubting houses
where laundry sways in the arms of your fragrant smoke on
sunlit roofs

Give me sanctuary, O you simple whole women
whose fingers delicately trace
the fetus turning
deliciously
and in whose opened blouses the air
forever mingles with the scent of new milk

What peak, and what heights?
Give me sanctuary, O glowing hearths—O horseshoe talismans—
And O, copperware in the kitchen's smudging work
and O, somber purring of the sewing machine
and O, endless campaigns of carpets and brooms
Give me sanctuary, O all you loves insatiable
whose throbbing lust for eternity bedecks the beds in which
you are possessed
by magic water
and drops of fresh blood

All day all day long
forsaken, as a drowned corpse forsaken
I marched towards that greatest of rocks
towards the caverns below the deepest sea
and the most fleshrending of fish
and my backbone's frail disks groaned
sensing death

I couldnt anymore, I couldnt
My steps echo on the denying way
despair vaster than my spirit can endure
And Spring, that delusion colored green
passing the window, says to my heart,

Behold,
you never went on
you were drawn down[56]

Alone and lonely, her vision caged in the vastness of a mirror, transformed by the bitterness of dreams become nightmares, a woman— also a poet—feels terrorized in this poem. In her cocoon of loneliness, her sense of success turns into failure. Overwhelmed by an agonizing feeling of emptiness, transfixed, and immobilized, she has no safe place to run away to. The transparency of her nightmares has invaded every inch of the mirror and, with it, the most inaccessible hiding places of her mind. She cannot seek refuge in oblivion, in lies, in deceits, in denials, behind the safe solitude of her eyelids. Kept awake by the glaring eyes of the mirror, she cannot take shelter in dreams. Surveying her life, going from room to room, from memory to memory, from experience to experience, she finds herself empty-handed.

When she looks in the mirror, she sees the face of a lonely woman looking back at her—two large eyes that stay open, see too much, and refuse to lie; two open eyes that pour out tears all day long and still cannot wash away the pain. This colossal pain stares back at her like the blinding sun, a pain so terrible that no kind mirror should ever remember it. But who said mirrors have to be kind? You look at them for too long and they open up old wounds—wounds that had closed in on themselves to alleviate the pain; wounds that, through layers upon layers of forgetfulness, had covered what was hidden underneath. That is the way it is with mirrors.

Under the dislocating influences of such a revealing and unkind mirror, in the harsh clarity of its spring-filled surface, nature's rejuvenation stirs up in this lonely woman the torrential enumerations of pent-up nostalgias. In the ritual marriage of the new year with the new sun, with herself in front of a mirror like a woman during her wedding ritual, she has to witness the absence of her "other half." She is a bride without the groom: only half of what she considers an entity.[57] With the onset of spring and the Iranian new year, in the season of birth and growth, she has to listen to her barrenness finding voice in the silence of the mirror. Loneliness blossoms all around her like spring flowers. Solitude buds. Sorrow burgeons. Silence, the hollow and long-lasting echo of the silence surrounding her, lingers in her ears and contrasts sharply with the reverberations of sounds coming from children playing in the street. Walled in, she watches the draining out of hope, the terror of illusions gone sour, the murder of dreams.

"Green Delusion" is a window thrown open to spring but also to the miseries of a woman poet. Although a hymn to motherhood, to woman's body as a source of nurturance and creativity, the whole poem resounds with frightful contradictions and contrasts: an inner autumnal melancholy against an outer regenerative spring, forces of song against silence, gestation against decay, success against failure. Here, in this mirror, a poet's long-cherished dreams are slain by facts. Here, in this jungle of regrets and retributions, a woman has to surrender to shattered ideals. Silent and listless, she has to awaken to the bitter reality of her betrayed dreams, the sacrifices she has to make, the loneliness she has to face. Trapped in the cocoon of her own making, all she can do is cry all day to her mirror.

Was Farrokhzad, the poet or the poetic personae, asking for too much? Was it because she demanded something so spectacular, so much larger than life, so inaccessible, that she needed to cry all day to her mirror, experience nervous breakdowns and attempt suicide? Apparently all she wanted and could never accomplish was the joys and comforts of family life and complete fulfillment of her talents. In contrast, in reading more than a thousand years of Persian literature, I have rarely come across men who have complained of the clash of their commitments between being a husband and a father and an artist. A man can choose marriage, fatherhood, and art. Women have not traditionally had such an option.

Farrokhzad tried hard to define for herself a new life as a woman and ended up paying dearly for her attempt. Her frustration is shared by other women artists inside and outside Iran. In *Fear of Flying,* Erica Jong writes:

> I would roam through the Metropolitan Museum of Art looking for one woman artist to show me the way. Mary Cassatt? Berthe Morisot? Why was it that so many women artists who had renounced having children could then paint nothing but mothers and children? It was hopeless. If you were female and talented, life was a trap no matter which way you turned. Either you drowned in domesticity (and has Walter

Mittyish fantasies of escape) or you longed for domesticity in all your art. You could never escape your femaleness. You had conflicts written in your very blood.[58]

Not that Farrokhzad regarded maternity as the only destiny for women. She never viewed art as a liberation from the demands of motherhood or as an incomplete substitute for it. She rejected the notion that giving birth is the hidden generator of woman's creativity. She did defend, however, the rights of motherhood, childbearing, and child rearing when they are a woman's choice.

But femininity was intricately and inextricably associated with woman's commitment to domestic concerns. Not surprisingly, the Persian word for woman, *Zan,* also means wife, just as *Khanum* [lady] also signifies wife. *Zan* and *Khanum* describe woman as a dependent. Woman is defined with reference to man, whereas man is described as a person and not with reference to her. Accordingly, *Aqa* means gentleman, sir, or master. *Mard* [man] and *Shohar* [husband] have distinct terminologies. As in marital vows in the West: "I now pronounce you *man* and *wife,*" women have no autonomy. "Wife" and "woman" are equated, made synonymous, submerged in each other.

Yet, despite the obstacles presented by a society that identified woman as wife and mother and idealized her invisibility and voicelessness, despite the anxieties of exposure and authorship, despite psychological dilemmas and cultural dislocations, despite accusations of shamelessness and charmlessness, toward the middle of the nineteenth century a tradition of women writers came to be established in Iran. Self-defining and self-articulating women such as Tahereh Qorratol'Ayn, E'tessami, Farrokhzad, and Daneshvar lifted the veil of secrecy to show the many faces of reality underneath.

The tradition of women's writing in contemporary Iran is thus one of radical dissent and questioning. It is the chronicle of an evolving consciousness, the testament of efforts to make lives according to new values and standards. It is the cries of mutinous women who suffered for their mutiny. Full appreciation of the problems these women confronted and the terrible odds against which they attempted to write reveals the strength and the value of their literary achievements. Perhaps that is why many Iranian women have rejected the possibility that their works can be understood in isolation from their restricting contexts—the hardships, sufferings, and anxieties that have dominated their lives. Daneshvar, for instance, emphatically maintains that "even the few writings we have produced are an accomplishment. Let Simone de Beauvoir come and live for a year the life I live and if she can still produce one line of writing I'll change my name."[59]

Although the path has been strenuous, the agonies and ambiguities that accompany change many, the rewards have been equally handsome. There is finally a tradition of women writers in Iran not only because there are a considerable number of authors and texts but also because there is a lineage. Women writers need no longer be compared to or evaluated in terms of an all-male community. They have a predecessor, a foremother, a legitimate and legitimized ancestry. They are no longer exiled from public life, either. If previously they could not speak in any public forum because both the content of any such speech and the act of oration itself would have been considered a transgression, even a sin, now they can articulate the previously unarticulated, name the once unnamed. Women, the ideally silent characters, have finally discovered surprising resources in their reappropriated voices and visions.

Women have literally transformed Persian literature in less than 150 years. They have desegregated a predominantly all-male tradition. They have reappraised cultural norms and patterns on a very intimate level. By achieving public, creative expression, they have delivered men from ceaseless soliloquies. Although men have lost exclusive control over public discourse, over the ability to define, categorize, and judge, they have, through women, gained access to dialogue.

Perhaps it is true that in a traditionally sex-segregated society women know far more about the world of men than vice versa. On the simplest level, men are raised by women. Furthermore, hidden behind their veils, women can have some access to men's world, whereas the opposite is not true. Also, men talk more or less openly to their mothers and sisters, whereas women have other women as their confidants and preferred interlocutors. For centuries, a cloak of secrecy excluded men from the private world of women. The female side of experience was like a terra incognita in Persian literature. Women writers have produced a key to unlock this riddle. The well-kept secret is finally being divulged. Woman is no longer the enigma she used to be, the veiled mystery, unknown and unknowable.

Indeed, the tradition of women writers in Iran is the chronicle of a presence asserted and inserted, of a body reclaimed, of a voice regained. It is the record of women's struggle to gain access to autonomous subjectivity, to become the speaking as well as the spoken subject. It is a rebirth of a sort. It is an attempt by women writers to establish dialogues with themselves, with other women, and with men.

> O friend, O brother, O blood of my blood
> . . . .
> Speak to me
> What does the one who offers you
> The kindness of a living body
> Ask in return
> Save a sense of life?
> Speak to me
> In my window's sanctuary
> I'm joined to the sun.[60]

PART TWO

From Tahereh to Tahereh

The Poets

4

Becoming a Presence

Tahereh Qorratol'Ayn

On a tombstone in the Shahzadeh Hossein Cemetery in the city of Qazvin is carved the gruesome image of a murder: a praying molla [a religious scholar] is being stabbed to death, from behind, by a masked man. A woman, semiconcealed behind a curtain, looks on. In her hand she holds a sheet of paper, incriminating evidence that she can read and write. The writings on the tombstone, carved over 150 years ago, make sure you understand what the image means: the "Martyrdom of Molla Taqi by a Babi Heretic."

The woman behind the curtain, overseeing and presumably masterminding the molla's murder, is the nineteenth-century poet Fatemeh Baraghani, better known as Tahereh Qorratol'Ayn. Her accuser, absent from the scene but pointing the finger through the image on the tombstone, is her husband and cousin, none other than the murdered molla's son. He remained unaffected by his wife's acquittal by a court of law, even after the confession of the real murderer.

It is unclear, given the iconography of the tombstone, which is the woman's greater crime: the murder itself, whether she has masterminded it or is its more passive accomplice; or her usurpation of the written word, the evidence of which we find in her own hand: the paper. Or it might be that it doesn't really matter which: the writing in her hand is as good as the dagger in the assassin's hand for achieving the same lethal end: death of the patriarch.

In the society of mid-nineteenth-century Iran, knowledge, like a child, was only legitimized if properly fathered by a man. In the hands of

77

a woman, it became an unnecessary tool, a dangerous tool, even a sign of the end of time, of apocalypse. The murdered Molla Taqi was heard to have said words to this effect, with Tahereh in mind: "When the signs of the promised One appear, the Zindiq [heretic] of [the city of] Qazvin will also appear, and the words of the Zindiq will be the words of a woman's religion! Now this woman and her religion have appeared."[1] To avoid such a disaster, observed Mirza 'Abdol-Vahab, Tahereh's brother, "the clergy have prevented all women from studying lest they should become believers like Tahirih."[2]

Clearly, then as now, such views were not held by all the clergy. Actually, one of the first schools for girls, *'Effatiyeh* [House of Chastity], was founded in 1910 with the help and encouragement of a high-ranking mojtahed [one with a high theological status who is allowed independent legal judgments] Sheykh Mohammad Hossein Yazdi. But Tahereh's father-in-law and her husband blamed her book learning for destroying her life. Since that time others have also argued that her access to books—especially dissident, Sheykhi books—made her go "mad" and abandon the sanctity of motherhood and the sacredness of home. (Sheykhism is a school of theology that grew out of Shi'i Islam. With its pronounced messianic expectations, it is the theoretical foundation for Babism, a religious faith proclaimed in mid-nineteenth-century Iran that called for spiritual and moral reforms and a new sociopolitical order. "The Bab" [the gateway, or the intermediary, between the Hidden Imam and the believers] is the title given to the founder of Babism.)

E'tezadol-Saltaneh believes that "her persistent study of Sheykhi materials and inquiry into their books totally absorbed her and slowly changed her whole life. It ultimately made her leave her sacred matrimony to wander from place to place."[3] Moshir-Salimi is even more explicit in his diagnosis: Tahereh's "sustained examination of and curiosity about Sheykhi works changed her life to the point that she dumped her sacred and simple married life. Basically, she could no longer agree with her husband's views or her father-in-law/older uncle's reasoning and values. Their discussions led to physical fights. Finally, in spite of having three children, she left home and her married life."[4]

If education can threaten some women with the loss of their natural place and position in society, if it causes violent disputes and eventually makes women leave their husbands, children, and the bliss of domestic life, it can also lead to women's madness. Kasravi, the famous historian, claims to know "the exact causes of Tahereh's insanity." While calling her a *Shir Zan* [a woman fearless and strong like a lion], or "one of the exceptional women of the whole world," he ultimately portrays her as a crazed woman, scurrying around, caught in her own self-destructive messianic ethos but above all ruined by her extensive readings. "We know of all of her readings and her knowledge," he writes, "her poems clearly indicate what her brain was filled with. It is exactly these things that toppled her."[5]

Why should this woman's education have provoked such a strong reaction and intense hostility? It is true that most of Tahereh's detractors seem to object to her reading Sheykhi materials in particular rather than to her pursuit of knowledge per se. But it is a fact that in her time, higher learning was basically a masculine prerogative. Women's reading was controlled if not discouraged. Even if unusual circumstances allowed a woman access to higher education, the outlets for public expression of such learning were severely limited. Women were excluded from the public domains of discourse. Theology was reserved for men. Most women neither had access to higher education nor were expected to learn Arabic, a necessary tool for the Islamic scholar. Their domestic confinement precluded the freedom to travel to centers of learning. Denied participation in disputation, they could not refine or exchange points of view. Barred from the pulpit and public preaching, they had no audience and could not propagate their learning.

Obviously, some women before Tahereh had written and spoken out on religious issues. It was not uncommon for some daughters of the clerics or the privileged classes to be highly educated, especially in religious matters. But normally, such competence, its expressions, and its audience were confined to the private and familial. Prayer books, books of religious instructions for women and children, were allowed; but sermons to men and doctrinal statements were not. Interpretative power was strictly a male prerogative. If in rare circumstances women attained the level of mojtahed, their decisions could not be binding on others. What was acceptable in the privacy of the home or in strictly female gatherings verged on insolence or even heresy when done in public. Women's learning could serve no public purpose. Silent in mosques and in mixed gatherings, women never preached or addressed "serious' religious matters beyond the home.

If a woman's place was only in the home as wife and mother, then

Tahereh was never satisfied with her natural domain. Even though a wife and mother, she also busied herself in libraries and classes, with talks and debates. By becoming a public scholar, she penetrated a male preserve. She was not writing or speaking only on private, personal matters, in private; on the contrary, she addressed theological issues in the public domain. She even challenged some of the most learned religious scholars of her time by inviting them to *Mojadeleh* [public rational argumentation]. She assigned herself a public role and a public place. A triple transgression—verbal, spatial, and physical.

Tahereh refused to be trapped by stereotypes, images, ideals, and stories foisted upon her by tradition. She wanted to take charge, be mobile, subvert the master narratives of her culture, write her own story, control the plot, and orchestrate a public image for herself and perhaps for other women as well. She succeeded to a large extent. Just as she refused to be silenced or pinned down during her life, she has continued to defy silence or categorization after death. She has proven to be too enigmatic a presence to be dealt with neutrally or to be ignored altogether. Her life is probably the best documented of nineteenth-century Iranian women, although it is fact and fiction compressed into one. She is saint, whore, sorceress, martyr, and murderer. Invented and reinvented, she is honored and dishonored.

It is unfortunate that this woman who unveiled herself so many years ago still lives such a veiled life in the memory of her own people. Her life story represents, in more ways than one, a kind of fantasy literature, a literature that has absorbed in itself disparate materials from dreams and nightmares, fears and wishes, fascination and terror. It is hard to discern who she really was amid all the adulation and hatred that have surrounded her during and after her life. Extolled as a saint, an exceptional woman, a miracle, she is also denounced as a lunatic, a dangerous woman, a heretic.

On the one hand, there are those Babis and Baha'is who have nothing but praise for her fervent involvement with and relentless advocacy of the Babi faith, her flawless character, and her martyrdom. They seem to miss or dismiss the moral and intellectual challenges posed by her personal life. They curiously ignore the significance of the private choices she made, such as leaving her husband and her three children, refusing to comply with prescribed norms of feminine comportment, and causing much agony to herself and to her immediate family, especially to her father and her children.[6] In a characteristic observation on her life, Edward G. Browne writes: "The appearance of such a woman as Kurratul'Ayn is in any country and age a rare phenomenon, but in such a country as Persia it is a prodigy—nay, almost a miracle. Alike in virtue of her marvelous beauty, her rare intellectual gifts, her fervid eloquence, her fearless devotion, and her glorious martyrdom, she stands forth incomparable and immortal amidst her countrywomen. Had the Babi religion no other claim to greatness, this were sufficient—that it produced a heroine like Kurratul'Ayn."[7]

On the other hand, there is a group that concentrates totally on its own version of Tahereh's private life and produces an avalanche of outrage against her personal choices. In *Baha'ism, Its Origins and Its Role,* she is claimed to put history to shame: "During 'Ali Mohammad Shirazi's [the Bab's] imprisonment, unpleasant events took place at the hands of Babis in [the cities of] Zanjan, Ghazvin and Mazandaran at foreign instigation and by the makings of people such as Mirza Hossein Ali [Baha'ullah] . . . as well as a prostitute by the name of Qaralein [Qorratol'Ayn]. History is ashamed to relate such events."[8] Presented as a blasphemer, Tahereh comes to be a symbol of spiritual and moral wickedness. Considered promiscuous, she is slandered as an advocate of promiscuity. Depicted with insatiable carnal desires, she is viewed as a woman with gargantuan sexual appetites, indulging indefatigably in earthly pleasures. The chronicler Mirza Muhammad Taqi Sepehr, amazed that this beautiful "girl who had a moon-like face and hair like musk"[9] could also be so knowledgeable, gives his imagination free reign:

> She would decorate her assembly room like a bridal chamber and her body like a peacock of Paradise. Then she summoned the followers of the Bab and appeared unveiled in front of them. First she ascended a throne and like a pious preacher reminded them of Heaven and Hell and quoted amply from the Qur'an and the Traditions. She would then tell them: "Whoever touches me, the intensity of Hell's fire would not affect him." The audience would then rise and come to her throne and kiss those lips of hers which put to shame the ruby of Ramman, and rub their faces against her breasts, which chagrined the pomegranates of the garden.[10]

Sepehr not only attributes to Tahereh the familiar powers of the woman as a body, as a sex object, he also maintains that she "counseled the marriage of one woman to nine men."[11] Quoting Sepehr, the historian Bastani-ye Parizi adds a zero to nine and increases the number of recommended husbands for each woman from nine to "ninety" men.[12] It is as if in not knowing what to say about such a remarkable woman, some historians just assumed she was promiscuous. What else could she be if she were beautiful and wished to appear before others?

Reactions to Tahereh have varied from repulsion to fascination, from horror to sympathy, from disgust to admiration. Any attempt to unveil her, to find the real woman beneath all the myths about her, inevitably leads to a struggle through a morass of contradictory information. Just as her dazzling complexity eluded her contemporaries, friends and foes alike, accounts of her life dissolve into legend. Now idealized, now demonized, now revered, now rejected, she provokes in her biographers and critics unrestrained creativity that often results in hagiography or demonology.

The mystery that shrouds Tahereh's life is quite different from the mystery she saw around her and tried to explain and understand. The first is like the veil she tried so hard to lift from her face. The second is the mysteries that impassioned her mind.

Snippets of information, sensational gossip that she has attracted through the years, haphazard interpretations of her poems, and rumors give Tahereh's life story an element of the fantastic, the surrealistic. Yet, although the information on her life is sketchy, often contradictory, underneath all the confusion and ambiguity one story emerges with clarity. It is the story of a woman who wanted voice, mobility, and visibility and succeeded in establishing and allocating her own space, the story of an absence who strove to become a presence.

Born Fatemeh Baraghani sometime in 1817 to a highly religious family, she was to have as many names as destinies. Om-e Salmeh, Hind, Zakiyeh, Noqteh [the point], Tuti [parrot], Zarrin Taj [crowned with gold], Qorratol'Ayn [solace of the eye], Tahereh [the pure one], Bent-e Taleh [daughter of evil] are only some of her acquired names, and perhaps a manifestation of attempts to make her disappear behind the veil of too many names. Ironically, the only daughter of this multinamed woman remains nameless. Islamic and, for that matter, Babi and Baha'i sources guard her name with silence. The only piece of information available on her is that "the girl died not long after the passing of her mother."[13] The life of this unnamed daughter, like that of almost all of her women contemporaries, remains a mystery, an untold tale, a veiled story.

Owing to happy circumstances of birth, Tahereh received the finest education available. Her father, Molla Saleh, was a liberal and broad-minded scholar of the Qor'an and the traditions and an influential high priest of his province. Her aunt, Mirza Mah-Sharaf Khanom, was so learned and accomplished in calligraphy that she "wrote most of the government's decrees in her beautiful hand."[14] First taught by her father, later by a tutor, Tahereh continued her studies in theology, Qor'anic exegesis, jurisprudence, and Persian and Arabic literature, an education quite unusual for a woman in those days. Pleased with the acuity of her insight mingled with her vast knowledge, Tahereh's father often discussed religious issues with her. But more importantly perhaps, he allowed her participation, from behind a curtain, in his classes and debating sessions.

Tahereh's thorough knowledge of scripture and the ease and eloquence with which she undertook theological discussions soon earned her a reputation. Her father, aware of the many restrictions placed upon women's access to religious authority, regretted his daughter's gender: "If she were a boy," he repeated, "she would have illuminated my house and come to be my successor."[15] His successor Tahereh could not become; she could not even further her studies at a theological school because such schools were barred to women. Instead, she followed custom and was married, by arrangement, to her cousin, when she was barely fourteen. Her husband, the son of a paternal uncle, Molla Taqi, soon left for Iraq, accompanied by his wife, in order to pursue his religious studies. Abbas Amanat, a notable historian specializing in modern Iran, writes that "for close to thirteen years the couple resided in Karbala [shrine city in Iraq]. Though Fatima [Tahereh] gave birth to two sons, Ibrahim and Isma'il, it appears that almost from the start the marriage was not free from domestic quarrels."[16]

Tahereh grew up in an environment of passionate debates and absorbed the controversial points of theology of her day. In Iraq, she gained access to more Sheykhi materials and perhaps even attended classes of the Sheykhi leader, Seyyed Kazem Rashti.

Upon her return to Iran, Tahereh was more than just a female orator.

She was a thinker in her own right. She was not only discussing and challenging religious issues with members of her extended family, she was now contradicting them. With a deeply held messianic vision of the world, she believed that a new era was in the making. Far from simply trespassing on male clerical terrain, she was challenging and subverting the dogma behind it. The orthodoxy of her family, especially her husband's, clashed bitterly with her reformist views. Consequently, she left her husband and her three children and accompanied by her sister and her brother-in-law, she returned to Iraq to join Seyyed Kazem Rashti, who in appreciation of her scholarship, had called her Qorratol'Ayn [solace of the eye]. But by the time she reached her destination, Rashti had died. Tahereh stayed in his home and eventually took his place. From behind a curtain, she began to teach the many students of Rashti. But her radical views, her refusal to be secretive and practice Taqiyeh [dissimulation of faith], and above all, her unusual assumption of a traditionally masculine position disturbed many. And perhaps justifiably so. Even today, no woman in Iran occupies her position—that of a teacher and a leader in centers of higher religious learning for men.

In Iraq, Tahereh stepped beyond Islamic and Sheykhi theology and proposed a break with past religious legacy. Although the sole woman among the first eighteen disciples of the Bab and the only one who never met him face to face, she soon became one of the most influential and controversial figures of that movement. Openly advocating and preaching the new religious faith of Babism and appearing at times without her face veiled at gatherings of her followers, Tahereh threatened deep-seated cultural, social, and religious norms. Her fiery oratory, knife-edged and eloquent, and her knowledge, vast and radical, captivated and shocked her audiences. Many considered her a troublesome heretic overpowered by satanic temptations and inevitably licentious. In response to such allegations of immorality, she pleaded her case in a letter to her father. "I plead with you! This humblest of people is your daughter. You know her, and she has been brought up and educated under your supervision. If she had, or has, a worldly love, that could not have remained a secret to you. If you want to inquire into her affairs, God who holds the scale and is the remover of the veils would testify for her."[17]

Some Babi disciples saw Tahereh as a challenge to their faith. Her social vision was far beyond her time, too radical even for some Babi converts and sympathizers. Rebellious as they might have been as Babis, more widely prevalent cultural ideals of femininity colored all their beliefs. Objecting to her conduct and attempting to purify the new faith of her harmful innovations, they complained to the Bab. Disapproving of their consternation and of their allegations of immorality, the Bab defended Tahereh unequivocally and asked them "to accept without questions whatever she might pronounce, for they were not in a position to understand and appreciate her station."[18] He also bestowed upon her the title Jenab-e Tahereh [His Excellency, an honorific male title with the attribute of purity].

Put under surveillance in Iraq as a result of her activities, Tahereh was eventually deported and ordered to leave Ottoman territory. Followed by some thirty Babis, she left for Iran around 1847. Throughout her journey back home, she never stopped advocating Babi faith, recruiting new members, and especially inviting highly respected theologians to public debates. In the city of Hamedan, one such gathering was convened. "Speaking from behind a curtain, Qurrat al'Ayn set three rules for disputation: reliance on prophecies; abstinence from smoking—a strict Babi prohibition; and most significantly, adopting decent language and avoiding abuse and execration. She unequivocally reiterated the basic themes of the early Babi doctrine: everlasting divine guidance, the progressive cycle of revelation, need for a new creed to meet the challenge of a changing age, and the legitimacy of the Bab as the sole recipient of divine inspiration."[19]

Tahereh's arrival in Qazvin caused an even greater controversy and a family feud. Her father and especially her father-in-law tried hard to convince her to stop proselytizing and to return to her husband. She refused both. All attempts to reconcile her with her husband proved ineffective, and she refused to give in to pressure to return home. Molla Mohammad eventually had to divorce her. It is around this time that Molla Taqi, Tahereh's father-in-law, who had intensified his public attacks on Sheykhis and Babis, was stabbed by a man named Mirza 'Abdullah Shirazi early one morning, while at prayer in his mosque. He died two days after the attack in September 1847. Accused of masterminding the murder of her father-in-law, Tahereh was arrested. Eventually released and put under house arrest, she soon escaped from her home and birthplace, never to return to either.

Spending almost a year in hiding in the capital city of Tehran, Tahereh left for Badasht in 1848, where she was to play a major and dramatic role in this first Babi convention. Before Badasht, no public claim had been made that the Bab was the inaugurator of a new faith. It was there, in northeastern Iran, that disciples superceded the Qor'an and Islamic rules publicly and collectively for the first time. They proclaimed Babism an independent faith rather than an offshoot of Islam. Actually, it was Tahereh who proclaimed the new faith and symbolically heralded the coming of the new era by her unveiling. In the words of 'Abdul Baha: "Tahirih, with her face unveiled, stepped from her garden, advancing to the pavilion of Baha'ullah; and as she came, she shouted aloud these words: 'The trumpet is sounding! The great Trump is blown! The universal Advent is now proclaimed!' The believers gathered in that tent were panic struck, and each one asked himself, 'How can the Law be abrogated? How is it that this woman stands here without her veil?' . . . and thus was the new Dispensation announced and the great Resurrection made manifest."[20]

Tahereh's unveiling of her face in Badasht, however much an iconoclastic act, conformed with her expressed views before and after that gathering. It presented no dramatic break with her past. Not a metamorphosis or a sudden reaction, it was simply a culmination.[21] If her unveiling was interpreted as an invitation to lust, her words were viewed as the destruction of all religious values. Indeed, she did preach the elevation of the individual's conscience above all religious ordinances and exempted the believers from any Islamic laws. "All religious obligations are abrogated today," she said. "All prayers, fasting, and salutation are futile. When the Bab conquers the seven kingdoms and unites all religions, he will bring forth a new set of rules."[22] The assembly was set in an uproar. Many, enraged by her act, left the premises as well as their newly embraced faith. Some called her a heretic. One man wanted to strike her with a sword, while another, one 'Abdol Khaleq Esfahani, "aghast and deranged at the sight, cut his throat with his own hands."[23] Shattered by her heresy, he could not allow the sanctity of his eyes or honor to be defiled, nor his newly espoused faith to be defamed. Directing his anger toward himself, "spattered with blood, and frantic with excitement, he fled away from her face."[24] The story of this first male casualty of women's unveiling in Iran remains to be written.

The conference at Badasht, with eighty men and one woman present, was by itself a novelty. Amazingly, it included a woman among its active participants. It is interesting to note that about the same time, on July 19, 1848, in another corner of the world, the first women's rights convention was convened. If in the small town of Seneca Falls, New York, women were busy working to amend the Constitution, in Iran, a woman was struggling to insert herself in the public sphere of debates. If the American feminists could seek women's active participation in their society and could try to change the terms of their social contract, their Iranian counterpart had to fight for the space to enter into the dialogue, for the privilege to be seen and to be heard in public.

Lady Sheil, the wife of the British ambassador, who visited Iran in those days, was so shocked by the total absence of women from the public scene that she hastily concluded: "In Persia a woman is nobody":

> Three easy stages over a very tolerable road, through valleys with mountains on both sides, sometimes near, sometimes more distant, brought us to [the city of] Tabriz on the 2nd of November. Here preparations on a grand scale were made for a solemn entry, from which I, however, as belonging to the inferior and ignoble class of womankind, was excluded, though I was permitted to gaze on the scene at a distance. It was difficult to say how many thousand people had assembled, or what class of persons had not come forth to do honor to the Queen of England's representative. There were princes and priests, and dervishes, and beggars; there were Koordish and Toork horsemen of the tribes, and soldiers, and Ghoolams; in short there was everything and everybody, but there was not a single woman, for in Persia a woman is nobody.[25]

Normally, women contemporaries of Tahereh were not allowed to be in the presence of men, let alone to participate actively in debates and discussions and hold key leadership roles. Perhaps that is one reason why the convention at Badasht is remembered not only as a celebration of heresy but also as a shameful orgy of sinful lust. Tahereh's voice, her sermons, her unveiled face became signs of contamination, tokens of an unleashed sexuality that was deemed dangerous. "When all those assembled at Badasht accepted the new faith of licentiousness," writes E'tezadol-Saltaneh, "men and women mingled and lived the legend of the Epicurus Garden."[26]

After some twenty-one days, the gathering at Badasht was dispersed by nearby villagers. Tahereh wandered for a while from village to vil-

lage, from one hiding place to another. She was finally arrested by government agents on charges of collaboration in the murder of Molla Taqi
and sent to Tehran. There, she had an audience with the king, Nasser
al-Din Shah, who is believed to have said: "I like her looks: leave her
and let her be."[27] Some sources even maintain that the king wanted
to marry her, should she stop believing in and advocating the new faith.
Her reply was a definitive, even though poetic, no:

> Kingdom, wealth, and power for thee
> Beggary, exile, and loss for me
> If the former be good, it's thine
> If the latter is hard, it's mine.[28]

Despite the king's ordinance, leave her they did not. She was once
again put under house arrest in the house of Tehran's chief of police.
And when, in August 1852, an unsuccessful attempt was made on the
life of the young monarch by three Babis, she was executed—a fate she
shared with many men accused of being heretics. Whereas the execution of all other Babis was a public and publicized affair, that of Tahereh
was shrouded in silence and secrecy. Consequently, accounts of her death
are as conflicting as those of her life. Differing on details, however, they
all agree on the broad outline: although in the Islamic precepts of apos-
tasy a woman should not be executed but rather imprisoned until she
regains her faith, she was executed by a governmental decree. There
is also little doubt about the method of execution: one summer night,
dressed in her best clothes, made up and perfumed, she was taken to
a walled garden, strangled to death, and thrown in a well, followed
by a heap of rocks. She was only thirty-six years of age.

The government of the time made a deliberate effort to conduct all
Babi executions in public. Torturing and killing them in cities and vil-
lages soon became a commonplace event. According to one source, "not
only the executioner and the common people took part in the massacre:
sometimes Justice would present some of the unhappy Babis to various
dignitaries and the Persian [recipient] would be well content, deeming
it an honor to imbrue his own hands in the blood of the pinioned and
defenseless victim. Infantry, cavalry, artillery, the ghulams or guards of
the King, and the guilds of butchers, bakers, etc., all took their fair
share in these bloody deeds."[29]

The Bab himself, executed two years earlier, did not fare any better than his followers. He was first carried around the city before being executed by a firing squad in public. Later, his body, along with that of his companion, was fastened to a ladder and dragged through the streets of the city of Tabriz.

Tahereh, the most outspoken, unrelenting, and controversial leader of this controversial movement, however, was handled quite differently. Concealed in a cloak of anonymity, her execution, like her life, was considered a private matter. In the society of her time, a woman's body—dead or alive—belonged to the privacy of the home. No forbidden eye was to be cast upon her. Even the body of an allegedly heretic woman could not escape this order of the day. Dead or alive, she had to remain concealed, hidden from prying eyes, privatized, veiled.

Accounts of Tahereh's death have an element of the fantastic to them. She seems to have died as she had lived, with an unswerving will and flamboyant originality. Lowell Johnson, quoting the son of the chief of police in whose house she was last imprisoned, writes:

> On the day that she was secretly killed, it seemed as if she had been told it was going to happen. Tahirih bathed, changed all of her clothing and came downstairs to see the family. . . . [She] called to me and asked me to go to the Chief of Police with a special request. "It seems that they wish to strangle me," she said. "Long ago, I set aside a silk handkerchief which I hoped would be used for this purpose. I deliver it into your hands and I want you to ask that drunkard to use it for the purpose of taking my life." When I went to the Chief I found him completely drunk. He only shouted at me, "Don't interrupt our gay festival. Let that Babi woman be strangled and her body thrown into a hole." I was greatly surprised by such an order, because it was exactly what she had wanted. I did not ask him whether he would permit the murderer to use the silk handkerchief. I just went to the two guards and they agreed that the handkerchief would be a good thing to use.[30]

Sources disagree on the logistics of Tahereh's strangulation. Some believe that a handkerchief was used, while others write that she was choked by a silk scarf. Still others claim that the deadly weapon was the green turban of another executed Babi convert—Quddus—alleged to be her lover.[31] The strangulation itself, however, remains basically an undisputed fact, although some sources contend that she was not yet dead when thrown in the well.

But the Persian term for strangulation, *Khafeh Kardan,* also means to drown and more commonly conveys "suppressing, stifling, silencing." Unlike the Babis who were executed in public, the method of Tahereh's death suited her offense. Her voice was silenced because she shouldn't have spoken in the first place. Her body was hidden because she shouldn't have unveiled it. Perhaps the Friday prayer imam of Qazvin, Molla Taqi's replacement, knew better when he reproachfully warned Tahereh's father: "No glory remains on that house / From which the hens crow like the cocks."[32]

The hen crowed like the cock; the private, the secret, leaked into the world of the public; the concealed became exposed; the absent became present; the seals dividing male/female, private/public broke down. Unveiling her face, as she unveiled her voice, Tahereh used her self as a medium, a text to break the silence. She asserted women's autonomy and distinctiveness in an age that demanded conformity and anonymity from its women. She wanted her face seen, her voice heard, her individuality known. She lifted the veil of secrecy and came out from behind the curtain.

Tahereh's contribution to the history of women's writing in Iran is invaluable: she proved that women could think, write, and reason like men—in public and for the public. Such actions set her apart from her contemporaries and confer upon her an inalienable precedence. The prominent woman novelist Shahrnush Parsipur allies herself to a limited historical tradition that includes Tahereh. In a detailed enumeration of prominent figures, she considers Tahereh a precursor of women's modern literary tradition.[33]

The corpus of Tahereh's poetry, like accounts of her life, remains scattered and the subject of opposing views. A collection of Tahereh's poems was published for the first time more than a hundred years after her death. Although some question the authorship of certain poems ascribed to her, others claim that many of her poems were burned and lost to us. Still others maintain that some of her poems, coming as they did from the pen of a woman considered a heretic, were assigned to others. Their authorship disguised, her poems could more safely circulate from mouth to mouth. "It must be borne in mind that the odium which attaches to the name of Babi amongst Persian Muhammadans would render impossible the recitation by them of verses confessedly composed by her. If, therefore, she were actually the authoress of poems, the grace and beauty of which compelled an involuntary admiration even from her enemies, it would seem extremely probable that they should seek to justify their right to admire them by attributing them to some other writer."[34]

Major studies of poetry barely, if ever, deal with the work of Tahereh. Keshavarz-e Sadr and Moshir-Salimi include her among other women poets, assigning no special place to her. They provide cursory biographical notations and a few samples of her work. Whether because she has been deemed too offensive, too dangerous, or too minor a literary personage, no article, let alone a full-length book, has been written either on her work or on her life as a struggle for gaining a public voice.

Some of Tahereh's poems are difficult to understand. Their language is rich in abstractions. She not only mixes Arabic with Persian but also makes repeated allusions to Babi jargon and codes. Her religious convictions saturate her poetry and set her verse on fire. They glow in her poetry like a flame that burns every obstacle in its way. The erotic-mystical imagery and language she uses reveal an all-consuming love of and an intense devotion to a divine manifestation.

> In pursuit of your love, O darling,
> Enamored of afflictions, I am
> Why do you shun me so?
> Weary of your separation, I am.
>
> You've veiled your face
> You've dishevelled your hair
> You've abandoned people
> Just as secluded, I am.
>
> You're the milk and you're the honey
> You're the tree and you're the fruit
> You are the sun and you are the moon
> A speck, an iota, I am.
>
> You're the palm and you're the date
> You are the nectar-lipped beloved
> A distinguished master, you, dear love,
> An insolent slave, I am.

> You are the Mecca and you are the One
> You're the temple and you're the shrine
> You're the beloved, the honored one
> The miserable lover, I am.
>
> "Come to me!"
> Love said alluringly
> "Free of pride and pretense,
> Manifestation of the One, I am."
>
> Tahereh is but floating dust at your feet
> Drunk by the wine of your face.
> Awaiting your blessing
> A confessing sinner, I am.[35]

Although the insignificance of the poetic persona is highlighted by juxtaposition to the virtues and holiness of the beloved, it is impossible to guess the sex of the beloved in this poem. Had it not been for the name Tahereh inserted in the last line, it would have been equally impossible to ascertain the gender of the poet. Ambiguity is compounded by the language itself, which is not gender marked. The second-person-singular pronoun *Tow* used throughout the poem can be either masculine or feminine. The terms used to address the beloved make the task of the curious reader interested in deciphering the sex of the beloved no easier. *Sanam* [idol], *delbar* [sweetheart], *shahed* [beloved] can be addressed to both men and women.

In this poem and others like it, the gender of the poet cannot be ascertained. It is incidental to the major theme, or message, of the poem. The following poem is a first-person narrative that establishes in its first line the gender of the poet: "Should I unveil my scented hair." The following four lines further describe the narrator. In the last two lines, however, the poem takes a surprising turn. Characteristic of Tahereh's poetry, it dramatizes a theological conviction that becomes the very focus of the poem.

> Should I unveil my scented hair
> I'll captivate every gazelle
>
> Should I line my narcissus eyes
> I'll destroy the whole world with desire

To see my face, every dawn
Heaven lifts its golden mirror

Should I chance to pass the church one day
I'll convert all Christian girls.[36]

If self-assertion is a cardinal tenet of Tahereh's life, self-denial and self-effacement are key elements of her poetry. The themes of love, union, and ecstasy relate to mystic and spiritual experience. The object of love depicted is an abstraction rather than a concrete and palpable portrayal. It is ultimately divine love or its manifestation on earth. The desire and passion portrayed are merely starting points for spiritual realization, vehicles of expression in a long-established tradition of mystical love poetry. Perhaps nowhere does Tahereh depict more eloquently the Sufi theme of separation than in the following poem. This is the articulation of spiritual exile, imbued with fervor and intensity.

I would explain all my grief
Dot by dot, point by point
If heart to heart we talk
And face to face we meet.

To catch a glimpse of thee
I am wandering like a breeze
From house to house, door to door
Place to place, street to street.

In separation from thee
The blood of my heart gushes out of my eyes
In torrent after torrent, river after river
Wave after wave, stream after stream.

This afflicted heart of mine
Has woven your love
To the stuff of life
Strand by strand, thread to thread.[37]

Although modern notions of feminist writing might not be quite applicable to Tahereh's poetry—she does not overtly assert her gender or the rights of women—she nonetheless challenged the social and lit-

erary conventions of her time. She questioned, problematized, and subverted the socially prescribed woman's place. She challenged the sharp
separation between public and private, male and female, rational and
emotional. She refused silence. By becoming her own public interpreter—a
body with a voice and a voice with a body—she refused to slip away
into silence. She defined the speaking subject as female and authorized
for herself a public life. She earned herself an identity in ways both sexual and textual.

It is true that Tahereh's concerns were strictly along theological lines,
but her explicit demand that she, a woman, be given the space to think
for herself, to express her beliefs, and to use her voice publicly was significantly to question the validity of the place assigned to women. As
an articulate theologian and poet, she challenged the silence and marginality that characterized the women of her era. Consciously or not,
she dispensed with existing sex roles in order to create new ones.

It may be misleading to express Tahereh's religious aspirations in
feminist terms. Whether she was a conscious champion of women's rights
we don't know. Such a movement was not yet conceived of, let alone
articulated.[38] Yet accounts of her life clearly indicate that even before
her conversion to Babism, repeatedly and openly she challenged some
of the most cherished and deep-seated norms of her society. Tahereh
might not have espoused feminism (if we can use such an anachronistic
term) as a cause, but she embodied it at every turn of her life. Her
whole life story is indeed the expression of dissent and of dissatisfaction
with the roles available to women. In fact, by her conduct, she subverted not only the established religion but the whole fabric of androcentric society. She rejected the traditional female occupations and the
attributes of femininity by departing from existing gender roles. She
eschewed the feminine virtues of submissiveness, domesticity, absence
from the public view, and silence. Articulate rather than silent, transgressive rather than obedient, mobile rather than walled in, she challenged the prevailing values of the established order.

Uninhibited by spatial constraints of femaleness, moving from one
city to another, crossing boundaries between nations and cultures, she
could not be pinned down. Now in Bagdad, now in Qazvin, returning
to Iraq, visiting Kirmanshah, Hamedan, Nur, now in Tehran, now in
Badasht, she embodied motion and vitality. In a culture that cements

women to the private sphere through walls, veils, and their attendant customs, a culture so terrified by women's movement that even to this day a woman needs her husband's written permission to be granted a passport, a culture in which the word *harja'i* [straying about] becomes synonymous with *prostitute* when applied to a woman, Tahereh resisted any confinement.

Aversion to and fear of women's mobility is not confined to any one culture or period. Perhaps the practice of footbinding in China best reflects the desire to confine a woman to the domestic sphere, to immobilize her. Or in the West, one of the major charges against witches concerned their ability to be mobile, to roam about. Condemned for their mysterious escapades, witches were thought to fly incredible distances through the air. "We," wrote the inquisitors in *Malleus Maleficarum* (Hammer of Witches), "had credible . . . information from a young girl witch who had been converted. . . . When she was asked whether it was only in imagination and fantastically that they rode, through as illusion of devils, she answered that they did so in both ways."[39] Dunking, a most common method of testing a witch, embodied society's fear of women's mobility: "The victim was stripped naked and bound with her right thumb to her left toe, and was then cast into the pond or river. If she sank, she was frequently drowned; if she swam, she was declared guilty without any further evidence being required, and so escaped drowning to be hung or burned."[40]

Tahereh's physical mobility parallels her metaphorical journey and her struggle to attain a voice of her own. Wherever she went, we are told, she attracted large audiences. Her physical presence, according to Babi/Baha'i and even Muslim sources, was irresistible. Her beauty, joined with her eloquence, it is said, was bewitching. She was endowed with personal magnetism. According to many, her power of persuasion caused many to convert to Babism despite the manifestly dangerous consequences of such a conversion. She was so charismatic a leader, it seems, that she not only recruited members but came to have a group of devoted followers known as the Qorratiyeh, that is, followers of Qorratol'Ayn.

Most sources claim that Tahereh's words did cast a spell. "In the small town of Kirand," writes Balyuzi, "her eloquence and the clarity of her disquisition so impressed the chiefs of that area that they offered to place twelve thousand men under her command, to follow her wherever she went."[41] According to Baha'ullah, in *Memorials of the Faithful,* her "sweet words" so mesmerized people that they preferred her talk to music in a wedding ceremony:

> It happened that there was a celebration at the Mayor's house for the marriage of his son; a nuptial banquet was prepared, and the house adorned. The flower of Tihran's ladies were invited, the princesses, the wives of vazirs and other great. A splendid wedding it was, with instrumental music and vocal melodies—by day and night the lute, the bells and songs. Then Tahirih began to speak; and so bewitched were the great ladies that they forsook the cistern and the drum and all the pleasures of the wedding feast, to crowd about Tahirih and listen to the sweet words of her mouth.[42]

The powers granted by Tahirih's eloquence were assumed astonishing for a woman, even for Babis themselves, for whom women's verbal expression was still a private matter. Although the Bab "allowed men and women members of an extended family to converse freely, he made it conditional on the topic being 'important and serious,' reducing the conversation to an exchange of no more than twenty-eight words if it was not."[43]

It is true that Tahereh's ideas provided mainly an alternative to the dominant religion. Yet, this stance allowed her further access to knowledge, organizational authority, and articulation of her ideas. It allowed her to reject some of the values of the dominant patriarchal society without giving up her strong and long-sustained religious beliefs.

The relationship between Babism and the women's movement has hardly been given an adequate treatment by historians. Though referred to in some works, it has not formed the focus of any extended research. Clouded by religious and political rhetoric, obscured by insufficient information about both movements, and somewhat crippled by a certain trivialization of both topics, the issue remains almost unexplored.[44] All one can say with certainty at this point is that Babism soon became a pejorative label used by antifeminists to justify their condemnation of those who struggled for equal rights and even for education for women. "In fact, the mullahs, led by Shaykh Fazlullah Nuri, a constitutionalist sympathizer who then became one of the most powerful opponents of the revolution," writes Bayat, "declared these schools and women's education in general, contrary to the Islamic law, hence *Haram* [forbidden], and denounced the whole project as a Babi conspiracy."[45]

Taj-os Saltaneh, who not only unveiled herself publicly but also used her autobiography to argue extensively against veiling, writes: "As I would start speaking my mind, mother said: 'You have turned Babi.' My relatives deprecated me. They avoided me and did not listen to me."[46] Taj-os Saltaneh was thus conveniently branded a heretic and isolated. She was neither the first nor the last to be so treated. "The pioneers of women's militancy," says another early Iranian feminist, "made tremendous sacrifices. They exposed their breasts to arrows of accusation and reproach flung by women and men of the common people, who denounced them as 'wantons,' 'Babis,' and 'apostates.'"[47]

As for the scholarly writing on Tahereh, one of its interesting features is the conspicuous lack of any major input by women — until almost a century after her death. The only woman contemporary who has written about her is a Westerner, Lady Mary Sheil. She spent a little over three years in Iran — from October 1849 to April 1853 — and dedicated a paragraph to her in her book entitled *Glimpses of Life and Manner in Persia:* "There was still another victim. This was a young woman, the daughter of a moolla in [the Province of] Mazenderan, who, as well as her father, had adopted the tenets of Bab. The Babees venerated her as a prophetess; and she was styled Khooret-ool-eyn, which Arabic words are said to mean, Pupil of the eye. After the Babee insurrection had been subdued in the above province, she was brought to Tehran and imprisoned, but was well treated. When these executions took place she was strangled. This was a cruel and useless deed."[48]

Muslim sources about Tahereh's contribution to women's writing or to the women's movement differ from published materials by Babis and Baha'is. Generally speaking, Muslim sources, until recently, if not critical of her, basically relegated her to oblivion.[49] Although Babi/Baha'i sources have not delineated her specific contributions to the women's movement, they have, for the most part, considered her a "forerunner of the modern feminist movement"[50] and "a woman who gave her life for her sister women."[51] Her role as a precursor of Iranian women's literary tradition, however, remains neglected.

Paradoxically, after long years of silence by women writers about Tahereh's literary contribution, the novelist Shahrnush Parsipur, in the Islamic Republic of Iran, pays her tribute. In her novel *Tuba va Ma'na-ye*

Shab [Tuba and the Sense of Night], published in 1989, Parsipur portrays Tahereh—without mentioning her name—as the first challenge to an age-old, male-centered, male-dominated belief system. "Haji thought to himself that women think. Unfortunately, they think. Not like ants or tree particles. Not like specks of dust. But more or less like himself. . . . After all didn't that rebellious woman cause a lot of trepidation and disorder during his childhood. They said she was a loose woman but a scholar too. A lot of rumors about her circulated around. He even recalled having heard a man tell his father excitedly that she is the Proof of the Age."[52]

Toward the end of her life, Tahereh lost faith in the efficacy of words to bring about the desired change. She became increasingly intolerant of views that differed from her own. Her desire to establish a dialogue, to challenge the established views through argumentation, proved too difficult to pursue, thwarted at each turn. Eventually, she realized words were too weak, unfit to guide, too soft, too ineffectual. According to Fazil Mazandari, the Baha'i historian: "Suddenly, Jenab-e Tahereh, a bare sword in hand, appeared and with her characteristic eloquence, courage, and authority declared: 'wrap up this spectacle. The time for prayer and liturgy is over. Now is the time for devotion and sacrifice.' . . . She wanted to say forget words and enter the battlefield of bravery and self-sacrifice."[53]

The poet, disillusioned with words, finally resorted to cross-dressing and the sword. And how different is this picture from the tombstone carving. If Tahereh was destined to view life from behind a veil, if even in depicting her crime, her husband had to place her behind a curtain—immobile, hidden, and mute—Tahereh stepped forward—articulate, mobile, and ready to fight openly for her message.

> O slumbering one, the beloved has arrived, arise!
> Brush off the dust of sleep and self, arise!
>
> Behold, the good will has arrived,
> Come not before him with tears, arise!
>
> The mender of concerns has come to you,
> O heavy hearted one, arise!

O one afflicted by separation,
Behold the good tidings of the beloved's union, arise!

O you, withered by autumn,
Now, Spring has come, arise!

Behold, the New Year brings a fresh life,
O withered corpse of yesteryear, up from your tomb, arise![54]

5

Revealing and Concealing

Parvin E'tessami

*I*n the summer of 1908, an American, Charles Mason Remey, accompanied by a friend, visited Iran. In his travelogue, he recounts a meeting he had with some Iranian women. The gathering was arranged by a friend who "had for some time past discarded her veil and with her husband received men in her house and garden, yet she was obliged, as she explained to us, to veil in the streets on account of attracting too much attention."[1] The hostess had a very specific aim in mind for that afternoon party. She wanted to encourage other women to "follow her example and unveil."

At the beginning, according to custom, two receptions were held simultaneously. "Twenty or more of us men," writes Remey, "were in one room, while in an adjoining room, separated from us by a curtain, was a party of twelve or fifteen ladies, our hostess slipping quietly from one room to the other, serving and entertaining her guests." Soon, the American guest was asked to talk a little about Western women, which he did "through the curtain to the listeners on the other side." As he spoke, the hostess

became more and more enthusiastic, until, finally, she went toward the doorway and, drawing the curtain, began speaking very earnestly to the people in the next room. I could not understand her words, but so stirring was the tone of her voice, that I caught the spirit of what she was saying. She was calling to her sisters to come forth and lift their veils, saying that it was a rare opportunity to do so then, for we from the

West were there, who were accustomed to seeing women's faces. At the expiration of several minutes her words had the desired effect, for the women arose and drawing aside their veils with one accord entered the room. The men made place for the ladies by retreating to the other side of the room, while the newcomers found seats. When the women had arisen to the situation, they were quite equal to it. Then it was the men who were ill at ease. In fact, their embarrassment was contagious, for even I began to be uneasy and scarcely dared to take a good look at the faces opposite. Sherberts and other refreshments were served. . . .

Bit by bit the men gained their ease, but, as their embarrassment passed, the women seemed to lose courage. Little by little the veils were drawn over their faces, until all were practically veiled. Then one who was seated near the door moved as if to leave, whereupon all arose and like a flock of affrighted birds fluttered from the room.[2]

Why the fear and the flight? Why the discomfort, the shame, the uneasiness, the embarrassment? What caused these "affrighted birds" to take refuge behind their veils and ultimately to flee from the mixed gathering? I suppose it must have been too great a change to make quickly and decisively. Or perhaps it was a reaction to men's ambivalence. The women must have felt helpless at suddenly being exposed to prying eyes, anguish at being abruptly revealed, even if they had wished for and expected it. It is exactly to overcome this serious problem of hesitation and ambivalence that the Women's Freedom Society was founded at the turn of the century "to accustom women to the appropriate deportment at mixed gatherings . . . and to help women to overcome shyness and embarrassment."[3]

Remey's eyewitness account of women's timidity and discomfort parallels the gestures of unveiled women in pictures taken immediately after the compulsory unveiling act of 1936. With their ankle-length skirts, full sleeves, loose dresses, these women seem to have lost the security of their portable walls. Placid and stiff-necked, they look embarrassed and shy. It is as if the difficulty of disclosing their previously covered and publicly invisible bodies translated into embarrassment and unease. Heads lowered, eyes cast down, scrunched up as if to claim as little space as possible, these women attempted to blur the outlines of their bodies. Uncomfortable with exposure, it is as if they preferred absence to presence, maybe because it was what they were used to.

I sense this same tension in the poetry of those women who first attempted to insert a woman's voice and vision into Persian literature. And indeed what is the difference between the woman who tries to conceal her newly exposed body from men's gaze and the pioneering poet who needs to hide her authorial identity from what she perceives as prying eyes and ears? For both, there has been a breach of propriety, an enormous change from the way things had been. The otherwise invisible has gained a body or the otherwise mute a public voice. The poetry of Parvin E'tessami expresses perhaps most eloquently the push and pull between self-assertion and self-denial, between self-revelation and self-concealment, that many women must have felt who wanted to unveil but could not do so easily or at once.

I do not intend to imply that there is a perfect solution somewhere out there, like perfect teeth, to which all women, especially the veiled ones, should aspire. Neither do I mean to imply that the contradictory mixtures of shame and boldness, revelation and concealment in the perceptions and attitudes of the women struggling with the question of the veil is something to be overcome, like a speech impediment or a psychological hang-up. We are all creatures of the half-light. We reject and cling to the veil simultaneously. We cast aside one veil only to weave it anew in a different and more complex form. We unveil only by spinning another veil. There is indeed always another veil to rend. The fact of the matter, however, is that the semiconcealed expressions of these unveiled women in photographs or in print should make us more aware of ambiguities. By interpreting a woman's relationship to the veil in a simplistic manner, we may miss the incredible richness and subtlety of meanings and functions of the veil, our own enigmatic natures, and Parvin E'tessami's shadowy world behind the veil and before it, in which a woman, and a poet in particular, finds herself "unhouseled," like the ghost in *Hamlet*.

It was a happy coincidence that Parvin E'tessami was born on March 16, 1907, into an affluent and cultured family. Her father, Yussef E'tessami, better known as E'tessam-ol Molk, was a man of letters. He wrote and translated several books and was interested in the plight of Iranian women. He not only included several articles on the women's issue in the journal he founded, *Bahar*, but also translated Qasem Amin's book *The Emancipation of Woman*, in 1900, one year after it was published in Egypt.[4] In this translation, entitled *Women's Education*, the author argues that women should be educated and given a greater role in the public arena.

Women's Education is the earliest book I have been able to locate in Iran, written or translated, entirely dedicated to issues or questions regarding women's status. According to Fatemeh Ostad Malek, it is only after the publication of this book that "a sector of the higher echelon of the society considered unveiling—beginning with the veil becoming less all encompassing and thick—as an important step towards women's emancipation. Under these circumstances, the first *Fatva* [a ruling on a point of religious law] by the constitutionalist *'Olama* [religious scholars] was issued in 1911 against unveiling."[5]

The prominent humorist-satirist Dehkhoda calls the publication of *Women's Education* "an example of an exceptional courageous literary act. . . . History testifies that Yussef E'tessami is the first person who raised the banner of [women's] liberation in Iran and planted the seed of this fruitful tree."[6]

It is not surprising then that E'tessami, with her remarkable education and with, more importantly perhaps, the unfailing support of her father, broke free from social confinement. As one of her brothers said, "Parvin lacked for nothing. In our quiet, unpretentious, and withdrawn family the parents and brothers turned around Parvin as moths do around a shining candle, full-heartedly trying to fulfill her wishes, even the unspoken ones. Perhaps hardly a girl may have enjoyed as much love, adoration, and respect from her own family members as did Parvin."[7]

First educated at home, E'tessami was later sent to the American Girls School, which, as mentioned earlier, was founded in 1874 by a group of American Christian missionaries. Only foreign and Christian girls attended the school until 1891, when two Muslim girls entered and completed their studies later. E'tessami graduated three years later from this school, in 1924, and taught there for a while after graduation.

The tender care and appreciation her father bestowed upon E'tessami helped her develop and nourish her poetic talent. Like Tahereh Qorratol'Ayn, she was allowed to participate—in person and not from behind a curtain—in her father's weekly literary gatherings. According to Nasrollah Taqavi, a family friend, "From her early childhood, Parvin joined us and with a diligence uncharacteristic of a child, she listened to our conversation. She composed her first poem when she was eight. At this age, she could already read and write Persian."[8] The poet Shahriyar also recalls E'tessami regular attendance at her father's literary meetings: "She would come from school, drop her veil, and then greet and join the gathering."[9] Perhaps there was a connection between E'tessami's artistic development and her not having been secluded and segregated as a child. She accompanied her father "on all his trips in Iran and abroad," and by force of circumstances, she was surrounded throughout most of her life by some of the foremost literary figures of her time.[10]

As a young girl, E'tessami had no problem publishing her poems. She was only fourteen when her first poems appeared in 1921 in her father's literary journal, *Bahar.* This easy access to publishing, however, was not to be enjoyed for long. As E'tessami approached a marriageable age, her father would not allow publication of her poems for fear that people would consider it an advertisement or a promotion in the marriage market. Women's marriage through the publication of their poems was not such an unheard of phenomenon. Badr ol-Moluk Bamdad describes the experience of Fakhr-e Ozma Arghun, the mother of the prominent poet Simin Behbahani, as a result of publishing a poem: "Fakhr-e Ozma Arghun was once moved to write a fiery patriotic poem with a verse saying that 'the blood of traitors must be shed, and stain Iran's soil tulip-red.' It was published in a newspaper named *Eqdam* [Action], which came out in 1923–1924. The poem shaped her destiny because it led to her acquaintance and marriage with the newspaper's editor, the journalist and novelist Abbas Khalili."[11]

Almost half a century later, Hadi Hoquqi, the editor of the Los Angeles-based Persian newspaper *Khandaniha,* still equates women's writing with only one objective: finding a husband. "Hengameh Afshar, like most Iranian girls, believes that at sixteen the mother and the sister of a suitor must ring the bell to their house. But when they lose hope, they resort to such professions as teaching, nursing, and office work to earn a living and to poetry, literature, journalism, and so forth for fame. All this is for one objective: to quickly get married."[12]

Unlike most of her female contemporaries, E'tessami was not married off at an early age. Actually, she was twenty-seven when she married, by arrangement, her father's cousin in 1934. Whatever the reason, and she never shed any light on it, the marriage lasted only two and one-half months, and E'tessami divorced her husband. However unsuccessful the marriage might have been, it was soon after, in 1935, that she published her first collected poems, *Divan.* The volume included

150 poems, of which only 12 had hitherto appeared in print. This was E'tessami's last and only attempt to gain wider recognition. Anguished and seemingly disappointed by the reception she received, she did not allow a reprint of her poetry collection in her lifetime, in spite of repeated demands. According to Dehkhoda, she also burned some of the poems she liked least a few years before her death.[13]

> O rose, what did you receive from the inhabitants of
> the garden, save the reproach and malevolence of thorns?
>
> O lovely diamond, despite your radiance what did you
> experience in the marketplace, save base customers?
>
> Into the garden you strayed; Fate caught and caged you.
> O captive bird, what have you ever known save a cage?[14]

Although disillusioned with her "base customers," E'tessami has always been popular with the reading audience in Iran. The first posthumous collection of her poems was a great success. It was published a few months after her early death in April 1941 of typhoid fever.[15] Expanded by fifty-three poems, it has gone through more than a dozen editions in the last fifty years. Indeed, E'tessami is not the kind of poet who needs to be unearthed or revived. Consistently, and for over five decades, she has had a powerful hold on the imagination of her amazingly large readership. Her poetry has survived the many ups and downs and literary fashions of contemporary history in Iran. Her reputation is as secure now, after the Islamic revolution, as it was previously. Neither has she been subjected to critical neglect. As a matter of fact, she has been and continues to be the center of literary and, at times, political debate. Her poetry receives an abundance of commentary and criticism in newspapers, literary journals, and books.

When E'tessami's poems first appeared in *Bahar*, they were considered a curiosity that could only be accounted for as some kind of aberration. Scholars debated back and forth on their authorship. Could a child —a girl no less—have written these remarkable poems? E'tessami herself tried to convince people that she was the author. In the following poem, she raises her voice in protest and denies the status of honorary manhood conferred upon her:

From the dust of false thoughts, the heart better be cleansed
So that the demon knows this mirror is not for dust.

Some literary persons believe Parvin to be a man
She is not a man, this riddle better be solved.[16]

The riddle was not to be easily solved. Suspicions and accusations persisted; denials continued. The author of E'tessami's *Divan,* many were convinced, was a man posing as a woman. Simin Daneshvar's account of the first memorial convention held for E'tessami at the University of Tehran is interesting: "While studying at Tehran University, I was appointed secretary of a literary club, with a male mathematics student as its president. We faced the death of Parvin E'tessami, a very prominent woman poet, and I suggested that we hold a memorial for her. I expected that since I was a woman I would be selected to talk about her or at least read several poems written by her. A poet-professor was invited to criticize her *Divan,* which he did, but in a very clever way he aroused suspicion in the audience's mind that most of Parvin's poems had been written by her father."[17]

Years later, 'Abdul-Hossein Ayati claimed to have discovered that three-quarters of E'tessami's poems actually belong to the male poet Rownaq 'Ali Shah.[18] And Garakani, the author of the first critical book wholly dedicated to E'tessami and written as late as 1977, is convinced that Dehkhoda is the real E'tessami.[19] He argues in some 140 pages that no woman, let alone Parvin E'tessami, who in his view was "kind of ugly, timid, and cross-eyed," could have written such good poems. The book is replete with arguments such as the following: "In principle, the usage of Arabic words and complex Persian vocabulary by a 'woman' or a 'youngster' is shocking. . . . That is why in a poetry collection attributed to a woman (and lacking as it does any poems other than maybe one or two that revolve around women's themes), citations from the Qor'an and the usage of so many difficult and uncommon words—and that at such a skilled and expert level—seem strange and indigestible."[20]

Parvin's vast vocabulary, both Persian and Arabic, is only one of the many points Garakani presents to support his contention that indeed she is not the author of poems ascribed to her and hence the title of his book, *Tohmat-e Sha'eri* [Accused of Being a Poet]. Other points are raised on an even more elemental level. With dazzling conviction, the author notes that E'tessami lacked the physical and emotional qualifications but above all the masculinity necessary for writing good poetry. Besides, "a woman's art is making an artist out of a man," he contends.[21]

Garakani's stance can perhaps be dismissed as too shrill, too extreme. But his views are not isolated. Even E'tessami's admirers, those who do not question the authenticity of her poems, cannot come to terms with her being a woman. To them, she is more like a man. In other words, even when men have celebrated her achievements, most have done so through a prism that either restricts creativity to men or acknowledges the value of E'tessami's creativity but unsexes and resexualizes her. Granted literary value, she is denied her womanness; allowed her gender, she is refused her talent.

For an explicit expression of the assumption that a good woman poet is some kind of a man we don't have to look farther than the introduction to E'tessami's own *Divan*. Malek-ol Sho'ara-ye Bahar, one of E'tessami's first staunch supporters, writes: "Like a man, she composes the poem called 'God's Grace,' and introduces the reader to loftier thoughts and truth."[22] The prominent literary critic, 'Abdol Hossein-e Zarrinkub, titles his article: "Parvin: A manly woman in the arena of poetry and sufism."[23] The poet Shahriyar describes her in a poem as manly because of her "big body."[24] And Manuchehr Nazer explains in his recent book, *Negareshi bar Ash'ar-e Parvin E'tessami* [Some Observations on the Poetry of Parvin E'tessami], why critics regard her "poetry as manly": "One of the reasons [for such a consideration] is the power and eloquence of her words. But this itself is the consequence of two other causes. First, it is because Parvin was a pious woman with a solid faith in God and creation. . . . As for the second and main reason, she paid attention to eternal and universal truth which does not discriminate between men and women and addresses the whole humanity."[25]

These remarks, far from being intended as a slight, are meant to compliment E'tessami. She is assumed to be more than just a woman, but a "manly" woman, a woman elevated to the level of a man. And yet E'tessami had a voice and a point of view of her own. She neither sounded like a man, nor looked like one, nor imitated male thought, tone, or ideology. Unlike George Sand, she never donned male clothing. Unlike George Eliot, she never chose a male pseudonym. Unlike classical male poets to whom she is compared all too often, she never wrote lyrical or panegyric poems. How then, we might ask ourselves, is she transformed into a "manly" woman?

Perhaps it is implicit in such a metamorphosis that only men reveal themselves in print. If it is a woman who reveals herself, ergo, she must be a man. The act of publishing is construed as a masculine act. If it doesn't turn a woman into a whore, then it must turn her into a man. One could also argue that the reality of a talented, prolific woman poet is shocking, too disorienting to a society without any such previous experience. Like the men in Remey's account, confused when confronted with this new sight of unveiled women, even those critics with the best of intentions became "uneasy and scarcely dared to take a good look at the faces opposite."[26] They could not find the right words to describe her. With no previous model, they had no mold to fit her in. She had no lineage. No past. No tradition. She was an anomaly and cause for deep confusion.

The literary scholar, Qazvini, who never wrote to E'tessami directly, expresses this astonishment in a letter to her father: "The more I read the poems, the more my admiration turned to astonishment as to how in the midst of such an acute shortage of [implied masculine] scholars and literati such a queen of a poetess could appear in the heart of Iran."[27] Bahar, known for his progressive views, is no less shocked than Qazvini. "It is no big surprise," he writes, "that in a country like Iran, a mine of culture and literature, a prodigious store of poetry written by men has developed. A woman poet, however, privileged with verve and talent, capable of writing excellent and pleasant poems, especially with such a mastery based on research and inquiry, ought to be considered exceptional and surprising."[28]

Perhaps the reality of a woman writer must be experienced for several generations before it escapes the brand of abnormality, transgression, transvestism of some kind or other. And I emphasize "generations" because, if we only look for isolated incidents, we find a number of women writers denied the support of a tradition and consequently metamorphosed into men. Here's Farid-ed Din 'Attar, the Sufi poet of the twelfth and thirteenth centuries, who needs to justify himself for having included Rabe'e ("the one set apart in the seclusion of holiness, that woman veiled with the veil of sincerity. . . . Lost in union with God; that one accepted by men as a second spotless Mary")[29] in his book, *Memoirs of the Saints:* "If anyone should ask me why I note her amongst the ranks of men, I reply that the master of all prophets has said, 'God looks not to your outward appearance. Attainment of the divine lies not in appearance but in sincerity of purpose. . . .' Since a woman on the path of God becomes a man, she cannot be called a woman."[30]

Several centuries later, the prominent fiction writer Mohammad 'Ali Jamalzadeh believed Daneshvar, the first woman novelist, to be a man. "Some twenty years ago," he writes,

> I started to communicate with the journal *Honar va Mardom* [Art and People] which was published in Tehran through the ministry of Art and Culture, and was indeed a valuable publication. Dr. Daneshvar edited this journal and I had thought that this distinguished person belongs to the masculine gender and is a man rather than a woman. All my letters and correspondences were addressed accordingly. Suddenly, I received a letter in Geneva from the late Jalal Al-e Ahmad which informed me that Dr. Daneshvar belongs to the fair sex, is a woman, and apparently his wife. I whispered so much the better to myself and from then on our relationship became friendly.[31]

E'tessami's literary excellence, like that of Rabe'e before her and Daneshvar after her, is not interpreted as evidence of women's potential, should they be given a chance to develop it. Instead, her poetry is considered as manly with the implicit assumption that men alone can write good poetry. If a woman accidentally or, to use Bahar's word, "miraculously" writes good poetry, she must be some kind of a deviation from the norm, a deviation that is quickly resolved by regarding it as unwomanly. It is difficult, it seems, if not impossible, to be considered different from men without automatically becoming "nonexistent." After all, the scale of measurement, the standard, and the norms are exclusively of man's making and interpretation.

As a "manly" woman, E'tessami is included, then immediately excluded; accepted, she is quickly branded as an anomaly of a sort. She cannot be accepted as a possibility actualized rather than as a miraculous phenomenon. Ultimately and at best, she is reluctantly or patronizingly included as a token woman in an all-male pantheon. If the cost she has to pay to enter this exclusive club is rather high (i.e., her becoming a man), the price other women have to pay for this tokenism is no less exorbitant. As Carolyn Heilbrun puts it: "Exceptional women are the chief imprisoners of nonexceptional women, simultaneously proving that any woman could do it and assuring, in their uniqueness among men, that no other woman will."[32]

The contention that E'tessami writes in a manly fashion appears not only in the works of her male traditionalist contemporaries. It also re-appears in the younger avant-garde critics—male or female. Ironically, the attitudes of young and old, modernist and traditionalist, religious and secularist, male and female, while sharply different on many grounds, are curiously similar in their assessment of this aspect of E'tessami's poetry. Now seen as compromising her femininity, now viewed as exceptional, she gets branded by both groups as masculine. Reza Barahani, despite his evident distress about women's silence and invisibility in Iranian history, overlooks E'tessami's major contribution to Persian literature in general and women's literature in particular. In *Tarikh-e Mozakar* [Masculine History], with an amazing certainty that takes the form of a self-evident truth, he writes: "Parvin's poetry is manly. It relies on age-old patriarchal morality. Surprisingly enough, it leaves championing women's rights to men. A certain Iraj Mirza should pop out of somewhere and talk for the first time about women's unveiling in Iran. As for E'tessami herself, she has not so much as a passing reference to woman's cultural oppression. If she does mention it at all, it is to accept it as fate, eternal and perpetual."[33]

Barahani is ignoring many facts even documented by the same history he criticizes as too overtly patriarchal. To cite just a few, Iraj Mirza is not the first one to talk about women's unveiling. Earlier, Mirza Aqa Khan Kermani, Malcom Khan, Akhundzadeh, and Lahuti, among others, repeatedly had condemned the veil on aesthetic, functional, and social grounds. Furthermore, we know of a woman, Tahereh Qorratol'Ayn, who as early as 1848, struggled for the option to unveil herself. She was followed by many other women. As for E'tessami, she did not rely on age-old patriarchal morality, as evidenced by the kind of poet she was and the kind of poetry she wrote. Besides, she made repeated explicit pleas for women's emancipation in her work. One has only to listen to them. In 1924, during her graduation ceremony, she said: "Women's lives in the Middle-East for long have been gloomy and afflicted, drenched in hardship and suffering, crammed with servitude and abjection. . . . It is our hope that through the effort of scholars and ideologues a spirit of perfection is created in the nation, and through education, important social reforms are brought about."[34]

More than a decade later, her attitudes toward women's issues remained basically unaltered and uncompromising.

> Formerly a woman in Iran was almost non-Iranian.
> All she did was struggle through dark and distressing days.
>
> Her life she spent in isolation; she died in isolation.
> What was she then if not a prisoner?
>
> None ever lived centuries in darkness like her.
> None was sacrificed on the altar of hypocrisy like her.
>
> In the courts of justice no witnesses defended her.
> To the schools of learning she was not admitted.
>
> All her life her cries for justice remained unheeded.
> This oppression occurred publicly; it was no secret.
>
> Many men appeared disguised as her shepherd.
> Within each a wolf was hiding instead.
>
> In life's vast arena such was woman's destiny:
> to be pushed and shoved into a corner.
>
> The light of knowledge was kept from her eyes.
> Her ignorance could not be laid to inferiority or sluggishness.
>
> Could a woman weave with no spindle or thread?
> Can anyone be a farmer with nothing to sow or to reap?
>
> The field of knowledge yielded abundant fruit,
> but women never had any share in this abundance.[35]

It is ironic that Barahani, who takes note of the silence of women and is apparently immensely disturbed by it, seems to have difficulty in hearing them when they finally speak in public. Unwittingly, perhaps, he imposes yet another form of silence on them. Although he may affirm woman's right to self-expression, her exercise of such a choice should conform to what he considers real femininity. Once again, a woman is sentenced to passive dependence on arbitrary androcentric definitions. She should say what she is expected to say; or, rather, she should have said what her critics, several decades later, wished her to have said. No wonder, the hen, "a captive in man's trap" in one of E'tessami's poems entitled "The Reproach of the Uncouth," bemoans: "Why tell our story? Nobody will listen / Why recount our life? Nobody will read it anyhow."[36]

It has been argued time and again that E'tessami carefully avoided any feminist stance. M. Ishaque claims that "it is rather strange that she has not wielded her pen in the cause of amelioration or uplift of her own sex. It was only when the abolition of the veil was enforced by an imperial Edict in 1936, that she gave full vent to her pent-up feelings in her *Ganj-i-Iffat* (Hidden Treasure of Chastity)."[37]

E'tessami regarded education for a woman far more important than forcibly removing her veil. Aware of gender inequities and concerned with discrimination, she never subordinated a woman's welfare to the symbolic significance of unveiling as a token of the modernity of the state. As a matter of fact, even in the "Hidden Treasure of Chastity" poem, she takes no clear position; a position that is either quite pro-unveiling or utterly pro-veiling. The complexity of the issue at hand did not allow her a quick and easy validation of either position. She did, however, refuse to consider the veil a sign of feminine modesty. As if predicting with remarkable astuteness the accusation soon to be brought against unveiling, mainly its equation with corruption and immodesty—cardinal sins for a Muslim woman—she argued in the last line of the poem that "a worn out *Chador* is not the basis of faith in Islam."

E'tessami has also been repeatedly stereotyped as a traditional recluse in the shadow of an overprotective, equally traditional father. This position is at times taken to the extreme of portraying her as a sensitive medium who merely and passively reflected the ideas and ideals of her father. "Didn't Parvin turn her father's ideas into poetry at the age of fourteen just as she had transformed into poetry his translations at the age of eight?" asks Fereshteh Davaran. "Parvin never disconnected her connecting cords to her father. She not only remained obediently loyal to E'tessam-ol Molk but also to the patriarchal tradition of Persian poetry."[38]

But the patriarchal tradition of Persian poetry demanded a woman's silence, her submissive domesticity as wife and mother, her authorial absence from the printed text, to none of which E'tessami, or for that matter, her father, complied. In the words of the literary critic Ahmad Karimi-Hakkak, "change is a process rather than an exertion of individual will, the result of constant cultural interactions between the poet and the culture that surrounds him or her. In the works of the poets of Parvin E'tessami's generation, the current running against the tradition of Persian poetry still runs below the surface, and thus remains invisible to the casual onlooker."[39]

These evaluations, divergent as they are, are similar in their inability or unwillingness to view woman as an autonomous individual, capable of choice, and credited for her achievements. Denied the privilege of a space in which she can be the actor rather than the grateful beneficiary, her uniqueness is neglected. She is forced to conform to a model conception of womanhood whether she is veiled or forcibly unveiled, whether she is living by the ethos of a traditional patriarchal culture or of a modern version of it. In the critical discourse, too, the age-old subject/object, active/passive dichotomies continue: critic the subject, woman the object; critic the arbiter, the judge, the actor, woman the judged, the recipient, the acted upon. One defines, chooses, categorizes; the other gets defined, chosen, categorized. And this either/or formulation leaves little room for appreciation of woman's limitations as well as her potentialities, even when actualized.

None of the many critics who have theorized about E'tessami, however, explain exactly what or how a woman of her generation and with her background should have written. They seem to approach women's writing exactly as legislators treat women's bodies. Both neglect the many invisible traces of centuries of institutionalized veiling. Both disregard the many implications and multilayered complexities of veiling and unveiling.

It did not occur to the legislators of either the unveiling act of 1936 or of the veiling law of 1983 that while the veil might be proclaimed illegal or obligatory by force, the gestures, behavior, and worldview attached to it cannot be transformed overnight. Likewise, literary critics, for the most part, seem to impose their own version of forced literary veiling or unveiling on women's writing. For centuries femininity as expressed, defined, and perceived by the male value structure was divorced from the realities of womanhood. Similarly, women's writing is made to fit the mold of theories about phantom femininity. If female stereotypes divested women of their particularity and of the specificities of their individual lives, this kind of criticism denies what a woman is in favor of what she ought to be. Wittingly or not, these critics grant their version of modernity and femininity a totalitarian role in structuring experience or in reflecting it in literature. Then or now, the attitude toward woman's rights and capacities for self-assertion or expression seems not to have changed much.

~~~~~

Paradoxically, what is called a "manly" body of poems constitutes in fact the burgeoning of a tradition of women's poetry, a tradition that strives to integrate a woman's self in its various aspects, including the public, with poetry. Parvin E'tessami is undoubtedly one of the pioneers of this tradition. She is a woman who refused anonymity, namelessness, and the masculine definition of reality and art. She used the mundane, the insignificant everyday details of domestic life as metaphors and allegories in her poems, deliberately breaking down the rigid separation of important and unimportant as defined by literary tradition.

E'tessami extended the field of rationalism far beyond the master discourse and used feminine experiences and images to enlarge the field of knowledge and rationality. In the poem "God's Weaver," the poet not only gives voice to one who has been traditionally suppressed but also questions the very validity of the value system that has so suppressed her.[40] The poem starts with the observations made about a spider.

> Stretched on the floor lay a lazy laggard.
> In good health, yet tired was he, lethargic, unwell.
>
> He spied a spider near the door, busily working,
> oblivious to everything round about it, good or bad.
>
> It toiled ambitiously as with a spindle,
> its mind bent solely on its work.
>
> Hidden behind the door, it constantly
> kept lookout, waiting in ambush for prey.
>
> It wove webs thinner and finer than gossamer—
> below, above, near, far, and everywhere.

It hung both visible and invisible curtains.
It spun ropes out of its own spittle.

Without the use of words it taught lessons.
It fashioned sensible plans out of raw threads.

It's the same with all work:
Don't quit the polo game while the ball can be hit.

The spider tore down its net,
only to build it up again.

Now dropping down, now climbing up,
down and up it went.[41]

Weaving and unweaving, laboring ceaselessly, speaking through her silent art, the spider is secluded in a corner. Master of fine designs, architect of masterpieces, the spider, this emblem for the woman artist, is vulnerable to the insensitivity and attack of the heavy-handed observer.

The work was well done without any tools.
Many circles were drawn without a compass.

Countless angles and triangles were executed.
Who taught the spider to make such designs?

It had toiled supremely and now owned a work.
It was the architect of that construction.

Such a profession no doubt brings great reward.
Each of its webs contains many warps and woofs.

Dancing upwards, dancing downwards,
now busily weaving, now skipping rope,

it was humble and unimportant, yet proud;
simple and uncomplicated, though a master.

A perfectionist at counting and drawing lines,
a deviser of flawless patterns and plans.

The observer, vain and arrogant, reminds the spider of the triviality of its work. He emphasizes in no uncertain terms the insignificance, worthlessness, and above all the unmarketability of the spider's art.

> The lazy fellow said: "What a superficial job!
> Heaven is in no need of such operations.
>
> There are mountains to climb in this world's workshop.
> Who'll ever exalt you, you wisp of straw?
>
> You spin threads for others to sweep away.
> You design plans for others to spoil.
>
> No one who is wise ever builds a house
> that can be blown to bits by a sneeze.
>
> You lay foundations on shifting sands.
> You draw nice patterns, but as if on water.
>
> Improve yourself; see if you're worth your salt.
> Weave brocade, if you have the skill.
>
> No one's ever made a shirt from your rotten fabric;
> nor did anyone ever thread your flimsy yarn.
>
> Who'll ever notice you there behind the door?
> You'll never be called an artist.
>
> A puff of smoke or wind, and you are homeless.
> A breath or bit of moisture, and you are engulfed.
>
> Who'd ever deliver you wool or yarn?
> Who'd ever ask you to make a cashmere?

The spider, assured its art would eventually triumph in mysterious ways, insists that one worldview—that of the man—is not enough to provide full understanding of the world. It is too narrow, too limited, too one-sided. It leaves out the perspectives of those behind walls and curtains who do not exercise institutional power; those immured in silence and allegedly unworthy of attention and recognition. The spider

insists that her perspective is valuable, that, in fact, it can be appreciated
in another setting. Backing its argument with indisputable logic—the
logic of the marketplace—it contends that its work is precious and brings
a good price in another realm where values are different.

> There exists another market, my dear Sir,
> where my fabric is well appreciated.
>
> No matter how great the customer, the gold treasure—
> neither can compare with the eye of an expert.
>
> You are blind to the curtains of my walls.
> How do you expect to see the veil of secrets?
>
> You keep cavilling me, the spider,
> when you've nothing to your name but arrogance.
>
> I've been a weaver from the beginning,
> and this I'll be as long as I live.
>
> I've taken every opportunity, used every chance,
> to weave, to weave, and to weave.
>
> This is my calling, important or not.
> I am the apprentice, time is the master.

Spinning, like weaving, has long been a symbol of woman's sanctified role and function. Spindle or needle in hand, a woman is within
her assigned arena of domesticity. Like Penelope (whose name also means
a Veiled One), Philomela (whose tongue was cut out), Mary, Queen
of Scots, and their many nameless Eastern sister weavers, women have
used their looms, thread, and needles silently to express the unexpressed.
In "God's Weaver," the feminine metaphor of spinning is elevated from
the level of mere duty and drudgery to the status of an accomplishment. Here, in this poem, art is not defined as an attribute of only
the officially recognized artists. The spider, secluded and concealed behind curtains, establishes the worth and value of her neglected, unpretentious artistry.[42]
Identifying with the spider, the poet dreams of a magic place where

she need not conceal herself and her art in obscurity; where, unlike Penelope, she need not undo at night all that she has achieved in the day because completion would spell disaster; where, unlike Philomela, she need not lose her tongue to be able to sing like a nightingale. Parvin E'tessami, like Emily Dickinson before her, who was not appreciated in her lifetime, identifies with and celebrates "the spider as an artist."

> The spider as an artist
> Has never been employed,
> Though his surpassing merit
> Is freely certified
>
> By every broom and Bridget
> Throughout a Christian land—
> Neglected son of genius,
> I take thee by the hand.[43]

E'tessami captured the spoken voice in the written word. She articulated the previously unarticulated. She commanded attention and achieved recognition. She appropriated a voice of her own, a voice normally muffled by inner or outer forces. Thus, the publication of her *Divan* may be acknowledged not only as the first major poetry collection ever published by a woman in Iran but also as a major act of unveiling.

The voice of Parvin E'tessami recounting, moralizing, and advising in public is the most original feature of her work. This voice is striking not only because of its continual confrontational tone. E'tessami asserts, though with awe and confusion, her voice in the public arena. Repeatedly, she includes her name in the poems by taking advantage of a well-established masculine tradition—*Takhallos*. In fact, the more people doubted her authorship, the more she seems to have felt compelled to thus sign her poems. If only one of the twelve poems published in *Bahar* bore her name, five of these original poems have her name attached to them in the *Divan*. Her proper name is no longer improper in public. She refuses to be a nameless presence, whether as a "mystery" or on the margins of masculine tradition.

In her personal life, too, E'tessami rejected marginality and invisibility. Unlike her mother, of whom we know nothing save her being a "selfless woman devoted to the happiness of her family" and surviving "her daughter by 32 years,"[44] E'tessami earned herself a more detailed public biography. Even in her youth, she expressed frustration at the limitations placed on women's lives. She refused to be kept in the women's quarter, in the kitchen, in the bedroom. Tying women's self-development to education, she not only repeatedly pleaded for its advancement but also became one of the founding members of *Kanun-e Banovan*, the Women's Center, whose primary objective was to promote unveiling and education among women. She moved beyond the acceptable categories of feminine status for her generation. In a culture where a woman's identity is defined relationally, solely with reference to the men in her life, where the word *Zan*, meaning woman, is synonymous with wife, E'tessami resisted such definitions. She escaped the prisonhouse of a bad marriage in spite of the social stigma attached to divorce. She left her husband, never to marry again. Neither a wife nor a mother, neither a lover nor the beloved, she established her identity as a poet.

If we approach E'tessami's poetry on its own terms, its salient features are different from those that critics have traditionally found in her work. In reappraisal, her poetics seem to arise from a mode of expression that is concrete and narrative rather than abstract and formal. There is a genuine appreciation for the complexity of people and situations. All presentations are contextual, based on the particulars of the situation. Like the break of dawn when light and darkness coexist, E'tessami's writing deals with mixtures and paradoxes. Free will and predestination, good and bad, power and powerlessness, freedom and necessity are held in a state of dynamic tension. Parvin manages to attend to voices other than her own and to include in her poems different and often divergent points of views engaging and disengaging moral and social issues.

Unlike many of her contemporaries, E'tessami was not committed to any particular dogma or political party. Her stands, as I see them, resist any categorical formulation. She avoided a hegemonic authorial voice and opted instead for multivocality.

Creating poems out of a polyphony of voices is one of the features of her poetry. Human beings, according to Mikhail Bakhtin, a leading Russian thinker of the twentieth century, are constructed out of a polyphony of voices that represent different discourses, from the political to the literary to the religious.[45] E'tessami refused to limit herself to a single narrative voice. Unburdened of any deep-seated need for a monolithic vision of the world and a mythical wholeness, free from dogmas that are believed to explain, order, and solve the complex and at times contradictory phenomenon of social existence, she presented opposing views, articulated paradoxes, faced reality in its multiplicity.

E'tessami portrays life from the vantage point of a woman. She creates a new literary language to express women's insights and experiences. Her repeated use of domestic images, her frequent references to pots and pans, beans and peas, thread and needle, and her sensitivity to and superb description of female bonds are clear indications of her attempt to integrate a woman's point of view into poetry. She uses new metaphors, considers new themes, identifies with the victims. Although she avoids involvement in conventional politics, she shows relentless sensitivity to, and rejection of, any form of violence. On the whole, her perspective is private and familial, her allegiance to the domestic sphere, her reasoning consistently based on interdependence.

In poem after poem, E'tessami ties the experience of self to activities that center or should center on care and connection. Her repeated explorations of emotional commitments are not adjuncts to the more universal issues of life and death but central to her worldview. Even though a preoccupation with male/female relations and romantic love is absent from her work, there is in it no general flattening of emotion. In fact, her poetry thrives on the portrayal of attachments to others, such as relationships between kin, between friends, between rulers and ruled, and especially between mothers and children.

Furthermore, E'tessami elevates women's vernacular storytelling to the status of a literary discourse. She uses anecdotes, allegorical tales, fables, strife poems *[Monazereh],* and parables to tell stories. She reproduces the voice of women storytellers in her written work, thus reversing an established order. Although storytelling has been traditionally within a woman's accepted discourse and well integrated into her life, she has only told stories. Men have written and composed them. E'tessami emerges from an oral tradition; but unlike her muted, anonymous mothers and sisters, she inscribes her signature on what she creates. She becomes a public storyteller.

Singing birds, as portrayed in Persian literature, have been traditionally male. For centuries, the courting bird has celebrated the beauty of his beloved—the Rose—and lamented her reticence, her silence. E'tessami reverses this tradition by making her bird female. In her poetry, the "caged bird" ventures into the traditionally forbidden garden. It is symbolically significant that the male nightingale — this age-old metaphor for the poet and the loyal lover of the Rose — after well over a thousand years of segregation in Persian poetry, is finally reunited with his female counterpart in her poetry. Aware of and disturbed by the fact that no mention was made of this female bird in the garden, E'tessami becomes one:

> A woman lived in a cage and died in a cage
> The name of this bird in the rose garden was never mentioned.[46]

The singing bird becomes a metaphor of poetic possibility for women, too.[47] Like her nightingale, Simin Daneshvar sees E'tessami as a poet "who proved to women that a woman can become a poet, and for that matter, a good poet."[48]

E'tessami simultaneously conformed to and subverted patriarchal literary standards. Not writing in a cultural vacuum, she had a tradition of almost a thousand years of male poets and masculine poetry to inspire her and was personally instructed and surrounded by male contemporaries. Although she transcended, in more ways than one, the social and literary conventions of her time, she also drew heavily from and depended on them. Writing in classical style, she showed little direct interest in modernistic experiments in form. Perhaps more than any other woman writer of contemporary Iran, her general outlook on life was stoic. Her belief that love, wealth, and fame are illusory, at best transitory, her perception of the ever-turning wheel of fortune, her detachment from many earthly desires, place her in a long and established tradition. She also never breaks through the barrier of impersonality— another literary convention. In fact, throughout the *Divan,* the narrator deliberately erases her personality. Because the inner landscape of the poet remains an absolutely private matter, there is little in her book that intentionally and directly addresses her life. She does not voluntarily commit much self-revelation to paper and keeps the reader at a strictly measured distance. She camouflages just as she expresses. She hides behind her art as she asserts herself through it.

In her nonliterary life, too, E'tessami was a private woman. Temperamentally, she is known to have been timid and withdrawn. She had few friends, and rarely did she confide in them. The details of her life remain a mystery to this day. She seemed to have been willing to pay with loneliness for her penchant for solitude.

Garakani repeatedly tried to establish some kind of dialogue with the poet while E'tessami worked as a librarian in Daneshsara-ye 'Ali, the University of Tehran, in 1939, but all his efforts proved unsuccessful. The Indian scholar Mohammad Ishaque was also denied an audience. "I twice visited Iran," he writes, "once in 1930, and for the second time in 1934. . . . On both occasions I failed to get into direct touch with the poetess, but I had the pleasure of meeting her father. . . . He received me with cordiality but felt different about introducing me to the poetess, perhaps owing to the system of the veil then in vogue."[49]

Although Vincent Sheean met E'tessami, he did not fare any better than the other two. "Parvin Khanum," he says, "exhibited an extraordinary timidity during the very lengthy conversation which I had with her. She sat in the darkest corner of the room, held her veil protectively across her face throughout the hour and a half when I was present, and nearly perished of the shock when I shook hands with her on departing."[50]

Residing in the darkest corner of her poems, holding her veil protectively over her private life, E'tessami hides herself from her reader as she hid herself from all those who wanted an audience with her. E'tessami risked exposure but was also disturbed by it. She unveiled and reveiled. She basked in her newfound voice but was also threatened by it. She presented herself as a woman-in-public but relentlessly kept her distance. She unveiled her poetic voice but covered the private details of her life.

E'tessami never wrote an autobiographical poem in the sense of openly and directly talking about her private life. Neither did she leave behind a memoir, a diary, or even a few letters. These omissions set her apart from many of the women writers who followed her, especially the poet Forugh Farrokhzad. Bothered by this detachment and self-concealment as opposed to Farrokhzad's blunt self-revelation, Barahani in *Tala Dar Mes* [Gold in Copper] claims: "Parvin is not revolutionary. She can never be passionate either. The love as well as the pure and transparent world of lovers didn't mean a thing to her. . . . Her poetry is neither exciting nor excited; neither startling nor moving."[51]

True, E'tessami's poetry, by today's standards, is detached and impersonal. While Forugh projects herself without reserve into her poetry,

E'tessami places barriers between self and direct expression of that self. The persona in Farrokhzad's poetry is both participator and observer. The "I" of the poem is not only the speaking voice but also the spoken, the "I" represented. E'tessami's language, on the other hand, her images and metaphors, her whole poetics create distance and concealment. If Farrokhzad's poetry is autobiographical, very little of E'tessami's poetry is even remotely personal.

But can we or should we expect all poetry to be autobiographical? T. S. Eliot, one of E'tessami's contemporaries, basked in a cult of impersonality that proclaimed that: "the more perfect the artist the more completely separate in him will be the man who suffers and the mind which creates"; and "poetry is not a turning loose of emotion, it is not the expression of personality, but an escape from personality."[52] It is also important to remember that this reluctance to address private matters in public is a cultural pattern rather than merely a stance devised by E'tessami to protect her privacy. In other words, apart from the subjective and personal inclinations of the individual poet, there exist cultural and social realities that leave their marks on the poem. A woman who has been taught to pride herself on her inaccessibility and modesty may have little interest or talent to reveal herself publicly in her cultivated poetry. She prefers to keep out of sight, covered up, concealed. By no small coincidence, more than forty years after E'tessami's death, traces of her personal life are decidedly scarce. Her friends and relatives, especially her family members, have meticulously guarded all information on her personal life even after her death.

The same push and pull between continuity and change, between transgression and submission, between compliance and resistance exhibited in E'tessami's life can be felt thematically in her poetry. In some respects, her poetry expresses the norms and values of a patriarchal culture. Time and again, it celebrates such traditional feminine virtues as modesty, a sense of devotion, and commitment to family. Sexual propriety rules supreme. Chastity and associated traditional ideals are the cornerstone of its value system. Even when the poet is attracted to women's independence and intellectual growth, this attraction remains, to some extent, confined within the limits set by tradition. Many of the social institutions, customs, and codes of moral behavior have an inherent, almost unquestioned validity for her, a validity that is repeatedly given priority over personal inclinations and dispositions. The poem entitled "Iranian Women," which E'tessami wrote to celebrate the mass unveiling of 1936, epitomizes this view. The poem expresses distaste for the *Chador* but wants to see it replaced with veiled hearts and eyes. Old sanctions remain untouched. Boundaries and enclosed spaces become more psychosocial than physical. The removal of the physical veil is compensated by the imposition of an invisible veil, faithfully carried on the shoulders.

> Only the robe of abstinence can mask one's faults.
> The robe of conceit and passion is no better than nakedness.
>
> A woman who is pure and dignified can never be humiliated.
> That which is pure cannot be affected by the impurities of incontinence.
>
> Chastity is a treasure, the woman its guard, greed the wolf.
> Woe if she knows not the rules of guarding the treasure.
>
> The Devil never attends the table of piety as guest.
> He knows that that is no place of feasting.
>
> Walk on the straight path, because on crooked lanes
> you find no provision or guidance, only remorse.
>
> Hearts and eyes do need a veil, the veil of chastity.
> A worn-out *chador* is not the basis of faith in Islam.[53]

If, in the words of Susan Juhasz, women poets in the West are caught in a "double bind,"[54] their Eastern counterparts have to struggle with a triple bind. The first, the difficulty of self-assertion for women; the second, the necessity for self-assertion for the poet; and the third, the cultural unfamiliarity with and unconventionality of public self-revelation. Torn between admiration for her poetry and scorn for its results, between such values as *Sharm* (modesty/shame) and self-expression, Parvin E'tessami in her poetry eloquently expresses the push and pull between self-acknowledgment and self-censorship. Indeed, the very ambivalence toward absence and presence, voice and silence is one of the central paradoxes of E'tessami's poetry. In one poem she calls herself a star in the firmament of poetry, in another she considers her work unworthy of scholars, a mere souvenir in a humble volume. The introductory poem to the *Divan,* entitled "In the Garden of Poetry," best exemplifies this ambivalence. On the one hand, her poems and words are nothing in comparison to the countless others in the literary arena. On the other hand, she entrusts her legacy to the judiciousness of time that eventually separates zinc from gold.

> In poetry's garden roses bloom and multiply.
> May my sapling gift bear some leaves and fruit.
>
> Though they be counted nought, my poems and words
> add up in numbers amongst others.
>
> May it please men of letters to approve
> what I attempted, hoping against hope.
>
> As a dust particle rises to meet the sunlight,
> so my longing rose but fell short.
>
> My heart's not troubled. I'm not dejected,
> for still some dust to light was attracted.
>
> This legacy I entrust to Time itself.
> Time is an intelligent assayer and critic.
>
> In Time's kiln copper and zinc do blacken,
> but gold untarnished stays when pure.
>
> The gardener of the world is a good one.
> He allows to die shrubs of thorn that bear no fruit.
>
> If my words are found unworthy, O men of excellence,
> take them as a remembrance collected in a humble volume.[55]

Ironically, the only two photographs of E'tessami included in her *Divan* delineate the layered complexity of personal expressivity—be it physical or verbal—for this pioneering poet. The first one pictures E'tessami with a headscarf looking you directly in the eyes. The other, unveiled, portrays her with eyes cast down. There is a certain sense of self-effacing timidity about this second picture. Perhaps it is her disinclination to see or be seen. Perhaps this inward pose is her attempt to close in, to disconnect herself, to cloak herself in an armor of self-detachment, to erect an invisible wall of separation, to limit contact—to veil.

6

Unveiling the Other

Forugh Farrokhzad

*T*oward the middle of the present century, a new tradition of women's poetry came into being in Iran; a tradition of women intensely involved in self-reflection and self-revelation, not sheltered or restrained by the anonymity or opacity of a veil; a tradition of women who not only revealed themselves but also unveiled men in their writings. The list includes, among others, Zand-Dokht Shirazi (1911–1952), Jaleh Esfahani (b. 1921), Parvin Dowlatabadi (b. 1922), Simin Behbahani (b. 1927), Lo'bat Vala Sheybani (b. 1930), Mahin Sekandari (b. 1940), Forugh Farrokhzad (1935–1967), and Tahereh Saffarzadeh (b. 1936).

These women wrote about hitherto private, autobiographical ideas and feelings, "facts." With body unveiled and pen in hand, they led the reader behind walls and veils to the domain of the private. They strove to reconcile the emotional, sensual, and social aspects of a female self. In their works, the authorial voice is neither subordinated to stereotypes nor hidden according to prescribed rules of psychological and social distance. Feelings are not rationalized, passions are not diluted, emotions are not flattened, details are not evaded, men are not absent. These writers created, to varying degrees, a sense of self divorced from the conventional definition of womanhood in Iran, a self that is all the more vulnerable in a society where walls and veils have been customary and censored communication the order of the day, where, in the words of the novelist Shahrnush Parsipur, "people whisper even behind tall walls."[1]

Most of these pioneering poets reject the silent whispers of a woman in the privacy of the home. Sharing their personal experiences with their readers, confiding to paper rather than to *Sang-e Sabur* [the patient stone], they speak the unspoken. They attempt to surrender neither to outside censorship nor to the self-censorship that develops in conjunction with it. Spontaneous and distinctive, they also refuse to submerge their voices in collective visions or aspirations.

Society's response to this new female voice and self has varied. To the Muslim fundamentalists, the rupture of tradition has consistently been more visible and least tolerable in the area of women's emancipation. Their stand has all along been unfailingly clear and uncompromising. They have reacted toward women's emancipation and desegregation, especially toward women's physical unveiling, with anger and hostility. To them, any deviation in traditional male/female relations implies debauchery and destroys cultural authenticity. It alienates the people from "true" Islam.

The modernized, educated elite, who claimed to support change, also could not reconcile themselves to the changes affecting women's status. Changes of behavior were felt to be threatening, especially with regard to sexual mores and conduct. The old ways retained the upper hand even for the liberated elite, who championed women's rights. 'Ali Shari'ati, a Western-educated ideologue/writer, especially popular among the educated elite, rejected women's oppressive condition and passionately condemned men for the subjugation of the female sex. In his view, "men have treated women as a savage animal which cannot be tamed, educated, or controlled. They have tried to control her by caging her. . . . Woman was like a prisoner who had no access to schools, libraries, or to the public domain."[2] But Westernized women appalled Shari'ati:

> These western-made dolls, empty inside, made-up and disguised, neither have the feelings of our own women of yesterday nor the intelligence of western women of today. They are mechanical dolls which are neither Adam nor Eve! Neither wife nor the beloved; neither housewife nor worker. They feel responsibility neither towards their children nor towards people. No. No. No. And no. They are like ostriches *[Shotor-Morgh]* who neither carry any load on the pretext that they are birds *[Morgh]* nor fly because they claim to be large like camels *[Shotor]*. These are a hodgepodge kind of a woman, assembled in local industries with a "made in Europe" sticker.[3]

Shari'ati's nostalgia for a past when authentic feminine identity and values were not compromised, when women were women, exemplifies the sense of loss and decline that permeates the works of many mid-twentieth-century writers — men and women alike. This mutant character, this bad imitation from the West, this unauthentic replica of traditional Iranian women — this hybrid — not only subverted male authority and control but personified the painful losses of cultural identity. Allegedly, according to many writers, the degeneracy of Iranian culture was brought about by this new "Westernized," "half-naked," that is, unveiled, and "corrupt" woman. Her "Westoxication" challenged all beliefs in fixed sexual differences: she disturbed "natural" sexuality and cultural stability; she threatened legitimate order; she challenged the very identity and integrity of the privileged term *masculine,* defined traditionally in its opposition to *feminine.* Hard to control, categorize, define, and spatially fix, this generic female didn't seem feminine at all.

The new order of things in which women made their presence felt seemed to be an absence of any order at all. Many people found themselves overwhelmed by the discrepancies between the reality of their lives or of the lives of those around them and their traditional ideals. Filled with nostalgia for a more coherent world and worldview and attracted to change, modernity, and democracy, they showed signs of contradictory and mutually exclusive aspirations. 'Ali Shari'ati, for instance, who rejected women's oppressive condition, had nothing but contempt for these mongrel women, the "ostriches." He called them "Zilch-women," that is, worthless, useless, senseless slaves of commercialism and consumerism, concerned only with appearances and gratification of their limitless desires. All their achievements, in his view, were like a string of zeros without another number preceding them. They amounted to nothing — zilch.

Clearly, Shari'ati was attracted neither to the traditional nor to the modernized Iranian woman. What gets blurred, however, is his portrayal of the ideal woman. On the one hand, he blames the media for not showing Iranian women portraits of liberated, educated, and intelligent women, such as Angela Davis, or of prominent women intellectuals and scientific figures of the West, such as Madame Curie. On the other hand, he offers Hazrat-e Fatemeh, the daughter of the Prophet Mohammad, as the role model to be emulated. His portrayal of Hazrat-e

Fatemeh, however, is quite limited and limiting. He assigns to her beneficent and instrumental roles, but mainly devotion and sacrifice toward the male members of her family: her father, husband, and two sons. The traditional ideal of woman as daughter-wife-mother remains the cornerstone of Shari'ati's value system. He can be, and indeed is, attracted to women's independence, autonomy, and intellectual growth; but he cannot resign himself to abandoning the traditional domestic virtues expected of a woman. Accordingly, he attributes the escalating loneliness in Iran to women's independence and to their involvement outside the family unit.

Shari'ati was not alone in his diagnosis. In a much acclaimed and controversial book, *Gharbzadegi* [Westomania], Jalal Al-e Ahmad considers women's emancipation as one of the "necessary conditions" for Westomania. In his view, "we [Iranians] have contented ourselves with tearing the veil from their faces and opening a number of schools to them. But then what? Nothing. . . . So we really have given women only the right to parade themselves in public. We have drawn women, the preservers of tradition, family, and future generations, into vacuity, into the street. We have forced them into ostentation and frivolity, every day to freshen up and try a new style and wander around. What of work, duty, social responsibility, and character? There are very few women concerned with such things any more."[4]

Implicitly, and at times quite explicitly, all the ills of the society were blamed on women's sexual promiscuity, which was soon to become synonymous with women's liberation. A passage from an article published in *Kar,* organ of the leftist Fada'iyan-e Khalq (minority) claims that "the toiling women of our homeland are well aware that the liberation promised by these supporters of the bourgeoisie, these lackeys of imperialism and the antipeople regime of the Shah, is nothing but the freedom to exploit more, and the liberty to sell the luxury imperialist goods at the expense of plundering the toilers; it is nothing but spreading the penetration of degenerate imperialist culture. Their defense of women's liberation means defending prostitution, drug addiction, setting up houses of lust and a thousand other manifestations of capitalist culture."[5]

It is no mere accident that, when prominent contemporary writers want to portray the plundering of their country by outside forces, they resort to metaphors of woman's virginity, its loss made to represent the loss of honor and national resources. Sadeq Hedayat's *Parvin, Dokhtar-e*

Sassan [Parvin, the Daughter of Sassan] and Saʿedi's *Dandil* are two such examples.[6] The focal theme of the first book is the revival of the Iranians' heroic struggle against Arabs and the invocation of their last moments of resistance. The Iranians' firm stand, although doomed to failure, is panegyrized and their battleground—this presumably last bastion of opposition against an invading culture—is highly revered. The ultimate moment of downfall, however, is when Parvin, the heroine of the drama, is raped by an Arab.

Dandil, a controversial short story by Saʿedi, the eminent playwright, published in 1968 and banned upon publication, has a simple plot. A fifteen-year-old virgin is taken to a brothel in the red-light district of a small town named Dandil. When the owner of the brothel searches for a prosperous client for her newly acquired merchandise, the local policeman suggests an American sergeant who "can spend money like crazy, provided he can have some fun."[7] The rich, fun-seeking, client is agreeable to all; and on the day of his arrival the Dandilians, filled with awe and anticipation, pour into the street. But delight soon turns to disgust, fascination to terror. To the amazement of everyone, the American soon leaves without even paying the customary fee. The cheated Dandilians, powerless and disillusioned, have to face a nightmare: gone is the girl's virginity; and gone with it, too, is their honor.

Women's claims to personal rights and independence created unprecedented problems in a society where the age-old male-centered values, especially in the sexual domain, had remained intact. Blurred now was the boundary between masculine and feminine realms, and blurred with it was any sense of stability. The clear distinction between maleness/femaleness, permitted/forbidden, purity/pollution, honor/shame had blunted. Women became the real challenge to men's sense of *Mardanegi* [manliness]. They called it into question, forced it constantly to prove itself, its bearing, its power, its control. Actually, upon women were projected the whole society's doubts about itself, about modernity, and about change.

Subject to their own mixed feelings, women also became subjected to mixed signals. Immersed in discontinuities, safeguarding many traditional ideals, yet fascinated by change, they shuttled back and forth between the old and the new: "Here would be ladies, dressed up in Parisian clothes, made up, playing bridge," says the American ambassador to Iran, Richard Helms, "but before they went on trips abroad, they would ship up to [the shrine city of] Mashhad in *Chadors* to ask for protection."[8]

This ambivalent state of mind at the crossroads of continuity and change—shared by men and women alike—is epitomized in the literary life of Forugh Farrokhzad. Not only is her work the *locus classicus* of incompatible aspirations but criticism of it elicited is also fascinating in its ambivalence. Whatever the forum, before her death or after, the main drift of criticism seems to revolve around the sensual-erotic nature of her work. Many translated and still translate her search for autonomy, growth, and love into predominantly sexual terms.[9] They disregard her struggle to change her world and her role in it in favor of the erotic themes in her poems.

It is true that love themes consistently form the core of Farrokhzad's poetry. But its treatment is not strictly sensuous. It entails a radical reordering of values, acknowledges the limitations and failure of conventional love to satisfy the poet, and appropriates new communicative and personal terrain denied women previously.[10] Farrokhzad explores the self both within and beyond heterosexual love relationships. This neither demands nor brings about a denial of her passionate relationships with men. On the contrary, it expands her loving potential. Indeed, the needs of friendship, communication, and growth are as satisfied as those of the body in some of her poems. Before Farrokhzad, this intellectual reciprocity, this commitment to the expansion of relational possibilities, was rarely described in modern Persian literature. In her own words, "modern Persian poetry rarely has known what it is to love truly. In it, love is so magnified, so plaintive, and so anguished that it does not match the nervous and hasty lines of today's life. Or else, it is so primitive and so full of the pain of celibacy that it automatically reminds one of male cats in season on sunny roofs. Love is not commemorated as the most beautiful and purest feeling of humankind. The union and mingling of two bodies, with its beauty resembling praise and prayer, is debased to the level of a mere primitive necessity."[11]

To limit critical analysis of Farrokhzad's poetry to an exclusive preoccupation with one aspect of love, mainly the erotic, is to trivialize or neglect its many other merits.[12] One subtle consequence of this excessive eroticization has been a dismissal of her poetry by some as "sentimental," "sensuous," and hence "unimportant." When in the mid-seventies I chose for my dissertation topic a feminist study of her poetry, I was totally surprised by people's reactions. The argument against that choice ranged from the purely paternalistic to the hard-core sexist. Some were genuinely concerned about my professional future. Others, amazed and amused, wanted to know if a Ph.D. could be granted for a dissertation written on a woman poet who herself could not even earn a high school diploma and who only talked about her carnal desires and adventures. The Indian scholar Girdhari Tikku was also "jokingly" challenged for his choice of Farrokhzad's poetry as a serious topic of inquiry:

> Back in the States that fall [of 1965], I read a paper on Farrokhzad's poetry at the American Oriental Society Meeting in Philadelphia. I claimed her as one of the most important poets of Iran in the twentieth century. The late Joseph Schacht of Columbia University, then the editor of *Studia Islamica,* expressed interest in my presentation and invited me to write an article on her for his journal. This was in total contrast to the remarks, albeit joking, of an Iranian colleague and friend, who will remain unnamed, who asked why I had selected a Judas among the Prophets. Traditional critics, of whom the unnamed Iranian colleague is one, did not hold Farrokhzad's poetry in high esteem.[13]

Searching for independence yet attached to traditional ideals of femininity, Farrokhzad worked with conflicts from within and sociocultural contradictions from without. She wrote in an atmosphere of encouragement and admiration mingled with bitter criticism and even contempt. Indeed, her poetry has seldom left its Iranian readers impartial, evoking either strong attraction or intense aversion. Denounced by some for its immorality and its advocacy of promiscuity, it has been celebrated by others for its distinctively female voice that challenges the dominant value systems of her culture. On the whole, however, a large number of avid and enthusiastic readers have consistently offered their faithful support to this poetry. With numerous reprints, her work has been among the most popular in modern Persian literature. The enormous appeal of Farrokhzad's books has baffled critics for several decades now.

~~~~~~~~

Forugh Farrokhzad was born on January 5, 1935, into a large family, the third of seven children.[14] After graduating from junior high school, she transferred to a technical school to study painting and sewing. She never finished high school. She was sixteen when she married Parviz Shapur, a distant relative, the grandson of her mother's maternal aunt. Unlike her predecessors Tahereh Qorratol'Ayn and Parvin E'tessami with their arranged marriages, Forugh Farrokhzad married a man with whom she had fallen in love. A year later, their first and only child was born, a boy named Kamyar. Farrokhzad's first collection, titled *Asir* [The Captive], appeared in 1955. It contains forty-four poems and tells the story of a frustrated woman and her sense of the limitations of her life. The very title of the collection indicates her feeling of entrapment and despair. The poetic persona of *Captive* is a confused young woman who has a hard time forging an identity for herself. She is caught between the seemingly irreconcilable demands of a woman-wife-mother and an autonomous poet.

> I think about it and yet I know
> I'll never be able to leave this cage
> even if the warden should let me go
> I've lost the strength to fly away.
>
> Every morning from behind the bars
> my child's eyes smile at me
> as I start to sing
> his kissing lips near mine.
>
> God, if I need to fly one day
> from behind these silent bars,
> how will I answer this child's wet eyes?
> Let me be, I am a captive bird![15]

After three years of marriage, Farrokhzad decided to leave her husband despite the numerous social, psychological, and financial hardships that would result. With much pain and grief, she lost the permanent custody of her only child and was even denied visiting rights. In September 1955, she suffered a nervous breakdown and was taken to a psychiatric clinic, where she remained a patient for a month. A year later, in 1956, her second poetry collection, *Divar* [The Wall], was published, dedicated to her former husband "in memory of our shared past, and with the hope that this worthless gift of mine can be a token of my gratitude to his boundless kindness."[16] In less than a year, her third book,

Esian [Rebellion], appeared and securely established her as a promising yet notorious, poet. Throughout the poems of these two collections, totaling forty-two, one notices a much stronger and more sustained sense of the poet's autonomy. She bitterly criticizes her society, especially its injustice against women. A sense of outrage and anger provides the impetus for the writing of many of the poems from this period.

Farrokhzad had many claims on her talent and energy. Barely twenty-four, with three poetry collections to her credit, she developed new interests in cinematography, acting, and producing. In 1962, she made a documentary movie about a leper's colony, titled "The House is Black." The movie was acclaimed internationally and won several prizes. Meanwhile, her fourth poetry collection, *Tavallodi Digar* [Another Birth], was published in 1964. With the intimate and the personal as an ever-present background, *Another Birth* celebrates the birth of a female character who rejoices in her new options, a warrior who has fought for every step in her path to freedom. She becomes her own model and gives birth to a self in the image of her own likings and aspirations. Her rebirth is indeed a self-birth.

> I know a sad little nymph
> who lives in the sea
> and plays the wooden flute of her heart
> tenderly, tenderly
> Sad little nymph
> dying at night of a kiss
> and by a kiss reborn each day.[17]

At the height of her creativity and barely thirty-two, Farrokhzad died of head injuries in a car accident on February 14, 1967. Trying to avoid an oncoming vehicle, she struck a wall and was thrown from her car. Ironically, this woman who escaped and avoided walls for a lifetime was eventually killed by one, killed at a time when she claimed to have finally found herself. She was buried beneath the falling snow:

> Perhaps the truth was those young pair of hands
> those young pair of hands buried beneath the falling snow
> and next year, when Spring

mates with the sky beyond the window
and stems thrust from her body
fountains of fragile green stems
will blossom, o my love, o my dearest only love.[18]

At thirty-two, Farrokhzad had produced four poetry collections, had won fame and awards, and had "grey hair and two large wrinkles in her forefront in between the eyebrows."[19] But above all, and in her own words, she "had found herself"—only to lose herself forever. This incompleteness strikes one in the life of Farrokhzad. Like a dream cut short by wakefulness, her life and her art, characterized by a breathtaking dynamism and mobility, are stamped with the finality of a premature death. She never saw the publication of her fifth collection, *Iman Biavarim be Aghaz-e Fasl-e Sard* [Let Us Believe in the Dawning of a Cold Season], which was published posthumously.

The whole canon of Farrokhzad's poetry can be considered, with modifications, as a kind of *Bildungsroman*. Though a genre of novel, and though its tradition is almost exclusively associated with young male characters, *Bildungsroman* best embodies Farrokhzad's emergence from cultural conditioning and her struggle to come to self-realization, warranting its adaptation to her journey and to her awakening. Her five books constitute the account of an apprenticeship to life, a personal history of growth and change. Farrokhzad explores and ultimately defies the traditional limits for a woman's life that seem to make *Bildungsroman* more suited to a male protagonist. For this literary genre, even in the West, has been an almost exclusively male affair. Goethe's *Wilhelm Meisters Lehrjahre,* Flaubert's *Education Sentimentale,* Dickens's *David Copperfield,* Joyce's *Portrait of the Artist as a Young Man,* are all typical apprenticeship novels with sensitive protagonists who attempt to acquire a philosophy of life and to activate their powers and their potentialities. Dorothy Richardson's *Pilgrimage,* Virginia Woolf's *Orlando,* and June Arnold's *Applesauce,* among a few others, are rare exceptions to this general rule.

Men have found themselves an ever-changing, dynamic reality. Mobility, in its literal and metaphorical sense, has been their prerogative. Religion, philosophy, and literature have provided them with numerous role models. Women, on the other hand, have been assigned traditionally static rather than dynamic roles. Farrokhzad rejects this immobility. Her poetry is the chronicle of an evolving consciousness, the testament of a growing awareness. It enriches the heritage of Persian poetry with the portrayal of a dynamic woman character whose definition of self cannot be restricted to relationships or to love plots, a character who transcends sex roles by discovering and defining herself, freed from preconceived suppositions and expectations.

Farrokhzad also presents the voice of the Other in modern Persian literature. By speaking as a woman, she literally creates an-other voice. If E'tessami inscribes women's stories in public, Farrokhzad goes through the stories to the storyteller herself. If E'tessami tries to include women's everyday concerns in poetry, Farrokhzad attempts to reconcile the sensuous, emotional, and physical dimensions of a female self with her literary presentation. If E'tessami literally effaces men, Farrokhzad uncovers them. Indeed, throughout her poetry, she puts herself as well as her vision of men into the text and contradicts prevailing notions of the feminine and the masculine. She is neither silent nor concealed, neither chaste nor immobile. She refuses to suffer and not complain. She does not endure restrictions and prohibitions with fortitude. She does not condemn self-gratification. She does not consider it improper to talk publicly even about men. She plays out her story, including her relations with men, on the literary scene. She laughs and cries in public and shares her many pains and pleasures with total strangers—her readers.

From the beginning of her career, Farrokhzad refused to evade her feelings. Her poetry reveals the problems of a modern Iranian woman with all her conflicts, painful oscillations, and contradictions. It enriches the world of Persian poetry with its depiction of the tension and frequent paralysis touching the lives of those women who seek self-expression and social options in a culture not entirely accustomed to them. It explores the vulnerability of a woman who rejects unreflective conformity with the past and yet suffers from uncertainties about the future. Quite simply, it embraces the daily reality of the emergent Persian woman.

Farrokhzad's poetry is an oasis of the conventionally forbidden: textual and sexual. From first to last, her poems, in spite of their varying content and form, have a certain rebelliousness in common. They portray an iconoclast making her self, not all made and finished by men; an uncompromising, unaccommodating sort of a woman; the kind that would rather break than sway with the breeze.

But it is not only the woman portrayed in Farrokhzad's poetry who is unconventional. Her men, too, break their conventional molds. They are no longer determined or confined by roles traditionally assigned to their gender. They are not so tightly wrapped in their masculinity as to be forced to hide their own needs and desires. No other Persian woman has offered a more detailed, individualized portrayal of men.

Virginia Woolf believed that "women have served all these centuries as looking glasses possessing the magic and delicious power of reflecting the figure of man at twice its natural size."[20] Perhaps in the West it is so but not in Iran, at least certainly not in Iranian literature. Before Farrokhzad's poetry, reflections of men, let alone "delicious" and enlarged ones, barely exist in women's writing in Iran. Wrapped in their cloaks of obscurity or reduced to abstract representations, the men whom women have traditionally written about lack uniqueness or characterological complexity. They are deprived of real emotions or expressions of unmanly pleasures or pains. They are captives of a cultural canon of masculine image and archetype. They are cardboard characters lacking depth, replaceable with each other in their flatness. They are, in effect, veiled. The only man who makes his individualized appearance in E'tessami's poetry, for instance, is her father, to whom she dedicates a eulogy.

> O father, death's axe struck its grave blow.
> By that same axe my life's tree was felled.
>
> Your name was Yussef; they delivered him up to the wolf.
> Death was your wolf, O my Joseph of Canaan.
>
> Moon you were in the firmament of letters; earth
>   now is your abode,
> the grave your prison, O my imprisoned moon.
>
> Thievish Fate took me unawares.
> It stole you away, and grins now impishly at my ignorance.
>
> He who bedded you down in the earth,
> would that he could settle my unsettled life.
>
> Your grave I visit and see that blessed epitaph.
> Woe is me! That inscription tells my destiny.
>
> You departed and left my days blacker than night.
> Without you I grope in darkness, O my shining eyes!

Without you tears, sorrow, regret are my guests.
Take pity, father, honor me at my banquet.

My face I hide from all eyes,
lest they read on it the lines of my distress.
. . . .
I was your singing bird, what happened
That you no longer listen to my song?

You called me your treasure. Why did you desert me and go?
O I wonder, who after you will be my protector?[21]

But although Iranian men have traditionally been denied a glimpse of themselves in female literary looking glasses, mirrors have been in their own hands. For several centuries, they had the virtual monopoly of literary representation, including self-representation. The pulpit, the pen, the brush, the chisel, the camera—all were under their control. Furthermore, in a sexually segregated society, a woman's knowledge of men is partial and somehow hampered. Charlotte Brontë, oppressed by the Victorian mentality, complained of her handicap in portraying men. "In delineating male character," she wrote in a letter, "I labor under disadvantages; intuition and theory will not adequately supply the place of observation and experience. When I write about women, I am sure of my ground— in the other case I am not so sure."[22]

Although men's power was partially based on their social visibility, their symbolic power derived, it seems, from their physical inaccessibility to female representation. And although they were burdened by the heavy load of their masculinity, they did not encourage female representation of themselves; they were unwilling to be stripped of their empowering veil of masculinity. After all, woman having been readily considered the inferior sex, the *Za'ifeh* [the weak one], it remained for the superior party to tenaciously prove and safeguard his superiority.

"A man is he who keeps his mouth shut and flexes his muscles," says an age-old Iranian proverb, capturing with breathtaking accuracy both the privileges and the restrictions brought about by man's self-imposed silence and image. Through the centuries, the Iranian man has been imprisoned in and empowered by patterns of *Mardanegi* [manliness]. He has not been encouraged to communicate or disclose his inner thoughts and feelings nor to see his reflection in the Other's eye. Traditionally, his silence has been the voice of authority, one that speaks all the more powerfully because it does not necessarily have to speak. Others, especially women, have to decipher his muted messages, respect them, honor them, and acquire the skills to decode them.

Such a cultural scene, with its various forms of physical and symbolic barriers between the two sexes, does not seem to be a proper place for the development of realistic portrayal of men by women or for that matter of realistic women by men. And indeed few women, and those only recently, have opted for breaking the ancestral silence.

In Farrokhzad's poetry man is stripped of this veil of mystery. He is presented in his all-too-human frailties and contradictions. At times, he is represented in exaggerated conformity to his own codes of masculinity. He is mystified, terrorized by signs of emotion, softness, and nurturing. He tries so hard to be a man that he becomes a caricature of masculinity. Full of pretences, he is addicted to approval. Intense anxiety and vulnerability lurk behind his façade of strength. He is "unfaithful," "egotistical," an "oppressor," and a "warden." A physical creature, he follows erotic instincts and retreats from intimacy. His capacity to shift his affections according to the moment disappoints the woman who asks for an emotional commitment to match her own. Farrokhzad writes:

> He was taught nothing but desire
> interested in nothing but appearances
> wherever he went, they whispered in his ears
> woman is created for your desire.[23]

Flawed relationships, failed love affairs, and disintegrating unions fill page after page of Farrokhzad's poetry. The lover and the beloved, the oppressor and the oppressed, the bird and the bird jailer, to borrow Forugh's own metaphor in the title poem of the *Captive,* both prove to suffer from their internalizations of prescribed roles. Master or slave, victor or victim, predator or prey, man or woman, each experiences his or her own brand of disillusionment and dissatisfaction.

At other times, the poet represents man as freed from masculine stereotypes and clichés. She portrays him with a distinctive individuality and physical presence. No longer a phantom personality, a dream, a figment of imagination, no longer a Prince Charming of the wildest fantasies, a prisoner of silence or invisibility, constricted in his emotional expression, no longer compromised in his capacity for intimacy, Farrokhzad gives this man new life by giving him clearer focus. After centuries of posing as the lover, man finally becomes the beloved. In the following poem, entitled "The One I Love," an interesting reversal of gender-bound representation occurs.

My beloved
is wildly free
like a healthy instinct
in the heart of a deserted island
he wipes the street-dust
off his shoes
with strips torn from Majnun's tent

My beloved
like the god of a Nepalese shrine
has been innocent from the start
he is a man of bygone centuries
a reminder of beauty's truth

He always awakens
like a baby's smell
innocent memories around him
he is like a happy, popular song
brimming with feelings and nakedness

He sincerely loves
life's atoms
specks of dust
human sorrows
pure sorrows

He sincerely loves
a country garden-lane
a tree
a dish of ice-cream
a clothesline

My beloved
is a simple man

a simple man
I have hidden
in between my breasts
like the last relic of a wondrous religion
in this ominous land of wonders[24]

The "beloved" in this poem transcends sexual roles ascribed by literary tradition. Majnun, the most stereotyped hero of classical literature, represents the perpetuation of a destructive romantic idealism. He can no longer serve as a role model.[25] The beloved wipes the dust off his shoes with rags of Majnun's tent. If Majnun had to remain the lover, he would become the beloved. If Majnun went mad from his frustrated love, he would grow in his love. He stretches himself and breaks down barriers. He does not need to be self-contained, in charge of himself and his surroundings. Neither remote nor given solely to thoughts rather than emotions, he can show pain and pleasure. He can love a "dish of ice-cream," be "full of feelings," be "free." To borrow one of Farrokhzad's own metaphors, he can be "brimming with nakedness." He can be the "beloved."

Traditionally, *Ma'shuq* [the beloved], which is a word not linguistically gender marked, has been uniformly a woman or an effeminized lover. Accordingly, all verbs referring to sexual relationships are transitive and have a female object. The emphasis is so much on male-centered action that the Persian word for lovemaking can be translated as "doing" *[Kardan]* for men and "giving" *[Dadan]* for women. Eslami-ye Nadushan, in his fascinating memoir of childhood, *Ruzha* [Days], focuses on the·many restrictions placed upon the full burgeoning of heterosexual relationships:

> Man/woman relations were either based on barter and settlement or on domination. There was no equality between the two sexes to generate love. Generally speaking, with the view a man held of a woman, he considered it below his dignity to feel himself obligated to satisfy her. In other words, he could not debase himself to the level of gratifying her. His fulfillment was bound with domination and possession, that is, taking by force and preponderance. This was called "enjoyment."[26]

Rarely a spectator of his own desirability, man is finally desired in a female-authored text. The poem titled "I Sinned," one of Farrokhzad's best-known and most widely anthologized early poems, epitomizes one such unprecedented expression of female desire. In this passionately sensual love poem, a passion both painful and delightful, a radical change occurs not only in the traditional notion of the boundaries of poetic content for a woman but also in the conventional heterosexual relationship.

> Beside a body, tremulous and dazed
> I sinned, I voluptuously sinned.
> O God! How could I know what I did
> in that dark retreat of silence?
>
> In that dark retreat of silence
> I looked into his mysterious eyes
> my heart trembled restlessly
> at the pleading in his eyes.
>
> In that dark retreat of silence
> I sat, disheveled, beside him
> passion poured from his lips into mine
> saved I was from the agony of a foolish heart.
>
> I whispered the tale of love in his ears:
> I want you, O sweetheart of mine
> I want you, O life-giving bosom
> I want you, O mad lover of mine.
>
> Passion struck a flame in his eyes
> the red wine danced in the glass
> in the soft bed, my body
> shivered drunk on his breast.
>
> I sinned, I voluptuously sinned
> in arms hot and fiery
> I sinned in his arms
> iron-strong, hot, and avenging.[27]

There are violations of many codes in this poem, subversions of power and propriety. Linguistically, the poem violates norms that define proper language for a woman. Woman—the respectable kind—would not openly address such sexual issues. "To express passion for one of us women," complains one of Tahereh Saffarzadeh's heroines, "is considered so repulsive and hideous that our desires suffocate under the bell jar of point-less prohibitions."[28] Even if a woman treats sensual themes at all, she would do it allusively, through metaphors or under the cover of sym-bols, games, songs.[29] But Farrokhzad's poem is intense and to the point. Its sexuality is not camouflaged by formulas, allusions, metaphors, sym-bols. It thrills in its directness and intensity. Its explicit imagery dis-courages multiple readings. This poem is not an allegory in which erotic love signifies love of God. Love here is human, not divine. Unlike most traditional love poems, it does not make extratextual pronouncements. Its very title, "I Sinned," suggests rejection of euphemism. It represents a self-assertiveness quite different from the self-effacing virtuousness of the ideal woman. "I Sinned" is the abandonment not only of body to passion but also of pen to tabooed expression. If this poet's sexual im-pulses cannot be contained within traditional boundaries, neither can her poetry. The adventurer in life becomes the adventurer in language.[30]

I spoke of subversions, and this poem is noteworthy for the way in which it subverts cultural codes. Farrokhzad, like other women, was taught that to succumb to the desires of her body is to condemn herself to everlasting notoriety in this world and to hellfire in the other. The novelist Mahshid Amirshahi explains with her own customary percep-tiveness how a burgeoning love relationship can be murdered in its in-fancy by bitter restrictions, internalized and metamorphosed into fear. The narrator of the short story "There and Then" recalls the story of her first love with a boy and their escapade in a movie theater — a tale of frustrated desires piled upon frustrated needs:

> But then fear sought me again. It came upon me because of love. . . .
> Fear lingered on — fear that I had done something wrong, something dirty, and it took away all the love. The only memory of love that re-mained was the film that I did not see and the ice cream that had melted in a cup. It all started with the eagerness of two shadows walking side by side to school and it ended in the union of two gazes and the touch-ing of two hands. It never reached the warmth of two breaths and the softness of two bodies. When mingling of breaths and bodies came, it came without love — with the Molla [religious cleric] and Arabic mar-riage vows.[31]

Farrokhzad does not eventually surrender to fear or shame. She breaks through the cultural barrier of experiencing and expressing, even if with much awe and confusion, feminine lust. Caught between two equally imperative and irreconcilable drives—fear and feelings of guilt on the one hand and the demands of a passionate body on the other—she chooses less and less to be ruled by the first. Her poetic persona indulges in what women were not allowed to do or express in public. She also subverts the sexual act. It is, for instance, only the prerogative of the man to choose his partner and to display his desire. He is neither chosen nor can he expect much display of sexual enjoyment from a woman who knows too well that to show interest in a man is improper behavior. Interestingly enough, whereas there is no acceptable and proper open admission of a woman's physical desire for a man, there is a commonly used term and even legal terminology for her sexual rejection of him: *'Adam-e Tamkin*, which literally means to disobey, has come to mean a woman's noncompliance with her husband's sexual wishes. Uninterested she is taught to be, and uninterested she pretends to be. It would not be exaggerating to say there are many Iranian women, including Farrokhzad herself in some of her early poems, who truly believe that once they prove their total interest in and desire for a man they have lost him for good.

> You, with a sincere heart, woman
> don't seek loyalty in a man
> he does not know the meaning of love
> don't ever tell him your heart's secrets.[32]

Sexual misconduct for a woman has been traditionally synonymous with total ethical lapse. Even male honor depends, to a large extent, on the chastity of his womenfolk. The worst accusation brought against a woman and, by extension, against her male kin is to associate her with illicit sexual behavior. But in this poem a woman publicly announces both her sexual misconduct and, worse yet, her enjoyment of it. Freed from false pretenses or strategic maneuvering, she allows her feelings to express themselves freely. She gives voice to her passion. She initiates it, enjoys it, even basks in it. She refuses to be only the object of desire. She feels triumphant in her ability to transform the "dark retreat of silence" to a flame of passion. She generates desire and takes pride in it. She further dramatizes her own desire by her persistent use of the first person singular throughout the poem. Indeed, the poem's autobiographical tone makes it exceptionally forthcoming in its expression of forbidden experiences and feelings of lust.

A curious poem this is, firm in its depiction of pleasure, daring in its revelation, yet confused in its feeling. It conveys delight mingled with guilt and doubt. Conventions struggle with passion. It is the tale of a woman frightened by the flowering of her passion but also fascinated by it. She may talk freely about her unconventional sexual experiences, but she considers them "sins" and herself a "sinner." The dominant standards and values of her society, although somehow disregarded, are absorbed by her in a subtle and inescapable way. Contradictory aspirations make her an intriguing blend of certainties and doubts. On the one hand, there are the burning flames of a body and a mind. On the other hand, there are the limiting social norms and sanctions, internalized. She can neither deny herself the privilege of listening to her adventuresome mind and heart nor can she free herself from what she has been taught in regard to self-respect and morality. She vacillates between two sets of values and aspirations, the old and the new, unable to relinquish either or to integrate the two.

> Bind my feet in chains again
> so that tricks and deceits won't make me fall
> so that colorful temptations
> won't bind me with yet another chain.[33]

Throughout the first three collections, Farrokhzad calls herself a "sinner," "notorious," "a foolish woman," and "undependable." Public opinion and her own internalized value system don't paralyze her, but they afflict her nonetheless. She becomes bitter and alienated, overcome by a need for seclusion.

> I shun these people
> who seem so sincere and friendly
> and yet, in an excess of contempt
> charge me with countless accusations.
>
> I shun these people who listen to my poems
> and bloom like sweet-smelling flowers
> but in their own privacy
> call me a notorious fool.[34]

Not only duplicitous readers condone and condemn Farrokhzad, her supporters also show ambivalence. If she believes herself to be a "sinner," even her most staunch advocate considers her a sinner, too. In the introduction to Farrokhzad's own poetry collection, Shoja'ed-Din Shafa apologetically reminds the reader: "The artistic confession of a woman and her ability to candidly portray her feelings are, I believe, what is truly new and interesting in this lady's poetry. Otherwise, the subject matter of these poems is nothing new per se to deserve commotion. It is a tale as old as man himself and shall remain with him till his very end. And let's face it, which one of us can deny having felt these unspeakable desires in our own hearts? In the words of Jesus, 'let he who has no sin cast the first stone at the sinner.'"[35]

What is truly new and interesting in Farrokhzad's poetry is actually much more than her ability to candidly portray her unspeakable desires. Perhaps what commands both attention and admiration among so many readers has something to do with the emergence of a significant poetic female character whose complexities defy easy categorization. What sets her apart from her predecessors and even from her contemporary women writers is her rendering of quotidian experience with no intention to guide, to educate, to lead. Hers was the subversive, the innovative text, not only in its language, technique, or point of view but also in its subject manner. The candor of these poems might allure readers unaccustomed to such frank self-revelation. The continuously rewoven webs of passion and love depicted in them might provide a cathartic release for what voluptuousness offers and puritanical morality withholds from many of her readers. Her simultaneous portrayal of the thrill of being free and fetterless and the anxiety and uncertainties attached to it might eloquently speak of a confusion that in many of her readers remains unarticulated. Indeed, far from being a personal history, this poetry is an accurate portrayal of the pain and pleasure of a whole generation undergoing radical change.

Liberated from conventional sex-stereotyped modes of thoughts and emotions, committed to the expansion of their possibilities and potentials, man and woman celebrate reciprocity in this poetry. Aware of the many limitations imposed upon them in the name of masculinity or femininity, they seek, and to a certain extent achieve, liberation.

Farrokhzad learns and reveals more about herself through her attempt to mirror the other. Her act of unveiling man is far more of a violation of feminine norms than the hackneyed image of gratified desire. Her curiosity about the real that lies behind the veil, whether it expresses itself in sexual imagery or not (and isn't it instead a reflection of those very checks and curbs placed upon her by society that censor and restrict and judge her in whispers and smiles and acknowledged notoriety, isn't it because of these impediments that she is compelled to express her act of unveiling the Other in sexual terms?), this thirst for and courageous desire for the naked truth leads her, finally, to a place of infinite loneliness and honesty: the homeland of all good poets. No wonder she needs to create, through poetry, her own utopic space.

The poem entitled *Fath-e Bagh* [Garden Conquered] is perhaps Farrokhzad's most elegant and engaging reappraisal of some of the deeply held norms of her society. It attempts radical reformulation of ideas, relationships, and norms. It is the mythopoeic enterprise of a woman who does not find an appealing paradise in the accessible mythology of her own culture. It creatively rewrites and subverts the Fall story, while using the familiar context recorded in the biblical/Qor'anic text.

> The crow
> that flew over us
> and dove into the troubled thoughts of a vagrant cloud
> whose cry, like a short spear, streaked across the horizon
> will carry our news to town.
>
> Everyone knows
> everyone knows
> that you and I gazed at the garden
> and picked the apple
> from that coy and distant branch.
>
> Everyone fears
> everyone fears
> yet you and I joined the water, the mirror, and the lamp
> and did not fear.
>
> It is not a matter of a weak bond between two names
> on the old pages of a registry
> it is a matter of my charmed hair
> and the burning peonies of your kisses

and the mutinous intimacy of our bodies
and our nakedness glittering
like fish scales in water
it is a matter of the little fountain's silver song
sung at dawn.

In the green, flowing forest
in the anxious, cold-blooded sea
in the strange, haughty mountain
we asked, one night
of the wild hares, the pearl-filled shells, the eagles
"What is to be done?"

Everyone knows
everyone knows
we found our way into the cold and silent repose
of Simurghs
we found truth in the little garden
in the bashful look of a nameless flower
and eternity in the never-ending moment
when two suns gaze at each other.

It is not a matter of fearful whispers in the dark
it is a matter of daylight, open windows, and fresh air
and an oven where useless things are burnt
and an earth pregnant with new crop
it is a matter of birth, and completion, and pride
it is a matter of our amorous hands
connecting the nights
with perfume's messages of breeze and light.

Come to the meadow
come to the large meadow
and call me from behind the breath of Acacia blossoms
like a deer calling his mate.

The curtains are overflowing with a hidden spite
and innocent white doves
from the heights of their white towers
gaze at the earth below.[36]

In "Garden Conquered," Farrokhzad clearly subverts the nature of the man/woman relationship projected by the myth in its religious or secular version. Here, in this Garden, woman neither speaks for the devil nor assists Satan. Undeceiving and undeceived, she is neither gullible nor weak in nature. If Eve seems to be a captive of the identity imposed upon her, if in her sins as in her virtues she proves to be unchanging and unchangeable, the woman in this poem is on a journey of her own. Her body, stretched to new experiences, refuses to return to its original dimension. Her mind, exposed to new horizons, refuses confinement. She is fluid like water, protean, changing and challenging ceaselessly, moving, growing, and learning.

Her companion, the man, is also far from being a conventional character. Not frightened of intimacy, he does not try to protect or preserve a false innocence. He does not find it necessary to blame the woman for deceiving him. He voluntarily picks from the forbidden tree and enters a Garden where he can choose and be chosen, desire and be desired, gratify and be gratified. He does not need to invade, to penetrate, or to attack. He knows how to love and be loved.

In this Garden, there is no Satan to lead either the man or the woman to their Fall. Without a scapegoat to mediate between innocence lost and sin accomplished, both voluntarily pick the apple and assume responsibility for their needs and deeds. This freedom explains why the pronouns "you" and "I" rather than "we" are carefully used every time a decision is to be made or a step taken. In this utopia, the man and the woman console, delight, and strengthen one another. Love is neither bought nor sold in the name of power, possession, or protection. Sex is not exchanged for loyalty or security. Pleasure is reciprocated in kind, and sexuality is not tossed on the bargaining table. This Garden is a place of trust where both partners can lower their defenses, revel in the nonutilitarian quality of their partnership, receive the full force of love, and welcome intimacy and dialogue. With their love-locked hands, they can even "bridge the nights." In this Garden, nakedness "glows." Walls are demolished, artificial boundaries destroyed, curtains pulled, veils cast aside. Transparency rather than secrecy is sought and valued. Here, feelings, like bodies, don't need a cover.

But this Paradise is surrounded by hell. It is a Garden enclosed in a hostile land, its paradisiacal aspect tempered by anger and anxiety. Even if it is a landscape of bliss, the site is not blessed. This Garden offers no privacy or repose. Ears and eyes grow on its trees, and birds tattletale with cries that cut the horizon like daggers. Gossip invades this utopic space. Uncalled-for visitors barge in. Intruders—real or imagined—haunt it. Crows, those ill-omened gossip mongers, visit it. This oasis of harmony between two lovers and nature offers no place of real comfort.

Feelings of dislocation and vulnerability lurk behind the festive mood of this poem. From the very first line, and at the ecstatic moment when the two lovers enter their paradise, the poet describes the crow flying over their heads, the crow that eventually will spread the news of their unconventional relationship. Anxiety breaks through from the outset. Guilt and suspicion set in. The couple, it seems, remain isolated, expelled as it were. This Paradise eventually turns into an exile—a willful self-exile at best. No wonder its inhabitants have to ask the hares, the shells, and the eagles, "What is to be done?"

Some of the submerged or implied feelings of "Garden Conquered" achieve explicit expression in other poems and especially in poems published posthumously. The bliss enjoyed in the Garden proves to be short-lived. Nakedness, however much valued, seems to cause agony, misunderstanding, and isolation. Passionate love proves to be a transient illusion. Images of Thanatos stalking Eros, of death of love and lust, of the sucking mouth of the grave, and, above all, of loneliness emerge.

> They carried the whole innocence of a heart
> to the castle of fairy tales
> and now
> how could one ever dance again?
> and toss her childhood tresses
> upon flowing waters?
> How could one crush
> the plucked and smelled apple?
>
> O Darling, O my dearest Darling
> what black clouds await
> the sun's festive day.[37]

Yet, crush the apple and leave her fairy-tale castle she must. Living on the fringes of her society, alone and lonely, a rebel conscious and perhaps tired of her rebellion, Farrokhzad foresees the coming of black clouds. An exile in her native land, she is "a lonely woman" suspended in the space of transition from one cultural pattern to another. Uprooted, she is certain only of her uncertainty. Deracinated, she personifies the pleasures of hybridization, of mingling the old and the new, but also of their pains and problems.

> And here I am
> a lonely woman
> at the threshold of a cold season
> coming to understand the earth's contamination
> and the elemental, sad despair of the sky
> and the impotence of these concrete hands.[38]

7

Negotiating Boundaries

Tahereh Saffarzadeh

*M*ore than twelve decades after Tahereh Qorratol'Ayn's voluntary unveiling, another woman, also a poet and also named Tahereh, voluntarily took up the veil. For Tahereh Saffarzadeh and for many others like her, the symbolism attached to the veil has become more complex than ever before. Wearing a veil no longer merely fulfills a religious norm or serves as a symbol of gender segregation and as a constraint on social intercourse. Instead, the veil has become a fortress of personal integrity, a shield against unwelcome intrusions, the proper way to communicate. The veil represents strong political and ideological connotations that challenge class privilege; sexual license; corruption; and, above all, rejection of Western domination.

Although for centuries the veil functioned as a means of segregation, paradoxically, for Tahereh Saffarzadeh and many other educated women, it now functions as a means of desegregation. In this multivalent context, many women veiled themselves voluntarily before the revolution. This willful and symbolically charged veiling was intended not to exclude them from the public arena but to facilitate their access to and participation in public life. No longer a sign of humiliation or disgrace, the veil returned to them the exalted and active position that women in their eyes rightfully deserved. Indeed, Saffarzadeh has been far more accessible to the Iranian readership since the revolution than before it.

If veiling appears to some people as a retrogressive step, a backward turning of the clock, or an alienated reaction against modernization,

153

to Saffarzadeh, a Western-educated writer, it is a valid assertion of independence and indigenous values. To her and to many others, the revival of Islamic values through veiling expresses a desire to create a new social order—just, honorable, and authentic. This revival stands for a new sense of mutuality, purity, and communal spirit to replace the excessive individuality, mistrust, and corruption of the preceding few decades, the same few decades that were marked by a sense of disturbing cultural void, felt especially by segments of the educated elite who saw Western influence as the cause of the degeneration of Iranian society.

It soon turned into a trite cliché that the aim of cultural imperialism is to deprive Iran of its native character so that it can be exploited better. Women became the potential or actual fifth column, the primary accomplices of the evil plans of superpowers to infiltrate Iran. With its strong symbolic connotations, the veil became, among other things, a revolutionary emblem to challenge and negate the West and its local representatives. It attained a level of political and nationalistic expression not previously achieved or even envisioned in Iran. Hence, the poet Zeinab Borujerdi says: "Isn't it true that Islam is the fortress, the shield, and the castle imperialists wish to conquer? Then what is better than to assault the very personification of this stronghold? Unveiling, in fact, is the most brutal weapon used to attack this fortress. It is the longest step imperialists have ever taken to invade our country and other Islamic nations."[1]

If in the thirties women's veiling symbolized the country's backwardness, in the late seventies and early eighties it quickly came to personify morality and authenticity. A veilless woman became a tool of imperialist conspiracies, her veillessness attributed to colonial plots of the West that allegedly, like termites, fell upon her vulnerable soul and little by little emptied it of content and resistance. Woman the temptress metamorphosed rapidly into woman the tempted, the easy prey, the docile victim, the obedient casualty open to alien "penetration." In this same spirit, the Women's Organization of Iran, its demands, and its leaders were the first to be dropped by the Pahlavi regime. Without hesitation, members were offered as sacrificial lambs on the altar of popular rage and revolutionary demands. Presumably, they personified corruption, pollution of indigenous culture, and Western infiltration.

The concern over the cultural penetrations of Iran can be seen throughout the literature of this time. This is not to say that the theme of loss of Iranian identity is anything new per se. Opposition and resistance to modernization and especially to Westernization have been historical constants in contemporary Iran. What differentiates these decades from the preceding ones, however, is that such hostility vis-à-vis the West attained a level of collective and political expression it had never achieved before. If traditionalists had been the ones who had obstructed or postponed reforms in the name of Western intrusions, now the secular intelligentsia showed resentment against the West as well.

The anger and disgust expressed by the general public against the West were redisseminated and reinforced by secular intellectuals, as, at the same time, they were more fully exploited by the clerical establishment. In fact, this strong anti-Western movement, characterizing the West as a fatal threat to Irano-Islamic vernacular culture, can be traced back to the midforties, when indiscriminate acceptance and emulation of Western models first elicited murmurs of discontent even from forward-looking, enlightened intellectuals.

Paradoxical as it may seem, it was in 1946, as Iran was rushing toward modernization, that a holder of a high position in the Iran-British Petroleum Company, a twenty-year resident of Europe and America, wrote a book dedicated in its entirety to the loss of Iranian cultural identity. Fakhr ed-Din Shadman, in *Taskhir-e Tammadon Farrangi* [Possessed by Western Culture], reacts bitterly against the blind imitation and idealization of the West by Iranians.[2] With passion, Shadman sketches the portraits of Westernized pseudointellectuals who personify nothing more than arrogance and ignorance. He presents them as lacking a firm grasp of their own culture or of that of the West, as perpetrators of trivialities and confusion. He argues that the only logical outcome of such mimicking will be an unstable community in conflict. Shadman sees the blending of Islam with technological advances and cultural self-assertion as the only salvation.

Possessed by Western Culture, however, was dismissed with a slur and sank quickly into oblivion. Although the core of the ideas in the book was picked up later by others and mingled with condescension, revulsion, and utopian zeal, the atmosphere of the time was not receptive to Shadman's arguments. The 1940s were indeed a period of intense thirst for everything Western, and the romantic attachment to the West could not be disturbed by such a sober, critical attitude.

The quasi-insatiable admiration of things Western was finally to come to a halt. Rejection and denunciation replaced admiration and imitation. Beginning in the sixties and gaining momentum, many writers, poets, and social critics began to focus on the degeneration of the Iranian culture as a direct result of Western infiltration. *Gharb Zadegi* [Westomania], written in 1962 by Al-e Ahmad, a prominent intellectual, best exemplifies this protest against further Western domination.[3] *Westomania,* as a term, was coined to describe a contagious disease that has infested, infatuated, and stupefied Iranians. It must be stopped before it is too late, argues Al-e Ahmad. Warning against the bewitching influence of this affliction, he proclaims that the only cure to the multifaceted ills of his society is a return to Islamic traditions. Overwhelmed by the discrepancies between the reality of his life and his traditional ideals; filled with nostalgia for a more unified, less chaotic society; witnessing a sharp increase in commercial and political ties with the West, and oppressed by a sense of political nausea, Al-e Ahmad resorts to traditional revivalism. For him Islam becomes the ideology of resistance — resistance to the West, to the shah, and to cultural alienation.

This rejection of the West that Al-e Ahmad proposes with such forcefulness and that had been in the making for years, even decades, suddenly took on disproportionate force. On the one hand, books and articles condemning Western imperialism sprang up like mushrooms after the rain, their authors trying hard to outdo each other in the finality and harshness of their judgments and condemnations. Indictments against the West quickly became a serious business; and with increasing doses of stimuli, the West, like all collective creations, took on an artificial, almost mystical quality. This reduction of an otherwise complex reality produced a murky atmosphere in which real issues were often distorted or avoided altogether. On the other hand, the revival of Islam became a means of finding something solid and enduring in the flux of undergoing vertiginous change. Islam became a political force, a potent weapon for the creation of an ideal society built upon the ruins of a decayed, Westernized one.

The ten nights of poetry reading held at the Goethe Institute in October 1977, one of the most creative and influential literary-political events of recent years in Iran, best exemplify how the crusade for freedom takes a palpably Islamic/anti-Western shape for some writers. Actually, an examination of the lectures and poems of two of the most important literary events of the last few decades invites an amazing, even bewildering, comparison. Indeed, one is reminded again of the abrupt alternations in Iran of periods of cultural borrowing followed by withdrawal. Whereas in the First Congress of Iranian Writers held in 1946 there was a complete absence of Islamic preoccupations coupled with a romantic attachment to and celebration of anything Western, during the ten nights of poetry reading, there were few references to the West and none of the idealization formerly displayed. If one out of the eight nights of the First Congress was dedicated in its entirety to Russian literature, almost no recognition was given to foreign literature during the ten nights. If numerous quotations from Western sources suggested in 1946 that the committed artist has "to carefully study works of Western writers in order to implement their methods in our literature,"[4] in 1977 such a study was seriously frowned upon and viewed with mingled suspicion and revulsion. Now, according to Gholam Hossein Sa'edi, a foremost writer, "a pseudo-artist is a boorish creature who can master, for good or for ill, one or two foreign languages. He can remember names of some Western artistic schools, which have nothing to do with us. In any time, any place, and under all circumstances, he shows off erudition with his flashy vocabulary and his gog and magog language polluted with foreign words."[5]

The use of religious themes, images, and language is an interesting feature of the speeches during the ten nights. Avoiding the risk of irreverence or irrelevance, many writers found themselves quoting from the Qor'an or the Islamic tradition.

It is significant, although not surprising, that one of the politically significant manifestations of the discontent with the West should assume a literary form. The links between art and politics in Iran, especially in the last hundred years, have not been fortuitous. Many writers and poets could barely remain neutral to the rapid turns of political events. Actors rather than spectators in the turbulent political scene, they saw their art and their lives interwoven with sociopolitical currents. Often politics took precedence over the intrinsic demands of art.

To many, disappointment with the West and Western-oriented, Western-educated leaders and intellectuals had produced a failing political system and disturbing cultural problems. Resentments escalated. A return to the past, the rushed escape from which had proved to be too unsettling, came to be seen as the only viable option. Islam became a popular political alternative. Many found in it an invigorating ideology and a catalyst for needed change. Tahereh Saffarzadeh is one such example. Her poetry can be seen as one of the most vivid chartings not only of an individual's experience but also of a collective history. To borrow her own words: "Good poets are the most honest historians of their times."[6]

A series of eclectic social, political, artistic, and spiritual journeys led Saffarzadeh finally into the arms of Islam. The failure of the earlier searches to provide a stable and unified meaning for her life drew her into an almost utopic zeal about the political implications of Islam. This became a major turning point in her work. It precipitated a metamorphosis, a revitalization, a reformulation of her views of the world. A Western-educated poet, in fact the first Iranian woman who had a collection of her poems published originally in English, a poet criticized bitterly for being over-Westernized, for using too many foreign words, and for being out of tune with Iranian culture in her early poetry, Saffarzadeh has become a major critic of the West.[7] Time and again, she condemns the West's unjust exploitation of Iran's major resources — material and spiritual. She associates the West with secularism and corruption and portrays it as chief villain and symbol of destructive alien interference.

～～～～～

Tahereh Saffarzadeh was born in Sirjan, near Kerman, in 1936. Unlike many of the earlier women poets, she enjoyed the privilege of a university education. Upon graduation from high school, she enrolled at Pahlavi University, in the city of Shiraz, and earned a bachelor's degree in English literature in 1958. Her only collection of short stories, *Peyvandha-ye Talkh* [Bitter Unions], and her first poetry collection, *Rahgozar-e Mahtab* [Moonlight Passerby], were published in 1963 under the pen name "Mardomak," which means the pupil of the eye. She was hired by the Petroleum Company, first as an office worker and later as an editor and translator of its publications section.

After divorcing her husband (about whom not much is known), quitting her job, and "saddened by the death of her only child,"[8] Saffarzadeh left Iran to work for a master's degree in creative writing and a minor in cinematography at the University of Iowa. In 1969, Windhover Press published *Red Umbrella*, a collection of fifteen poems in English. After a little over a year in America, the poet returned to Iran and published in rapid succession *Tanin Dar Delta* [Resonance in the Bay] in 1971 and *Sad Va Bazovan* [Dam and Arms] in 1972 and started teaching at the National University of Iran. After some six years of silence, *Safar-e Panjom* [The Fifth Journey], published in 1978, became a big success. According to Saffarzadeh in a 1987 interview, the collection was an immediate best-seller: "With their popular support of *The Fifth Journey*, which sold thirty thousand copies and went through three printings in two months—the highest circulation in the history of [Persian] poetry—people showed their kindness to their poet."[9]

Starting with this last collection, the poet's preoccupations seem to have shifted. She began to write another kind of poetry, which found its culmination in *Bey'at ba Bidari* [Allegiance with Wakefulness] in 1980. Soon after the revolution, Saffarzadeh announced her candidacy for the parliament. She adamantly supported women's rights and wanted to see them clearly spelled out in the country's new constitution, but she was not elected. In 1987, two other poetry collections came out. *Didar Dar Sobh* [Morning Visitation] contains thirty-eight selected poems written between 1980 and 1986. *Mardan-e Monhani* [Curbed Men] contains hitherto unpublishable materials. According to Saffarzadeh: "This book is a collection of poems that were not allowed publication and inclusion in *Resonance in the Bay* and *The Fifth Journey* or did not integrate well with poems of *Allegiance with Wakefulness* which belonged to the revolutionary period. The interview titled 'The Arduous Phases of Being a Poet' was eventually deemed more appropriate for inclusion in a book rather than in a newspaper due to its length, technical nature, and some other considerations. It was filed away with other 'unpublished materials' until it finally found its rightful place in the present volume."[10]

Growth and change are the hallmarks of this prolific writer. Daring in her use of taboo subjects, Saffarzadeh has consistently challenged the dominant value systems of her society in order to assert her own sense of autonomy. Her work, the account of an evolving consciousness, can be divided into three distinct periods. The first consists of poems and short stories published before her departure for the United States. Characterized by a subjective lyricism, the work of this period is the rebellious cry of a woman who feels severely constrained in both her feelings and her experience, a woman who frantically seeks to emancipate herself from restrictive social codes and connections. She resents the structure of male domination and sexual segregation. She lashes out at the man at the center of firmly rooted conventions. Following is the poem entitled "Stranger":

> I am a pantheon of feelings,
> and I will not hold you—snowdrift of lies—
> I fear you will turn to ice the memories I cherish,
> remembrance of humanity.
> I am that lonely one who understands
> the agony of loneliness,
> the silence of the tolerant,
> the wrath of the inflamed.
> But I never understand you
> —all insouciance and silly cheer—
> I love more the self-made man's bitter smile
> the man who works with mind and muscles for tomorrow,
> more handsome than the glare of your wealth,
> more precious than your legacy of riches,
> which you guard like a dragon
> ceaselessly
> day in and day out.
> I am unfettered by desire
> or the clanking chains of fame.
> I have no need of people
> my life companions are God and poetry.
> You will never taste the freedom I taste
> as you join without a thought your destined peers,
> loaded with jewelry,
> colored with deceit,
> drained of human passion.
> Go marry the bride you have never met
> and follow in the footsteps of your countless ancestors.[11]

The inner experience conveyed through this early writing is one of frustration. It is the embodiment not of wholeness but of separateness, not of integrity but of alienation. All ten short stories of *Bitter Unions*, too, revolve around the theme of loneliness. The impulses and aspirations of the female characters depicted in these stories, like the poetic personae in *Moonlight Passerby*, collide with existing social codes and norms. Their relationships with men end in failure: bitter unions. They voice distress and agony rather than joy and gratification. None of the women protagonists are sucked into the solaces of conformity or domesticity; instead they experience a dilemma in its crudest form. On the one hand, they don't feel at ease with traditional roles and relationships. On the other hand, they find themselves imprisoned in depressing, mismatched alliances. Acquiescing to the limitations placed on them, they spend their lives mourning their lost freedom. Seeking refuge outside conventions, they find themselves paralyzed by doubt and guilt, disillusioned by the discrepancies between their romanticized expectations and their real experiences. The poem titled "Lone Tree" from *Motion and Yesterday* epitomizes the forlorn and solitary tone prevalent throughout the work of this period.

> A lone tree I am
> in this far reaching desert
> on this sorrowful plain
> I have no soul mate
> no one whose steps tread in unison with mine
> the friendly murmur of streams
> the happy rush of springs
> die in a space far away
> and my ear
> fills with parched strains of solitude
> In this desert
> I have terrifying companions;
> hail of pain, cloud of fear,
> and wild downpour of sorrows
> within me howls the clamor of
> wolves of loneliness.
> In this darkness of night
> my heart does not quicken
> with thoughts of tomorrow.[12]

A sense of incompleteness—void—fills page after page of the works of this early period. The author seeks freedom that slips through her cupped fingers. Alienation, fragmentation, and a search for autonomy are by far more forcefully realized here than is the ideal that the poet longs to compass. But as frustrated as she may be, she still refuses to conform, to stagnate, or to be silent. She resolves to take fuller control of her life, and her restless pursuit of self-discovery leads her to new ways of experiencing life and art. In an attempt to tend her poetic inclinations further, she resigns from her job and joins a creative writing program in Iowa. This trip to America proves to be a formative influence. In her own words: "I must say my knowing and living with foreign poets in American educational surroundings—along with my contact with a lively and fervent artistic milieu—had an incredible impact on me. Witnesses to the evolution of my poetry were those contemporaries of mine who did not suffer from sexist, nationalistic, or narcissistic hang-ups and viewed my poetry with a healthy and objective attitude."[13]

Indeed, in *Red Umbrella* we witness a change occurring in the technical form and poetic content as well as a corresponding change in the poet's relationship to herself. She not only talks freely about her unconventional experiences and desires but also deliberately disregards the dominant standards of her society. If in earlier poems the spontaneity of emotions was refined by reason or by social prescriptions, the poems of this second period are characterized by a certain intensity and candor in self-revelation.

The character that emerges from these poems is far from the woman portrayed in earlier works. Guided by her own needs, relentlessly resisting uncritical adherence to her society's dominant moral codes, she is a woman who wants to develop a self in the image of her own ideals. She is far more uninhibited in expression of sensual themes. Actually, never again will Saffarzadeh make such open references to lust and celebrate physical love. Perhaps her being away from home, having a different category of interlocutors, and experiencing the release afforded by a foreign language that does not invoke internalized taboos all account for the explicit voluptuousness of these poems.

> invite me to a sandwich of love
> I am tired of all the big lunches
> the big preparations
> the big promises
> remember I am not the woman out of Maugham's Luncheon
> I am the traveler
> who has experienced the weight
> of too much baggage
> who only thinks of

a light snack
light stomach
light memory

invite me to a sandwich of love
serve me in your hands
wrap my body
in the warm paper
of your breath
at the table of this cold winter night.[14]

Or, again, in "Love Poem," she writes:

we travel towards the enjoyment of salty waters
in a boat with no compass, we travel from nowhere to somewhere from
    somewhere to nowhere
cruising in the song of our bodies
my breasts trust every word that your hands
— hands with suppleness of the gentle heart — whisper

we drive we drive towards a hot summer noon
and yet men are shivering in their heavy coats
waves transcribe our gestures in the water's cloudy avenue
thirst is blowing our breath in all directions
we will die in a moment
we die in a moment of perfumed humidity and sun[15]

Resonance in the Bay and *Dam and Arms,* published after Saffarzadeh's return to Iran, testify to the poet's new adventure in both life and art. They chronicle her personal and artistic growth. They are characterized by the poet's desire to bring language and experience closer together than ever before. Wanting to embrace life on different levels and to include new themes, the poet comes to feel the need for new avenues of expression. She relinquishes classical rules of versification. The inner landscape of each poem as it reveals itself determines the poetic form. Anger, outrage against the unequal treatment of men and women provide the impetus for writing many poems of this period. Revolt seems to be the galvanizing principle behind them. In their consciousness of and attention to the fact that women have been and continue to be underprivileged, the Other, and in their attempt to expose the double standards and prejudices of a patriarchal culture, these poems are significant feminist achievements. They show resentment against the structure of male dominance that has pushed women to live on the outskirts of society. The poem entitled "Pilgrimage to My Birthplace" best expresses resentment toward society's injustices even at the moment of a girl's birth. This poem moves beyond the earlier sense of confinement and pulsates with fury and a will to change. The path pursued by the traditional mother—her acceptance of her lot, her inaction—is rejected by the speaker, who, in the character of the daughter, seeks to appropriate a new version of life and identity.

> I have not seen my birthplace
> where my mother deposited under a low ceiling
> the heavy load of her insides.
> It is still alive
> the first tick-tick of my small heart
> in the stovepipe
> and in the crevices between crumbling bricks.
> It is still alive in the door and walls of the room
> my mother's look of shame
> at my father,
> at my grandfather,
> after a muffled voice announced,
> "It's a girl."
> The midwife cringed, fearing no tip
> for cutting the umbilical cord,
> knowing there'd be none
> for circumcision.
>
> On my first pilgrimage to my birthplace
> I will wash from the walls
> my mother's look of shame,
> and where my heart began to pound,
> I will begin to tell the world
> that my luminous hands have no lust
> to clench in fists,
> nor to beat and pound
> I do not yell,
> I do not feel proud to kill,

I've not been fattened
at the table of male supremacy.[16]

Generally speaking, the subdued reaction to the delivery of a baby girl sharply contrasts with the jubilation expressed on the occasion of the birth of a boy.[17] Girls are, more often than not, greeted at birth with a sigh of regret, shame, or resignation. At best, consoling statements are offered the mother: "Thank God, she is healthy." "What is wrong with a baby girl?" "God willing, the next one will be a boy."

To say that baby boys are expressedly preferred to baby girls does not necessarily mean that daughters are not treated affectionately by their parents. In fact, most often, owing to the mother's identification with her daughter and the father's concern over her future, a particular attachment develops between them. Treated most lovingly by her family, Shusha Guppy compares her father's reactions to her sister's and her own birth to those expressed upon the birth of her two brothers:

During my mother's labour, my father was in his study, praying for a safe and speedy delivery. Nanny rushed in with the news and was given the traditional tip—a gold sovereign. Later, when the room had been tidied and Mother put to bed, he came in to see her. My parents had already three children, two boys and a girl. When the boys were born, Father congratulated Mother with a quotation from Firdowsi's *Book of Kings:* "Sufficient unto women is the art of Producing and raising sons as brave as lions." My sister was a welcome variety, and "such a pretty little girl." I just happened.

Would Father have preferred a boy, as men always did in those days? I once asked him: "Not because boys are better, but because women suffer more. One worries about their future; one wonders into whose hands they will fall."[18]

And here is Mahshid Amirshahi recalling the birth of her sister:

Then the nursemaid came in. I was happy to see her and jumped into her arms. But unlike usual, she didn't pay much attention to me and just talked to Dad.
"Is it over?" He put out his cigarette and lit another.
"Yes." She lowered her eyes.
"Is this one a girl too?"
The nursemaid kept silent.[19]

And the sociologist and editor of the feminist journal *Nimeye-Digar,* Afsaneh Najmabadi, was reminded time and again by her mother of her descent "into darkness":

> I wondered where I was supposed to start. Surely not with my physical birth; although if it were up to my mother, that is where she would start. She has never tired of telling and re-telling my birth story, my birth into darkness, or rather darkness descending on her upon my birth: I was the third female child she gave birth to, to the despair of my paternal grandmother who thereupon ordered all the house lights turned off. As if to make up for this original journey into the night, she resolved to give me the most enlightened upbringing she could.[20]

"Pilgrimage to My Birthplace" is about these lonely moments of silences, muffled voices, lowered eyes, turned-off lights. It is written in a reflexive, retrospective mood and carries with it a sense of power and strength. It reaffirms the bonds between two victims, mother and daughter. The poem does not simply bemoan the injustices of a patriarchal culture; it forcefully attacks those injustices. It does not perpetuate a lonely desolation or a bitter endurance. It reinforces the urgency of action. This metaphorical journey into the past is not only a revival of an all-too-common scene. It is a reexamination, a revision. It is a second visit with a specific plan. It is an attempt to "wash from the walls" the shame of a woman who continues to suffer silently the "shame" of having given birth to a girl—a girl who refuses passively to accept her lot; who, unlike the mother, is molded and defined by society; and who wants to establish her equal worth and value.

Thus, the first part of the poem renders the moment of a girl's birth, whereas the second portion portrays a vigorous struggle against its lingering aftermath. The earlier objective and representational tone quickly turns into anger and militancy. Again, unlike the mother, the daughter refuses to be an observer, a passive bystander. She becomes a participant. The poet, too, declines merely to record. She becomes a participant through her obvious subjectivity, attains a personal sense of identity and strength, and develops her personal context for power. Through words, she becomes a survivor and, as a victor, witnesses her rebirth— a birth not into silence, muffled voices, lowered eyes, turned-off lights, but a birth into light, into poetry.

Throughout, the poetry of this second phase combines Eastern and Western symbolism and mythology. We witness the poet building up, piece by piece, a new set of moral and spiritual codes for herself. If Islam enters into these poems at all, it is not as a passive imitation of traditional observances but as a new interpretation, an adaptation to new realities. Relevant to the changing conditions of the time, Islam is an effective guide to action.

> The crisp sound of Azan can be heard
> the crisp sound of Azan
> is like the hands of a pious man
> which frees my healthy roots
> from feelings of isolation and seclusion
> no longer an Island
> I go towards a mass prayer
> my ablution with city air and dark paths of smoke
> my Mecca, events to come
> and my nail polish
> no barrier
> for prayer chanting
> prayer for miracle
> prayer for change.[21]

An element of corruption governs the world around Saffarzadeh. She can neither ignore it nor evade it. She wants to see it changed. Surrounded by people worshipping material luxury, "curbed slaves / bent under masses of payments / monthly, yearly, eternal payments," she laments the spiritual wasteland of her milieu.[22] And as she becomes more disillusioned, she rises further in defense of religion. Deeply disenchanted with the West, she wishes to redefine and reformulate the process of modernization. She is not opposed to modernization, but she refuses to equate it with Westernization. In Islam, she finds an invigorating ideology of freedom and equality and views it as a revolutionary banner to mobilize people. She turns to Islam as the sole viable cure for all the ills and afflictions of her society and voluntarily veils herself. Again, this reveiling is not to segregate, to seclude, or to embrace silence. On the contrary, it is to allow her easier access to and participation in public life.

Surely, Saffarzadeh's interest in Islam is not only tactical but motivated by deeply felt personal needs and convictions. "My life companions are God and poetry" she says emphatically in one of her first poems.[23] But although in the early poetry religion is individualized, personal, in her later poetry it is institutionalized, politicized, a potent weapon to create a just society on the ruins of a decayed, corrupt one. Religious beliefs, although not totally absent in the early poetry, do not have the intensity of their later expression. They exist on the edges of her work, which is centrally occupied with different themes.

Saffarzadeh herself claims that this upsurge in religious interest comes out of opposition. In an interview with Mohammad-'Ali Esfahani, the poet associates her increasing interest in Islam with "my own anti-oppression, non-compromising, and justice-seeking stance and the justice-seeking, uncompromising nature of Shi'ism and the oppressiveness of our time which inevitably provokes a righteous person to rebel and increases religious inclinations."[24]

The following passage from the poem "Passageway of Torture and Silence" epitomizes this militant view of Islam.

> We were sound asleep
> so fast asleep
> that the footsteps of thieves
> —internal and external thieves—
> couldn't wake us up
> God itself wanted wakefulness for our people
> and a mountain of a man
> sustained us
> and the height of faith
> directed us toward
> struggle and martyrdom[25]

The religious and the political mingle in the poems of the third phase, that is, *The Fifth Journey* and later poems. Although the poet's revolt expresses itself in religious terms, the main focus remains the injustice, corruption, and materialistic tendencies that need to be challenged and changed. A vigorous espousal of political activism characterizes these poems.[26] The volcanic energy of the previous rebelliousness finds specific targets: the Pahlavi regime and the West. And as the problems become more concrete and tangible, so, too, the victories. Attacks on the West, its decadence, its exploitive nature, its muddled values, and its association with Pahlavi rule and secularism form an important part of these poems. They present Islam as the natural ideological base from which to fight both inner and outer enemies.

If Saffarzadeh's earlier poetry sought and celebrated the gradual breakdown of authority or status quo, her later poetry portrays the emergence of a new kind of authority. In a poem offered to Ayatollah Khomeini in *Allegiance with Wakefulness* she writes:

> Never was night followed by such awakening
> never did night see so many keeping vigil
> Enemy of sleep
> Soul of God spreading justice
> you are the ancestor of all heroes
> the hero among prophets
> in an era of temptation and greed
> in an era of ubiquitous murder
> an era of conniving imposters
> of bribe-givers and night-seekers
> in the darkest night of history
> you are the East in every universe
> with nothing between you and the sun
> and your movement
> is the movement of sun's hours
> with freedom and power
> and no leave from anyone.[27]

The poet who maintained that "attention to reality should not eliminate poetic imagination, otherwise journalism, reporting, and poetry will be synonymous"[28] sacrifices now the very vitality of her art to revolutionary proselytizing. A poetry that expressed the self with all its ambiguities, its aspirations, and its responses to complex outer realities becomes a hasty chronicle of daily events.[29] The observing eye and the narrating voice no longer intertwine in the aesthetic of these issue-oriented poems. They are clear-cut statements of intent. At times, they present an imagination denied its previous complexity, flattened to the level of mere slogans.

Walls have started moving
walls have started talking
walls of silence and surrender
walls of servitude that hold up castles
bent walls of government.
From the blessing of the attack of the masses
old walls
and middle-aged
these blind witnesses of yesterday's disaster
these mute witnesses of oppression and torture
have just started talking
they have just started walking
but how fast they can walk,
these children,
who have just started talking
these old people
who have just started walking.[30]

The poet's desire to be readily comprehensible makes her rely on the familiar, the unambiguous, the cliché. By pushing her work into political events, she actually pushes political poetry out of her poems. The following poem, dedicated to revolutionary guards, typifies the dominant mood of this volume of poetry.

O Guard
in the heart of night's cold
you watch as if from outside
the house of your own body
with tired eyelids
— a night nurse —
so that the wounded city can rest
from the plunder of death.
Your wakefulness comes from earnest faith,
your sincerity and Al-'Asr.
Stories of your martyrdom
like martyrdom of the people
remain unheard
they have no voice, no image, no date,
they are unannounced.
O light of the eyes

O good
O my brother
O watchful one
as your bullets in the air
break my sleep,
as if by reflex, I pray for you,
guardian of the liberating Revolution
O lonely hero,
watching against the nightly enemy
let God safeguard you from calamity.[31]

It should be noted that, although religious passion animates most of the poems of this third phase, there is a big difference between *Allegiance with Wakefulness* and the other three books. It is only in this collection that despair and disillusionment are left behind. The Islamic revolution seems not only to guarantee an ideal sociopolitical order but also to redeem the poet's inner world. The poetic persona depicted here seems to have been saved from the burden of swimming against the current, saved from doubts and contradictions. Technically speaking, the poems in this collection do not embody the earlier careful manipulation of formal elements combined with economy, precision, and thematic expansion.

In Saffarzadeh's later poetry, and especially in *Allegiance with Wakefulness,* her previous feminist voice is suppressed. The earlier lingering resentment of a rebellious woman disappears. One no longer hears the woman outraged at imposed gender limitations. Her femininity is submerged in a neuter persona, if not discounting, then at least hiding her sex behind an asexual façade. In these gender-indistinguishable poems, the peculiarities of the self are transformed, harnessed into the revolutionary social system, where there is no space for personal, especially feminist, demands. One no longer finds any concern over the fate of woman, let alone any protest over her condition.

The poet who earlier basked in her unique female voice becomes the mouthpiece for the downtrodden, the martyrs, the faceless crowd. If earlier, to borrow her own metaphor, she was "veiled in her nakedness,"[32] she is now covered, concealed, her personal life almost inaccessible to her readers. If in earlier poems she held the hands of her lover and blissfully sang: "Cruising in the song of our bodies / my breasts trust every

word that your hands / —hands with suppleness of the gentle heart—
whisper,"[33] she now extends her hands beyond the boundaries of time
and space to hold the hands of martyrs:

> O, you martyr
> hold my hands
> with your hands
> cut from earthly means.
> Hold my hands,
> I am your poet,
> with an inflicted body,
> I've come to be with you
> and on the promised day
> we shall rise again.[34]

Thus, in her later poetry, not only is the poet Saffarzadeh veiled but
so, too, is her poetic persona. If earlier the self was at the center of
the perceived world, it now has moved to the periphery. If earlier she
portrayed herself from within, in the privacy of her innermost feelings,
she now presents herself from without, submerged in a collective self.
Self-effacement emerges. Her self is masked, veiled, as it were. Here,
religious passion submerges lyrical metaphors of love and lust. Socially
validated codes of conduct now substitute for individualistic, idiosyncratic tendencies. Slogans suffocate details. Religiopolitical fervor sup-
plants intimacy. This genderless poetry with an asexual voice is distanced.

I do not mean to imply that an overriding concern with the private
self and womanhood should continue to be the focal point of Saffarzadeh's poetry. Just as I argued in the case of Parvin E'tessami, we cannot
expect all poetry to incorporate autobiographical material or to be "personal." Neither do I intend to deny the choice of a woman poet to write
from a male or from an asexual point of view. My point is that one
cannot help noticing in this poet's work an abrupt change of theme,
concern, and language. It is not a mere shift of emphasis, a refinement
of style or ideas, but a reordering of values, a sudden concealment of
the poetic persona. It is a metamorphosis.[35] The poet no longer needs
to distinguish herself from the whole. Now she wants to remain within
the confines of her cultural context. She assigns little value to personal,
idiosyncratic experiences or to their expression. The poet who had pre-

viously assumed the difficult task of defining her uniqueness in a society that values anonymity shows now a reverent acceptance of and a commitment to a model conception. Gone are her concerns with expression of distinctive personal experiences. Gone, too, are her attempts toward discovering and uncovering her feminine self.

The previous despair and disillusionment of the early periods are also left behind in these later poems. Loneliness no longer holds sway. The experience of conflict has disappeared, and especially the poems of *Allegiance with Wakefulness* are alarmingly free of friction and discord. A world that in the earlier poetry was an empty wasteland is now, for the most part, redeemed. The clouds of frustration that hung over her previous books have evaporated into the thin air of sunny skies. The poetic persona has become prescriptive, fitting a ready-made, utilitarian mold. Its previous isolation from the world has disappeared. She has given up her individual self, and she need not feel alone and anxious anymore. She feels like others. Inner pain is transformed into something more objective and less personally threatening. If earlier she relied on inner directed motives and rules, she now relies on given codes of conduct and shared beliefs. Freed from an independence that both limited her and gave her individuality, she finds comfort and refuge in her revolutionary zeal. The adventurous Saffarzadeh need no longer reassess; standing inside the system, she is no longer the outsider struggling for her rights.

But from first to last, a sense of movement and energy pervades the poems of Saffarzadeh. Indeed, the whole canon of her work can be seen as the account of the apprenticeship of a woman who attempts to restructure her life and her society according to a new vision and ideal. *Curbed Men* cannot be viewed as the conclusion of this journey. Saffarzadeh's original indefatigable striving toward *Azadegi* [liberation from the tyranny of and attachment to such worldly issues as money, power, or social station], replaced by her later more narrow concept of *Azadi* [that is, a sociopolitical state comprising an institutionalized (patriarchal) power], seems to be emerging once again. The order of the day is being challenged again in its most intimate and personal levels. Interestingly enough, even in its very title her last book returns to a prerevolutionary theme. In the poem entitled "The Millennium Journey" and dedicated to 'Ali Shari'ati, the emblem of the time is the image of the curbed man "who has bent down / to pick up coins."[36] And again, in the long poem entitled "Love Journey," in *Curbed Men,* she returns to the same image:

Life devoid of faith is a kind of death
even if all the windows are opened
even if all the doors are opened
O slave curbed
under the weight of payments
monthly, yearly, eternal payments
do you have a posture to show?
Do you have a voice to sing with?[37]

If in *Allegiance with Wakefulness* clenched fists, scores of martyrs, and numberless zealots ready to die did not leave much room for previous concerns, the last two collections present them again in their manifold disguises. Saffarzadeh cannot be pinned down. The fascination with movement and mobility never ceases for her. In her own words:

This is the nature of the walk:
to go
to turn
to return
to view and to review.
Going leads to the road
Staying joins stagnation.[38]

Saffarzadeh's journey will not stop here.

PART THREE

Shaherzad's Daughters
The Storytellers

8

Overcoming the Blank Page

You want a tale, sweet lady and gentleman? Indeed I have told many tales, one more than a thousand.... It was my mother's mother, the black-eyed dancer, the often-embraced, who in the end—wrinkled like a winter apple and crouching beneath the mercy of the veil—took upon herself to teach me the art of story-telling. Her own mother's mother had taught it to her, and both were better story-tellers than I am. But that, by now, is of no consequence, since to the people they and I have become one.... I beg of you, you good people who want to hear stories told, look at this page, and recognize the wisdom of my grandmother and of all old story-telling women!... We, the old women who tell stories, we know the story of the blank page.[1]

If the veil concealed their bodies and silence muted their voices, the blank page covered the storytelling craft of Iranian women. For centuries, female narrative talent was mostly channeled away from public forms of written self-expression. Veiled women storytellers know best the story of the blank page. It is their uncontested territory, their tale, their fate. It is the destiny they share, their kismet. It signifies a present absence. It indicates a violated space, several appropriated tales. Just as their great grandmother, Shaherzad, was not allowed to perform her art publicly, they, too, until recently, were denied access to the forum of the written word. Veiled women were the authors of unwritten books and the unacknowledged authors of many written ones.

Storytelling, traditionally the province of women in Iran, has been a form of discourse well integrated into their lives. Considered a safe and domestic craft, it entertained children and entangled them in webs of stories, it kept them away from trouble, it controlled them. Women

177

held the key to the magic world of tales. We surrendered our childhood
to their titillating accounts of adventure and romance, blending the real
and the fantastic. Their captivating stories could cast a spell to prevent
ruthless kings, monsters, and intruders from executing evil designs. We
basked in their fancy and trusted their mystic and dreamlike qualities
that opened vistas of beauty, adventure, and splendor in our bewildered
minds. Our childhood was impregnated with and transformed by these
tales, which like those told by Shaherzad to tame the enraged and violent king, consoled, distracted, delighted, and engaged the imagination.

Storytelling was not only an outlet for women's creativity, it was
also an artistic arena in which they found an expression for their life
stories. Their unwritten tales were handed down orally from generation
to generation. "My mother, in common with most Eastern women and
perhaps even women of the West," says Salman Rushdie, "was the keeper
of family stories. . . . She knows them like an encyclopedia. All family
stories, not just our own. Telling family stories is one of the ways by
which we define ourselves. Those stories become you. Because it is the
women who keep those tales, it passes through the female line, going
from mothers to daughters. I still hear some I haven't heard before, so
she hasn't run out."[2]

Storytelling was also a strategy for survival. It saved Shaherzad, who
spent her wedding night telling stories in order to escape the fate of
her predecessors, the many virgin girls who lost their heads the morning after. *A Thousand and One Nights,* better known in the West as *Ara-
bian Nights Entertainment,* exists because women knew of the transformative and liberating power of storytelling. The frame story of this
folkloric tale captures with breathtaking psychological and social accuracy key functions of storytelling in women's lives.

Betrayed once by an adulterous wife, the king in *A Thousand and
One Nights* vowed never to be betrayed again by a woman. He knew
from his own and his brother's experience that danger and hurt arise
from intimacy with women—the danger of dishonor, the hurt of betrayal,
the pain of humiliation by deceit. Feeling defenseless against the pains
caused by women, the king devises the only viable alternative he can
think of. Unwilling to take the risk of intimacy with anyone who has
the power to hurt him, King Shahriyar chooses aggression and destruction. By framing his urge for union in separation, he marries a virgin

every night and has her murdered in the morning. Thus, he never allows women the chance to deceive him. To him, only a dead wife makes a loyal wife.

On the surface, Shahriyar is a paragon of political and sexual power. He is the king, God's shadow on earth. A virile man, he has the power to "deflower" and "penetrate" a virgin girl every single night and have her murdered the next morning. Shaherzad, on the other hand, personifies powerlessness and female vulnerability. She can have her head chopped off just because she is a woman. At the mercy of a merciless husband, her only weapon is her craft of storytelling, upon which she relies to disarm the brooding and ruthless king, to transform her relationship with him to its opposite. Through the magic of storytelling she reverses the relationship of domination and subordination. She becomes the active agent, the narrator, while he turns into a passive and addicted listener. She appropriates the sovereign prerogative, the discourse, and tames the sovereign. The king's desperate search for autonomy versus women, his wish to gain control over the object of his desire, only gives way to more dependence. She tells, he listens. She mesmerizes, he is mesmerized. She controls, he is controlled.

Thus, through the oral tradition of spinning tales, a woman could attract an audience and achieve merit as a storyteller; but it was difficult for her to write them down or to gain recognition beyond the confines of her family and circle of friends. She was scarcely recognized in her own time, let alone later on, beyond the walls of her house; and her stories seldom directly reached an outside audience.

Women told their tales while men wrote them down—not only a manifestation of literacy inequality but also an indication of the literary appropriation of the female voice.[3] Behind many written stories stand women storytellers. There they are—secluded, unacknowledged, confined, colonized. Literally and literarily, they are erased from written texts and barely given due recognition for their highly skilled craft. After all, who finally wrote down the many stories Shaherzad spun for one thousand and one nights? The conclusion to the book is quite explicit about it: "In due time King Shahriyar summoned chroniclers and copyists and bade them write all that had betided him with his wife, first and last; so they wrote this and named it *The Stories of the Thousand Nights and a Night*. The book came to thirty volumes and these the

King laid up in his treasury." And who spreads these delightful stories "over all lands and climes?" Once again another "wise," "keen-witted," and "just" man is credited with this task:

> Then there reigned after them a wise ruler, who was just, keen-witted and accomplished and loved tales and legends, especially those which chronicle the doings of Sovrans and Sultans, and he found in the treasury these marvellous stories and wondrous histories, contained in the thirty volumes aforesaid. So he read in them a first book and a second and a third and so on to the last of them, and each book astounded and delighted him more than that which preceded it, till he came to the end of them. Then he admired whatso he had read therein of description and discourse and rare traits and anecdotes and moral instances and reminiscences and bade the folk copy them and dispread them over all lands and climes.[4]

Centuries later, Shaherzad's daughters were still erased from the text, exiled to oblivion. For instance, in the early 1970s, at the height of Iran's drive toward modernization, the Cultural Council of the Ministry of Arts and Culture prepared a list of the great figures of Iranian cultural history.[5] This concentrated history of greatness tolerated the presence of only four women. Lost in the illustrious company of three hundred kings, generals, statesmen, philosophers, scientists, writers, artists, calligraphers, and musicians, these four lonely women—all poets— revealed, among other things, the strength of the ties between women and poetry in Iran and the total neglect of women storytellers, in spite of the cultural centrality of storytelling.

But what about women prose fiction writers? They, too, are conspicuously absent from this honorary inventory. Have women never written down their oral narratives even when they could? Take Shaherzad, the ultimate storyteller. She is the classic case of the closet artist. Her own father, the vizier, was not aware of her talent. Even when her art was discovered, she was not allowed an audience of more than two. Night in and night out, she told her stories, but only to her husband and sister. No *Namahram* [forbidden man] ever heard Shaherzad's voice. Her ceremonies of storytelling might have gone on for one thousand and one nights, and through her art she might have transformed the vengeful and embittered king; yet, her lifesaving art was accorded legitimacy only within the privacy of her home. Time and again, Shaherzad proved the triumph of her art and her domesticity (and domestication). And although she managed first to postpone and ultimately to nullify her death verdict, she could never turn her stories into written texts or transcend the role that propriety allowed. She was resigned to her role as a dutiful housewife, a private storyteller. She had no other options.

It is not surprising, then, if the appropriation of fiction writing by women is a recent phenomenon in Iran. Whereas unveiled women had produced significant short stories and novels during the last few decades before the compulsory veiling act implemented by the Islamic Republic, veiled women had not written — or more precisely, published — works of fiction.[6] And whereas women's contributions to poetry, even if few and far between, go back to the beginning of Persian literature itself, women's presence in prose literature is less than a few decades old. The fiction-writing pen was in the hands of men, and it was not until 1947 that the first collection of short stories, *Atash-e Khamush* [Fire Quenched] by Simin Daneshvar, was published.[7] It did not attract much attention. Published in limited numbers, it was never reprinted. Although Amineh Pakravan, a lecturer in French language and literature at Tehran University, wrote a number of historical novels, they were all in French. Daneshvar's *Savushun,* the first novel by an Iranian woman, was finally published in 1969.[8]

Simin Daneshvar was born in the southern city of Shiraz, the third of six children, on April 28, 1921.[9] Her father was a physician, and her mother, who was a painter, also directed an art school. Daneshvar grew up in her native city, enjoyed the best available education, and was surrounded by books from her father's library. She moved to the capital in 1942 to attend Tehran University. There, she studied Persian literature, wrote her dissertation on beauty as treated in Persian literature, and received her doctorate in 1949. Her dissertation committee was directed by Fatemeh Sayyah, who had become Iran's first woman university professor when the chairs of Russian language and literature and comparative literature at Tehran University were awarded to her.[10] Sayyah, born and educated in Russia, accompanied her family back to Iran in 1942 when she was hired by Tehran University.[11] Her impact upon the aspiring young writer was enormous: "I worked with her for five years,"

writes Daneshvar, "whatever I have accomplished I owe it to her, whoever I have become I owe it to her. When I read to her the first short
story I ever wrote, she said: don't become a scholar, don't work for
a Ph.D. in literature, don't talk about other people's work, let others
talk about your stories."[12]

Confronting an economic crisis brought about by her father's death,
Daneshvar started to work. First, she became an assistant in foreign relations at the Ministry of Foreign Affairs and later wrote articles under
the pseudonym *Shirazi-ye Binam* [an Anonymous Person from Shiraz].
She was paid seventeen *Toumans* [the equivalent of three dollars] for each
article. *Fire Quenched* was published in 1947. Three years later, Daneshvar married Jalal Al-e Ahmad. He was a fellow student she had first
met on a bus traveling from Shiraz to Tehran. Jalal's father did not ap-
prove of his son marrying an unveiled woman. In protest, he did not
attend the wedding ceremony and "left town for [the shrine city of]
Qom. For ten full years after that, he did not set foot in his son's house."[13]

Marrying a man with whom she had fallen in love rather than one
chosen by her family, Daneshvar also managed to keep her independence
both as a woman and as a writer after marriage.[14] "When Jalal and
I decided to marry," she writes, "my only condition was that I will
remain Simin Daneshvar, not being identified as Mrs. Al-e Ahmad, and
thus I would keep my freedom, my philosophical aspects, my ideology,
my style of writing . . . and several male friends (not lovers) I have."[15]
It is within the framework of this unconventional marriage, for the
time, that Daneshvar could go abroad for two years to pursue higher
education, unaccompanied by her husband.

Shortly after her marriage in 1952, Daneshvar traveled to America
on a Fulbright Scholarship to study creative writing at Stanford University. The impact of this trip can best be appreciated when *Fire Quenched*
is compared with later works. Although there is no abrupt change of
theme or of concern, there is a noticeable shift of emphasis; a cultivation of style; an increasing command of language; an intensely developed use of colloquialism and folk idiom; but, above all, a refinement
of technique. According to the author herself, "Thanks to Dr. Wallace
Stegner, in charge of the Creative Writing Center at Stanford University (1952–1953), I learned to improve my technique by using fewer
adjectives and adverbs, to make my style more powerful with nouns
and verbs. He also taught me to show events instead of narrating them."[16]

Upon returning to Iran, Daneshvar first taught in the Tehran Conservatory. Later, in 1959, she joined the Department of Archeology, Faculty of Letters and Humanities, at Tehran University, as an adjunct professor. Although highly revered and liked by her students and qualified academically, she was never promoted to a tenured position. She finally resigned in 1979, disillusioned and disappointed: "One of my wishes was to become a University Professor. I had this academic ambition which was never realized. . . . Actually, Savak [the internal security agency] never allowed it to happen although I well deserved it. The Review Committee had given me 104 points while normally 50 to 60 points were enough for tenure. Later, Dr. Negahban showed me a copy of Savak's letter. It read like this: 'No! This woman does not deserve professorship. Slowly phase her out.'"[17]

Daneshvar may not have achieved tenure at Tehran University, but she certainly has earned a special place in the pantheon of Persian literature. *Savushun,* a best-seller for over two decades, has been reprinted fifteen times. Unrivaled in Iran in its popularity, it has been translated into English, French, Russian, Japanese, Uzbek, Polish, and Turkish. No other novel in the history of modern Persian literature, whether written by a man or a woman, has sold more copies than this book, which reportedly had sold about 400,000 copies by 1984.

According to Daneshvar, her *oeuvre* is slim mainly because of economic hardships.[18] Like almost all Iranian writers, she has never been able to support herself by her creative writing. While teaching full time, managing a house full of guests (students, colleagues, and friends), she also translated several books as another means of support.[19] Her creative writing suffered. After years of silence, finally in 1961 she published a collection of ten short stories called *Shahri chun Behesht* [A City like Paradise].[20] *Savushun* appeared in 1969, when Daneshvar was forty-eight years old, only a few months before the early death of Jalal Al-e Ahmad. *Be Ki Salam Konam?* [Whom Should I Salute?] and *Ghorub-e Jalal* [Jalal's Sunset] were published in rapid succession after the Islamic revolution.[21] *Jazireh-ye Sargardani* [Island of the Lost], her second novel, is forthcoming.

Daneshvar is not only Iran's first woman novelist but one of the country's leading writers. For over forty years, she has been a key figure in the unfolding of modern Persian literature. She was one of the founders, in 1968, of the Writers' Association of Iran, a member of its executive committee, and a signatory to all the open letters written by the association in defense of writers' professional rights and of protection of freedom of expression (e.g., 1968, 1977).[22] As a teacher and as a pioneering woman, she has also influenced many younger writers. The short-story writer and Daneshvar's own niece, Leili Riyahi, admits in a beautifully written article entitled "A Letter to My Rediscovered Mother" that "it was in the warm hearth of your house that I ripened and got formed. . . . I owe you both my B.A. and M.A. degrees as well as all the books I have ever read."[23] And this is how the poet Partow Nuri-'Ala acknowledges her gratitude: "I offered my first book of poems, *Sahmi as Salha* [Fragments from Years] to Daneshvar. I dedicated to her the one single thing that I owned and that was dear to me."[24]

Daneshvar's thirty-six short stories and her novel portray women's experience and establish her as a significant pioneer, refreshingly absorbing in the detail and range of her vision. She tightly weaves woman's life and fiction together. She creates remarkable female characters who are neither idealized nor caricatured. In effect, she reclaims the verbal space denied to women in Persian prose and, through her female characters, attracts attention to realities habitually relegated to the periphery of literary expression. Her work offers insights into the lives of women with little ideological or sexual stereotyping.

Until the middle of the twentieth century, Persian literature was conspicuously lacking in realistic portrayals of women protagonists. Stereotypes proliferated: women as types rather than finely detailed or differentiated individuals. By whatever names they were called, if they had names, most of these women were abstract, allegorical figures, deprived of characterizations that would do justice to the emotions or events of their bodies; denied the expression of unfeminine pleasures or pains; portrayed without emotional, intellectual, and moral complexity; and overshadowed by male heroes. They lacked dimension beyond a male-intoxicating beauty; a limitless nurturing capacity; a naïve innocence; or conversely, a seemingly endless potential for destruction, harm, and repulsiveness.

It might be argued that masculine as well as feminine stereotyping is likely to be narrow and limited and that Persian literature also abounds in male stereotypes. The warrior, the sagacious wine seller, the carefree drinker, the fair youth, the *Luti* [an urban Robin Hood type] are all stock characters with feelings, ideas, and destinies predetermined by the genre. Still, a significant body of literature presents man as possessing a dynamic existence, both transcendent and fluid. Heroism and projection of his self into the world are his prerogative. Even when he is framed by a stereotyped characterization, he serves purposes other than those of his female counterpart. The latter is essentially a fantasy, the reflection of male desires and fears, the very vessel for the qualities men traditionally wish women to have or not to have, the source of man's highest ideals or, conversely, of all his problems.

Even folk literature, in which women enjoy relatively fulfilling social functions and are granted some autonomy and self-assertion, defines and limits women characters much more than male heroes. In her interesting study of women in Persian folktales, Erika Friedl points to the subsidiary roles of women:

> In the tales, a woman's fate is usually dependent on the actions of men who have authority over her, like a father or husband, while a man's fate is either directed by his own actions or the actions of one with superior power. . . . Women can act in altogether fourteen roles, seven of which are based on consanguineal or affinal kinship. Men, on the other hand, fill forty-three roles, of which six are based on kinship. Men's roles and occupations span a wide range of familiar traditional and modern occupations, from dragon and king to teacher, doctor, and even migrant worker. . . . Except for maid, there is no occupational status described for women.[25]

An overview of the major genres of Persian literature proves that it lacks dominant and pivotal women protagonists. There are indeed only a few exceptional characters whose existences do not wholly revolve around their relationships with men and who are allowed some autonomy and mobility beyond the domestic sphere. Self-reliant, independent, strong, courageous, these exceptional heroines counter the stereotyped images of women.

Perhaps more than any other literary woman, Vis enjoys characterological complexity. As the heroine of the romantic epic *Vis-o-Ramin* [Vis and Ramin] (1054), she is not only endowed with beauty but also with spirit, passion, and intelligence.[26] Among the numerous Persian romances, few possess a heroine with such self-will, such repugnance for blind obedience, such insistence on dignity, and such claims to feelings and passions. She longs for amorous adventures, refuses to be imprisoned in a marriage arranged by her mother, insists on her liberty, and throughout the book maintains her pride and vitality. She is also privileged with a fervent, admiring narrator/creator who does not ultimately punish her for her traditionally punishable freedoms. Unlike other heroines (or women) of her kind, she is neither ostracized by her society nor condemned to death nor driven to suicide or madness nor imprisoned in a life of seclusion and loneliness. She marries the man she loves; enjoys prosperity, health, and happiness; and lives for eighty-two years.

Daneshvar adds a few remarkable women protagonists to the slim repertoire of such women in Persian literature. Indeed, her literary work is a celebration of the feminine—her taste for love and life, her art of endurance and strength.[27] She also takes pride in her attempt to give voice to women whose voices have gone unheard, their feminine identities veiled. She explores the daily lives, physical experiences, emotional states, and values of ordinary women within the frameworks of family, marriage, kinship, friendship, art, politics, and community. She reports the inner landscape of a woman's being, written from the center of feminine experience and revolving around it. It is one of her contributions to Persian literature that she was able to capture women's issues with such subtlety, familiarity, and abandon.

In her writing, we encounter a wide range of women characters, from traditional to modern, educated to illiterate, rich to poor, beautiful to ugly. Exploitive and exploited, victimizing and victim, powerful and powerless, they represent the many intricacies of man/woman relationships and transcend the customary idealization or demonization of women.

In Daneshvar's writing, women are not portrayed as mere extensions or powerless victims of their environments. They are active agents who work their way around prevailing norms to maximize what power they have. I do not mean to imply that the society depicted in this body of writing is unpatriarchal or egalitarian. Far from it. In effect, Daneshvar depicts a male-dominated, male-centered society in which women are oppressed and suppressed. Yet, in her works, the extent of male domination is not overrated. Daneshvar assesses man's power dialectically—as a reciprocity of influence. As men control certain aspects of women's lives, they in turn are controlled by women. This dynamic depiction of power and patterns of authority gives women more psy-

chological, emotional, and relational depth and discloses sympathetically many vulnerabilities of both men and women.

Daneshvar views herself as a mouthpiece for Iranian women, especially the ordinary kind: those of the lower classes, and those who have
little feminine charm to mesmerize. "I have noticed," she says in one
of her first short stories, "that the heroines of love stories are always
beautiful women. No one has yet written about the destiny of those
who are no beauties. Perhaps ugly women don't have any destiny!"[28]
Persian literature is indeed obsessed with women's beauty, a tediously
stereotyped kind of beauty: youthful, black-haired, moon-faced women
with almond-shaped eyes, peachy complexions, pistachiolike mouths,
jujube-colored lips, hazelnutlike noses, reddish applelike cheeks, and
lemon- or pomegranatelike breasts—a mobile green grocery, if you will.[29]

The experience of ordinary women, with their distinctly feminine
problems and points of view, is of central significance to Daneshvar. Perhaps more than any other contemporary Iranian writer of fiction, she
has proven that the portrayal of women's experiences, as opposed to masculine fantasies of womanhood, can be the stuff of novels and short stories
and, for that matter, of good ones. Although many of her female protagonists are alienated individuals, they reveal both the limitation and
the potential of their lives. They refuse to be purposeless and functionless beings or marginal, stylistic supporting casts; instead, they are pivotal
characters who offer vivid and captivating understandings of their lives.

Although the world of men stands in authority over that of women,
Daneshvar's fiction is set in a woman's world, where feminine concerns
and aspirations govern. Men's presence, although vital and visible, is subordinated to the universe inhabited by women. Even in the short story
entitled "Sutra," from *Whom Should I Salute?*, Daneshvar's only story
dealing mainly with a man, the very lack of a female protagonist comes
to dominate the unfolding of plot as its central problem. Daneshvar's
work thus displays a distinctive role in a predominantly male concep-
tual currency. It deliberately challenges the supremacy of the masculine
point of view by focusing on feminine perspectives. By depicting the
unfolding of women's lives in the overwhelmingly minute details of
everyday life, it portrays a view of the world from beneath rather than
from above. It trespasses boundaries vertically.

Daneshvar has also consistently refused to accommodate her work
to the dominant standard of political engagement. She has never sur-

rendered to the established prescriptions of serious themes and concerns (in effect male paradigms for the aesthetic, formal, and thematic elements of literature). Although she belongs to an age when unwritten laws have developed to communicate to every artist the expectations of the avant-garde intellectual community, she has managed to ignore them. She has disregarded the corpus of literary strictures that insist that only certain kinds of experiences, characters, and views of society are worthy of serious consideration. Those authors who have violated these norms of sociopolitical engagement have faced social and literary stigmatization, slight, or neglect. If they have not been labeled as puppets of the regime, dealers of art willing to sell themselves for a cheap price, then they have been branded unimportant and apolitical; they have been considered *Gheyr-e Mote'ahed* [noncommitted], a term much used, misused, and abused.

Obviously, Daneshvar's aversion to party politics or to strident ideologies does not mean that she has produced an apolitical literary discourse. On the contrary, the mere act of appropriating the fiction-writing pen and creating a literature that represents women's life in a hitherto male literature ought to be construed as political.[30] By validating the personal, the intimate, and the previously unacceptable subjects of explorations and points of view as literary themes, Daneshvar not only turns women's daily lives into a public performance, she also delegitimizes patriarchal patterns of power and authority. She presents an expanded vision of politics in which not only external, political issues are discussed but internal relations of domination and power are also portrayed. The collision of the two, the tension they create, and negotiating boundaries are the stuff of her writings.

Daneshvar's literary career, like that of most women writers, testifies to her sustained refusal to buy approval, fame, or critical acclaim by adoption of certain stands or certain topics. She has believed in her art, respected it, cherished it. It has taken precedence over any externally imposed literary standards or expectations. Living in a milieu where it was considered the right thing, almost a necessity, to belong to a political group or party, Daneshvar never belonged to one. As she herself has cogently pointed out in the epilogue written to her translation of the short story "Narges," "desiring to be an artist, one has to be free—free from politics, free from the pressure of the politicians and the programs they arrange to produce artists according to their own models and then to seal their foreheads with the sign of their own fabric of ideas."[31] Art has always been Daneshvar's overwhelming concern, though she is not untouched by ideological convictions or concerns about the many ailments of her society. As she argues in the same appendix to "Narges," "Iran is a country of contrasts. . . . Here live the people who are deprived of the elementary means of living, strangers to those who have whatever their hearts desire. I dedicate my pen (if there is any talent in it) to the first mentioned; the rich in Iran have no need of me. Their tragedies seem to me comic, their problems funny, nothing more than hidden love affairs, gambling losses or uncertainties about how to treat spoiled children."

Besides abstaining from militant political stances, Daneshvar has refused to follow the popular trend, typified by M. E. Beh'azin's *Dokhtar-e Ra'iyat* [The Serf's Daughter] (1951) and Samad Behrangi's *Mahi siyah-e kuchulu* [The Little Black Fish] (1968), of portraying the triumph of idealistic dreams over social actualities. No little black fish of hers is sent to the sea to meet the pelican with its wide pouch, the swordfish with its sharp jawbone, or the heron with its long beak, ultimately presaging victory for all the fish in an ocean of danger. Hers is a world where ruthless wolves devour idealistic sheep, where wolves often wear sheep's clothing. Rhapsodies of utopian longing catering to the longings of her readers have no value for this author. She sees no illusory romantic turning point in revolutionary changes; instead, she cherishes and explores sustained, even though undramatic, efforts to change. "No sheep has ever devoured a wolf," she writes, "the point is how long one can resist."[32]

Refusing to conform to the dominant literary standards and expectations of her time, writing as a woman and about women, Daneshvar was amazingly neglected for a long time by the critical establishment. For many years, she was missed or dismissed in most books of literary criticism, periodicals, and anthologies—inside or outside the country. No critical analysis in the form of articles, let alone a full-length study of any of her books, was undertaken. Even *Savushun*, the most popular Persian novel ever, was slighted. Altogether, it attracted a handful of short reviews, mostly by other women.

Critics hardly ever referred to *Fire Quenched*, the first published collection of short stories by an Iranian woman. Although it is true that Daneshvar herself critically denounced the book and never allowed its reprinting, although it lacks the aesthetic, thematic, and emotional complexity of her later work, still it calls for more attention because it is the first attempt by an Iranian fiction writer to integrate a feminine self with prose. It is not only the fertile soil from which Daneshvar's later work grows, it also provides a key to the development of skills and themes in her fiction.

It is interesting, although not surprising, that even when critics could no longer ignore Daneshvar's literary achievements and ever-increasing popularity, the belated recognition offered her was overshadowed by her relegation to the status of the wife of the famous writer Jalal Al-e Ahmad. The ten nights of poetry reading at the Goethe Institute in October 1977 is a good case in point. The frenzied applause of an audience aroused by Daneshvar's speech was explained, or rather explained away, by the chairman of the meeting as an outpouring of the accumulated admiration of those present for Daneshvar *and* for her late husband.[33] Even the unrivaled popularity of *Savushun,* unabated to this day, is miraculously associated with Al-e Ahmad. "What do you think is the reason behind *Savushun*'s popular appeal?" an interviewer asked the author while volunteering immediately a possible reason: "Haven't your concealed and eulogized references to the late Al-e Ahmad influenced it?"[34] *Savushun* was published a few months *before* Al-e Ahmad's early death.

This overvaluation of women's relationship to men is, of course, not confined to Daneshvar. Numerous critics have diligently and repeatedly sought for and noted the centrality of a man's influence on women's literary development. In Parvin E'tessami's case, it is her father, E'tessam-ol Molk. With Forugh Farrokhzad, it is Ebrahim Golestan, her friend and lover for the last eight years of her life. Sadr-ed Din Elahi repeats a dominant view when he claims: "One can say that Forugh was a motionless 'feminine pond' with no wave or mobility. Ebrahim fell into that water like a luminous stone and replaced the deadly calm and quiet with lively stirring and motion."[35]

Never was Farrokhzad a "feminine pond" (do ponds have a sex too?), inert and immobile. As a matter of fact, throughout her writing she is a dynamic character who assumes responsibility for an ever-changing and developing self. Her poems have always expressed a clear repugnance of the unchanging, the stagnant. Ironically, the image of lagoons and swamps recurs frequently in her poetry and always with negative connotations.

When in a lagoon water loses its flow
It stagnates and it sinks low.
Its soul turns into the empire of decay
Its depth becomes the grave where fish decay.[36]

Women, it seems, barely manage to achieve unqualified critical attention on their own. With men, personal relationships are considered a private matter, unrelated to their works; with women, they assume disproportionate significance. Only in recent years has Daneshvar emerged from the shadow of her husband's fame and popularity and from the need of critics to locate a man at the center of her artistic creativity and development.

Ironically, one of the characteristic features of Daneshvar's literary career is her independence of thought and character. If Al-e Ahmad was a trendsetter for many writers of his generation, he had no such impact on his own wife. During the seventeen years of their marriage, Al-e Ahmad wrote several popular and provocative books that further established his reputation as a foremost engagé writer and social critic. With his ideological tendencies, his reliance on abstractions and absolutes, and his amplifications of his readers' social and political frustrations, he came to be applauded as a notable literary figure with an ever-increasing popularity. Daneshvar's courage to go against the dominant trend set by her husband is as triumphant as it is rare among Al-e Ahmad's friends and colleagues. In her own words: "I had studied Persian masterpieces, both in prose and poetry. The prose I derived from my studies was not appropriate for writing fiction, and I didn't want to imitate anybody's prose, including my husband's, which was fashionable. It took time, but with enough practice and effort, I achieved a prose that neither continued the traditional nor imitated the Modernists, but which was at the same time nourished by both."[37]

Daneshvar reaches the height of her power as a craftswoman of Persian prose in *Savushun*. This novel is one of the masterpieces of modern Persian prose in terms of style, structure, and substance. It presents a world in which not only do the characters function fully and have the freedom and the ability to speak for themselves but the plot is also highly plausible, culturally, socially, and historically. *Savushun* is the story of a family, and by extension of a nation, caught by surprise by an uninvited and unwelcome guest: the Allied Occupational Forces. Although it is a political novel, it is not doctrinaire.[38] It chronicles a sad historical event with the least amount of explicit analysis or direct commentary. Although it brings to the foreground the intimate and the personal (relegated normally to the background), it blends the private and the public, the personal and the collective, the female and the human.

Zari, the heroine of *Savushun*, is an ordinary woman caught off guard by extraordinary events. She is a talented woman who wants to develop a self in the image of her own ideals but feels severely limited in experience and development. Although gifted with grace, courage, patience, and intelligence; although loving and loved; and although a successful housewife and mother; she is not a contented woman. She tries hard to live up to patterns created for Iranian women but cannot silence an inner voice pushing her in another direction. Although all her activities seem to revolve around her family, which defines not only her identity but also the contours of her fate, she secretly cherishes independence and self-actualization. She celebrates her family life and yet simultaneously represents its engulfing, encapsulating, nature. She shuttles back and forth between moments of elation and of depression. On the whole, freedom and independence seem to slip through the fingers of her cupped hand. At times, her children; the splendor of her comfortable life; her beautiful house and garden filled with flowers; and, above all, her husband seem like obstacles that keep her from herself. She consistently mouths her protests only to mute them immediately.

Zari experiences herself in terms of and in response to masculine-centered values and definitions, including those she has absorbed by osmosis from her surrounding culture. As she grows and the range of her activities and field of experience widen, she has to curb her spontaneity. Although there is an acute tension in her between her taste for freedom and the life she leads, she still adopts the patriarchal framework. A preoccupation with man-centered feminine ideals orders her priorities and clashes head-on with her desire to forge an identity of her own. Throughout her married life, she becomes a dependent figure, pliable and limited.

However much imprisoned in her femininity, Zari is far from what one can conveniently call a traditional woman. As a young girl, she enjoyed personal freedom. She was guided by internal standards, privileged with the best available education. She relentlessly resisted uncritical, passive adherence to social proprieties for women. Her childhood impulse to struggle, revolt, and oppose is later on matched by her desire to move beyond conventional definitions of womanhood. Most traditional women around Zari, like those in her society at large, seem to assume their traditional roles to be inherently fulfilling and life sustaining. They barely, if ever, openly question their validity. They consider these accepted roles as the norm; and it would be unusual to admit, publicly, any basic dissatisfaction with them. Zari, however, has basic doubts about some of the cornerstone values and patterns of her society. She questions, for instance, the very institution of marriage. "For a split second she even thought that marriage is basically wrong. It is not right for a man to be chained for a lifetime to a woman and to a bunch of children nor is it right for a woman to be so attached to a man and a few kids that she cannot take a free and deep breath."[39]

In spite of the rather unusual element of free choice in her selection of a husband, Zari still cannot find the emotional intensity and spontaneity she desires in her relationship with her husband, Yussef. Her relatively happy marriage has not only denied her the intellectual stimulation and independence of her school days, it has also forced her to curb her thoughts and feelings. Like many others, Zari finds herself surreptitiously sweeping her real emotions under the carpet. This ideal wife and mother cannot speak her mind even within the confines of her own home. Sporadic seclusion becomes an oasis in which she can take refuge from the frenzied and heavy load of her duties and delegations and accompanying frustrations and discontents — a sanctuary, or rather a safety valve, for her boiling, yet silenced, protestations.

To continue her life-style, Zari has to keep up the image of a happy, harmonious woman. Her supposed sunny disposition, however, fades in moments of anger and crisis, showing something very different through the cracks of the armor she has built around herself. Like a volcano, Zari only reveals her content when she erupts: "She collapsed in a chair and started to cry. She thought no one in the whole world was as fatigued and as depressed as she was" (p. 130). Beneath the surface of the calm woman, what we find is frustrated passion, sometimes accidentally released, sometimes deliberately unleashed. She can threaten herself as much as her husband with the simple yet frightening question: "Do you want to hear the truth?" (p. 130).

Zari tries hard to maintain an appearance of mastery over her desires and inclinations. On the surface, she seems quite comfortable in her roles as wife and mother. She idolizes her husband, adores her children, and engages in no rebellion of an overt kind. Covertly and repeatedly, however, she resents the loss, or rather the counterfeiting, of her true self as she sees it. In a moment of anger and loss of self-control she admits to her husband, as much as to herself, "I have so much compromised myself with you that concession has become my habit" (p. 130).

It is only after Yussef's assassination that Zari's rage becomes palpable. Finally, Zari confronts the repression she has suffered throughout her life. The cathartic release of this anger is enormous. It brings to the surface anxieties that had not yet reached the level of consciousness or of articulate emotions. After a short experience of insanity, a new peace, a new sense of serenity come upon her. The suffocating clash of commitments and ideals seems to disappear. Zari enters a new phase of life, redefines her role, and discovers new dimensions of experience and autonomy. Freed at last from self-mutilating compromises, from the necessity for lies and concealment, she can take charge of her life and escape even the final course of a woman's destiny: dependence upon her son.

Most marriages in Daneshvar's fictive world involve concessions, self-control, and contractual role playing.[40] Conjugal bliss of a truly satisfying nature is rare here. According to Daneshvar, "heterosexual relationships are altogether sort of sick in Iran. They are patriarchal and androcentric. Most marriages in our country are unsuccessful. Two individuals with two different backgrounds, educations, and customs have to endure one another for a lifetime. Well, this very tolerance creates hatred."[41] Like Daneshvar, other contemporary women writers have also attacked the submissiveness and acquiescence of women in marriage. Forugh Farrokhzad, in a poem entitled "Wedding Band," rebels against the restrictions placed on women in the name of marriage.

> With a smile,
> The little girl asked:
> "What is the secret of this wedding band
> Circling me tightly on my hand?"
>
> Years later, one night
> A sad wife gazed at that golden band,

And saw in its glowing design
Wasted days, wasted
In the hope of a husband's loving hands.

Anguished, she cried
Out loud, and said:
"This luminous and glowing band
Is the band of tyranny and commands."[42]

Although the first strophe celebrates the cheeriness of the smiling
girl, the bride-to-be, the second half, gloomy and troubled, mourns her
irrevocably lost freedom. The transition between freedom enjoyed and
freedom lost is as abrupt as the acquisition of a wedding band. A sense
of inertia and stasis governs not only the life of the married woman
but the entire poem. The only movement is the irreversible passage of
time. The innocently happy girl, now a distressed woman, can only
age and come to the bitter realization that her life has been wasted in
servitude and submissiveness.

No less painful than Farrokhzad's poem[43] is Mahshid Amirshahi's
description of her own marriage in the short story entitled "There and
Then."

I went to the new house but there was nothing new in there except
new fears for me.
"Why did you say that?"
"Why did you see that?
"Why did you do that?"
   I was afraid. I was afraid of fights and recurring fights. I was afraid
of loveless jealousy, habitual kinds of jealousy, pathological jealousy,
grudging jealousy. I was afraid that's what life is all about and not much
more.[44]

And so it is that a characteristic feature of women's writing in contemporary Iran is a ceaseless search for real love. This recurring theme
in female-authored fiction is more than a thematic motif. It is one of
the central issues and a manifestation of critical concerns women bring
to Iranian fiction. Houri, the heroine of Shahrnush Parsipur's beautifully written novel *Sag va Zemestan-e Boland* [The Dog and the Long
Winter], is a case in point.[45] Houri loves to love but cannot find an

object for her love. Actually, she is in love without knowing with whom. Her heart basks in that love and agonizes over the absence of the beloved—any beloved. In despair, she reviews all possible candidates, young male relatives and boys in the neighborhood. Anyone capable of love and of filling up that empty space would do. But Houri's desire, in all its modesty, remains unrequited.

The majority of Daneshvar's women characters are disillusioned and disappointed with love or the absence of it. Although they don't view marriage as their sole prerogative, they cannot find other viable options. They seek independent identities beyond those as daughters, wives, or mothers. Most dread becoming like their mothers but cannot find ways to avoid it. They don't enjoy the benefit of positive role models for their rebellion against the conventions binding their lives as women. Their choices, more often than not, turn out to be blind alleys. To most of them to remain unmarried means to be held in contempt, or worse, to be pitied, to lose one's sense of self-worth and confidence. Inevitably, they end up in oppressive marriages. Dissatisfaction piles upon dissatisfaction, and a whole network of frustration is constructed. This dammed-up energy frantically seeks new channels to release the undischarged tension.

Children become the supporting pillars for the broken and shaky relations—bait on a hook. Above all, woman's procreative power it seems remains insurance for mismatched alliances, with the failure to produce a child, preferably a boy, a cause for severe anxiety and desperation. Perhaps the heroine of the short story "The Snake and The Man," from *Whom Should I Salute?*, best represents the potential catastrophe of a woman's sterility.

Nasrin, the protagonist in "The Snake and the Man," is held responsible, without proof, for her incapacity to produce an heir. She succumbs to the pressure. After having tried to follow the advice of numerous well-wishers to no avail, she resorts to the supernatural. On her pilgrimage to the shrine city of Mashhad, she meets a Gypsy who assures her of a cure. Following the Gypsy's prescription, she inserts a snake's egg, without knowing what it is, into her vagina. Impregnated by the snake, her relation to her husband improves amazingly and, after nine months, she gives birth to a snake.

Children, who are not snakes, pay a high price for growing up in this atmosphere of frustrations. Whatever society and men deny women, women demand from their children, especially from their sons, with accumulated interest. Zari, for instance, until the very last pages of the novel, relates to her son in a vampiresque fashion. If she cannot show anger when frustrated, if she cannot achieve her dreams, if she feels limited and weak, she can live vicariously through her son. She literally feeds on his accomplishments, his anger, his power, and his defiance of rules. She has to make her son strong and rub off strength from him.

Spontaneous affection and true friendship are rare in the many heterosexual relationships Daneshvar portrays. Although her fictive world is not built on aloneness, it is crowded with loneliness. It is a world obsessed with relationships, even though the majority of them speak of a silent bafflement and bitterness between the sexes. Truncated at best, destructive at worst, these relationships betray a progressively deteriorating sense of understanding, passion, and compassion. Truly, neither men nor women flourish within these unions. Living in mutual miscommunication, men and women exchange mistrust, frustration, and misunderstanding.

In *A Room of One's Own,* Virginia Woolf remarks that women are rarely portrayed in relation to other women in male-authored fiction. In *Savushun,* there is a clear shift in focus that allows Daneshvar to study relationships between women. In fact, female friendship becomes a saving grace in the everyday lives of many of Daneshvar's women characters. The relationship between 'Ammeh [the aunt] and Zari in *Savushun* is one such celebration. These two women identify with one another, love, cherish, and respect one another. They unhesitatingly share their innermost thoughts and feelings with one another. 'Ammeh and Zari, when together, conquer loneliness. Their caring for each other is a sufficiently flexible love to allow autonomy for both. Although they find, time and again, solace and happiness in their female we-ness, they nonetheless keep their distinct identities. No basic compromise is requested in this relationship, no forfeiting of real feelings, no caging of spontaneity, no hiding of individuality. Theirs is a genuine friendship, a system of mutual support and respect, a compassionate kind of caring.

A frantic search for meaningful heterosexual relationships is a characteristic feature of Daneshvar's characters — male or female. Perhaps

"Sutra," her favorite and most successful short story, best echoes this quest. The story is a creative rendition of spirit possession. "I went to [the city of] Bandar-e 'Abbas for two weeks," said Daneshvar in an interview, "and became acquainted with Captain 'Abdul. I also attended a *Zar* [exorcism] ceremony. This story is to a great extent real and a true account of 'Abdul's life."[46] Through its vivid description of the *Zar* cult, "Sutra" portrays a quintessentially Daneshvarian passion.[47] It is a cry from the heart, an eloquent yet enraged protest against the nature of heterosexual intimacy as it exists in Iranian society.

Captain 'Abdul, the hero, or, rather, the antihero, is diagnosed as being possessed by intrusive spirits. The story begins with the exorcism of his evil spirit, with drums beating and 'Abdul gently swaying his body to their rhythms. As the beats quicken, his movements become more violent, until he falls into a trance. The spirit possessing him can now be approached and asked what gifts he desires in exchange for leaving 'Abdul's body. Unlike most spirits, who ask mainly for gifts of clothing, food, or jewelry, this spirit asks only for love: a gratifying relationship with a member of the opposite sex.

If 'Abdul cannot air his grievances openly or express his desires directly, the spirits offer a medium for oblique expression. Though expression of his interests and dreams in the face of social constraint, formal modes of discourse, and codes of moral propriety is impossible, his trance is an approved cultural outlet. Through the spirit invading his body, Captain 'Abdul not only demands an emotional space denied men and women, he also protests against the culturally prescribed silence shrouding the issue. His forbidden desires and needs are given full public expression. Now, through the mouth of spirits he can discuss his frustrated love and passion for women. Possession constitutes a symbolic rebellion for 'Abdul, a rebellion in feeling and words (if not in action).[48] In the grip of strong feelings of deprivation, he attacks man/woman relationships and offers a well-formulated and drastically different alternative.

Starved for love and affection, desperate to find the female companion denied him in real life, he creates a phantom personality, an imaginary partner, a mermaid, who soon becomes real and indispensable to him. "I can't understand," laments Captain 'Abdul, "why the doctor, the exorcist, and friends all try to deprive me of the most exquisite pleasure I've ever experienced in my life. What harm does it do and who in this world suffers from it if I've met a mermaid who happens to be a compassionate, kind woman, who doesn't nag me; whom I care for, whom I never want to enslave or be enslaved by."[49] Captain 'Abdul is not looking for a larger-than-life kind of love. Modest as his demands are, all alternatives have been closed to him. He has to rely on his imagination and create a phantom relationship.

For 'Abdul, as for many of Daneshvar's characters, as indeed for most prominent women fiction writers in Iran, there is a sense of loss and corruption surrounding personal relations. Mahshid Amirshahi, Goli Tarraqi, Moniru Ravanipur, Shahrnush Parsipur, and Farkhondeh Aqa'i, each in their own special way, represent in detail this social malaise. They depict the conflicted state of characters in a transitional society, their compulsion toward self-fulfillment and individualism, and their attraction toward traditional values incompatible with them. They depict the tensions between the sexes and the generations in a world in the throes of radical change, where old values are disintegrating and new ones have not quite arisen. They examine with passion and wisdom the life of their times.

Four decades after the first text of women's fiction in Iran, there is an unprecedented flourishing of women's fiction writing. Women have finally found an authentic and familiar voice in the novel and the short story. They have carved out spaces of their own in the traditionally male cultural strongholds. Since the revolution, a remarkable shift has occurred in women's fiction. For the first time, women have found a more powerful voice in prose than in poetry. Women's concerns, their points of view, the details of their personal lives, formerly taboo topics, are now being discussed openly, subjectively, unformulaicly. Perhaps the novelist Sharhnush Parsipur does not exaggerate when she claims that writing has become a "historic imperative" for women: "If twenty years ago, you would have asked me why I write, I would have probably answered, I write because I want to be someone; or I protest without even knowing why. Today, however, at the age of forty-one, forty-two, I can say I write because the course of events has suddenly pushed my generation in the crossroad of events. It seems as if writing now is a historic imperative."[50]

Fiction writing now, like storytelling then, is indeed a historical imperative for Iranian women. It not only pulls the women storytellers out of anonymity, it also proclaims voice, visibility, the mobility afforded by and through writing, and the right of access to writing. In the good old tradition of Shaherzad, it is a transformative act of celebration and survival.

9

Disclosing the Self
Autobiography

*E*rased from the public scene and privatized, the Iranian woman has for long been without autobiographical possibilities. Textual self-representation of individuals is not divorced from their cultural representation; and in a culture that idealizes feminine silence and restraint, not many women can or will opt for breaking the silence. Most will not name the formerly unnamed, move beyond the accepted paradigms of female self-representation. In a sexually segregated society where access to a woman's world and words is limited, and the concept of honor is built around woman's virginity (proof of her inaccessibility) women's autobiographies, with their assertive self-attention and self-display, cannot easily flourish, and they have not.

This reluctance to talk publicly and freely about the self, however, is not confined to women. Iranian men have also shunned self-representation. Even in the few published autobiographies available, authors often suppress their uninhibited, unformulaic public self-disclosure. Captive of the image they present, they are poised to keep honor in view and their virility intact. Concerned with their *Mardanegi* [manliness], they seem to form a barrier as solid and as forbidding as a veil around their private selves. After all, a "real" man is expected to be self-contained, in charge of himself and his surroundings, serious, invariably ceremonial, remote, given more to thoughts than emotions. Crying, getting emotional, are for women and little girls, as is confiding.[1]

Iranian male cultural heroes have amazing interlocutors. Hazrat-e 'Ali, the First Imam of Shi'ites, talks to a well. The pre-Islamic mythic hero

201

Rostam confides in his horse, Rakhsh. Dash Akol, the epitome of honor and manliness in modern literature, confesses to his parrot. Nasser al-Din Shah Qajar (r. 1848–1896) chats with Babri Khan, his cat (allegedly executed in secret by a syndicate of the king's co-wives who envied the animal's favored position and "through womanly ploys and extravagant expenditures, stole the unfortunate cat and threw him in a well").[2] Mohammad Reza Shah Pahlavi (r. 1941–1979) kept his cancer a secret for a long time, even from his own wife.[3] No wonder there is no tradition of and relief in confession (in its Catholic sense) or in its secular, modern counterpart, psychotherapy.[4] In fact, both practices are considered means less of gaining relief than of causing trouble by exposing the unshielded and unsheltered inner self.

Modern Persian literature, which has incorporated many Western literary forms, has avoided to a large extent one of the West's most popular genres. Avoiding voluntary self-revelation and self-referentiality, most Iranian writers have turned their backs on autobiography.[5] Clearly, whether writers choose to write and publish their life stories is a matter of personal choice and taste. Yet, when the whole panorama of a national literature ever so fascinated with the West lacks the genre, the issue deserves more attention.

As Georges Gusdorf rightly points out: "The genre of autobiography seems limited in time and in space. It has not always existed nor does it exist everywhere. . . . It asserts itself only in recent centuries and only on a small part of the map of the world."[6] Nor is any judgmental comparison with any other culture implied here. Furthermore, no self-concealment (or self-revealment) can be complete or permanent. Perhaps the harder the individual's attempt to conceal the self and to deflect intrusions, the stronger the impulse of the society at large to uncover and expose what it considers private. The restrictions on open verbal disclosure increase the need for alternative mediums of communication: eyes with an almost X-ray vision pry, penetrate, infiltrate; mouths compulsively spread rumors; for as the old saying goes, "City gates can be controlled but not people's mouths." Crows turn into gossip mongers, unruly tattletales; and walls — those armors for protection — grow ears. After all, as an Iranian proverb warns, is it not true that "walls have mice and mice have ears?" It is not surprising then if Persian miniatures are crowded with voyeurs and eavesdroppers.

I also believe with Paul John Eakin that "autobiographical truth is not a fixed but an evolving content in an intricate process of self-discovery and self-creation, and, further, that the self that is the center of all autobiographical narratives is necessarily a fictive structure."[7] Self-representation is an extension of fantasy rather than a platform of Truth; it is a play with relative uncertainties rather than the expression of revealed absolutes. The epistemological difficulty of what Truth is, the fiction-making processes of the mind, the failings of memory, the creativity of the imagination, not to mention all that is repressed or suppressed, make any faithful and unmediated reconstruction of a past an impossibility. Perhaps it is true that no one knows oneself better than oneself; but then, too, no one else is as apt to be biased. Who can serve oneself better than oneself?

A lived life is not a collection of immutable facts that might be objectively recorded. Looked at from different perspectives, life is infinitely varied and inexpressibly volatile. It is evanescent. It is also symbolically significant that we can see anything and anyone within our field of vision, but we can never see ourselves completely. We are captives of images, reflections, illusions, words. All of this suggests the inherent limits to autobiographic narratives that speak of the elusiveness and perhaps even fictiveness of any drive toward self-representation. The self simply refuses to be fully narrated, to become a text. It declines to be reduced to a language construct. It cannot be fixed, framed, or condensed. A suitable visual analogy for writing a self is looking at oneself in running water. Even with clear vision, the reflection is dim, diffuse. It is vague. It depends on the light and the angle. It is "I" but not quite so; the double, but in a somewhat scattered way. The outlines are almost familiar; but the details are blurry, twisted, distorted, spread out. Now flattering, now disfiguring; now formed, now deformed; it ceaselessly changes. Like the self, it is protean, often fleeting, frequently dispersed. In other words, standing as the observer and the observed, the narrator and the narrated, the creator and the created, and all the while subject to the temporal stream, the autobiographer has the quixotic task of reconciling the otherwise irreconcilable.

Aware of the inherent fictionality of any self-representation, Roland Barthes wrote on the inside cover of his autobiography that "tout ceci doit être consideré comme dit par un personage de roman." The autobiographer alerts the reader, whose expectations are thus diluted from the very beginning, not to take the fiction of his self as fact. By posing as a novelist, he undermines the notion of a true self. In his view, the autobiography constructs and is even constructed by a fictional self.

> All this must be considered as if spoken by a character in a novel—or rather by several characters. For the image-repertoire, fatal substance of the novel, and the labyrinth of levels in which anyone who speaks about himself gets lost—the image-repertoire is taken over by several masks (personae), distributed according to the depth of the stage (and yet no one—*personne,* as we say in French—is behind them). . . . Nothing is more a matter of the image-system, of the imaginary, than (self-) criticism. The substance of this book, ultimately, is therefore totally fictive."[8]

Salman Rushdie, with his customary brilliance, talks of memory's truth "because memory has its own special kind. It selects, eliminates, alters, exaggerates, minimizes, glorifies, and vilifies also; but in the end it creates its own reality, its heterogeneous but usually coherent version of events; and no sane human being ever trusts someone else's version more than his own."[9]

Just as there are fictional elements in autobiographies, there are also autobiographical elements in fictions. Flaubert claimed that "Madame Bovary, c'est moi." Dostoevski called himself a "biographer" in his introduction to *Brothers Karamazov,* and Charlotte Brontë gave her widely acclaimed novel *Jane Eyre* the subtitle "autobiography." Engels claimed to have learned more about the nineteenth-century French society, even in economic details, from Balzac "than from all the professed historians, economists, and statisticians of the period put together."[10] Nietzsche went even as far as saying that "it has gradually become clear to me that every great philosophy has hitherto been: a confession on the part of its author and a kind of involuntary and unconscious memoir."[11]

Having said all this, there is still a fundamental distinction between autobiography and fiction. It is autobiography that generically claims more than any other literary form the correspondence between the writing and the writer. It is, one is led to believe, an attempt to express the biographical reality upon which it is based. It poses as a personal-historical document. Even if it doubts the possibility of fully recovering the past, it still recounts the events of a life and presumably portrays the autobiographer rather than a fictive character.

Autobiography demands to be acknowledged as a personal document.

The gap between its avowed intention and the end result notwithstanding, claims of self-referentiality are the sine qua non of this literary genre. This explicit authority, this posing of the author as the best available source on the subject of inquiry, generates a different kind of expectation in readers. The unwritten yet confirmed contract between reader and writer, what Philippe Lejeune calls the autobiographical pact, is one important distinction between fiction and autobiography.[12] It is this pact between author and reader, rather than the facticity or fictivity of autobiographies, that I wish to address here. The autobiographical stance, the generation and reception of autobiographies, in short the mind-set and psychosocial attitudes that allow the birth and growth of life narratives are my primary concerns.

Paradoxically, if from autobiographies we expect a certain self-reflexivity whereby the self is a problem unto itself and thinks about itself, Persian literature abounds in it. Sufism, the Islamic/Iranian form of mysticism, not only allowed the most radical breaches of public convention and formality, it also demanded the most intense forms of introspection. If from autobiographies we accept a certain self-glorification and a self-congratulatory mode of discourse, then again Persian literature contains a generous supply of that genre, too. I am referring to *Rajaz-khani,* for instance, which is the ritualized boasting of heroes in epics, or the *Takhallos* tradition, which allows the poet ample space for open expression of self-praise and self-satisfaction. Why then, we might ask ourselves, have Iranians not cultivated until recently public self-disclosure in life narratives in spite of their fascination with Western literature and their long tradition of self-meditation and self-glorification?

Many factors have undoubtedly contributed to the scarcity of this literary genre. Traditionally, Persian art has been impersonal. "The first special feature which must strike anybody who views an exhibition of Persian art," writes Richard Ettinghausen,

especially after having first visited the other sections of a museum containing Western art, is the recognition that basically the Iranian artist has an entirely different objective. Instead of primarily producing paintings, usually of rather large size, or statuary using the human figure, the Iranian artist through the ages has dedicated himself to the making and beautification of objects and in a majority of cases of objects for very specific uses in daily life. . . . Of course the human figure is not excluded, but it has, on the whole, only a secondary significance. In addition one finds, too, that the human figure is usually highly stylized or rendered in such a way that its features have the aspects of caricatures, while in still other cases painted figures are given in a disembodied, flat manner, which makes them appear to be without corporeal substance.[13]

In Iran, where not only has art been mainly impersonal but also where an individual's identity is closely tied to the community and where use of the first-person-singular pronoun is still hard for people and is often diffused a bit by *we,* writing an *I*-book is not an easy task. A most popular explanation offered for not writing autobiographies is a certain sense of humility, a shyness about one's own importance and accomplishments. Significantly enough, *Mahjub,* the Persian term for "shy," also means "veiled," "modest," "bashful." Even in the West, with its long tradition of autobiography writing that has now turned into the favorite and the "commonest" of literary pastimes,[14] a sense of self-aggrandizement is still associated with the genre. In her introduction to Carolyn Heilbrun's recent book, *Hamlet's Mother and Other Women,* Nancy K. Miller praises the author and writes: "But despite the fact that to many of us Heilbrun seems to fit the category of exemplary women, she has resisted the impulse to mythologize herself. In fact, even in the current moment when autobiography has become fashionable, Heilbrun continues to prefer to write about the lives of others."[15]

Many Iranians have openly refused to embark on an autobiographic enterprise. At the end of a short life sketch, the foremost novelist of modern Persian literature, Sadeq Hedayet, writes, "There is nothing outstanding in my biography—nothing has happened in my life which might be of interest. I neither occupy a high position, nor do I hold a degree. In school, I was never an excellent student; on the contrary, I was pursued by failure. Everywhere, wherever I worked, I was always a forgotten, nameless employee; and my superiors were dissatisfied with me—they were glad when I left. Altogether, I am quite a forgotten creature, a good-for-nothing: this is the judgement of those around me. Perhaps it is true."[16]

Yahya Arianpur, the respected social/literary critic, also argues that there is not much of value in his life to be transformed into a piece of writing and offered to the reading audience for consumption. "You wanted me to write a sketch of my life. But now that I turn the pages in my book of life, I don't find anything of value to mention about my past or my present."[17] The painter Homa Partovi, praised by the interviewer for her self-reflexivity and self-knowledge, has only this much to say about herself: "Self-knowledge is beautiful and I believe in it. But this doesn't mean I could expose to others the self that I have come to know. I can talk to you about my work, but talking about myself is always extremely hard, almost impossible, for me. Perhaps my appearance doesn't show it, but inside I am an extremely shy person."[18]

'Abdollah Mostowfi, who wrote *Sharh-e Zendegani-ye Man* [An Account of My Life], uses the same line of argument for avoiding details of his daily, private life in his autobiography. In the introduction to the book, he writes: "An account of my personal life offers nothing worth reading. My main intention here is to describe the social situation and particularly to shed light on governmental and administrative operations in the course of the sixty or seventy years of my life."[19] And, indeed, the book covers almost the whole reign of the Qajar dynasty and is replete with historical facts. From Mostowfi's involvement in administrative branches of the government to the details of his political life, most of his writing focuses on the supposedly verifiable. At its best, his life narrative imitates social history. It rarely, if ever, emphasizes introspection, moves from historical information to personal revelation. Even if there are bursts of emotion, inklings of relationships with women or children, they are quickly concealed behind a mirage of historical facts. Brief allusions to private matters, questions about feelings, are quickly obliterated.

On the whole, desiring to record their part in contemporary history, men have preferred to write memoirs, travelogues, and diaries rather than to present their own inner experience of life. Although in their views of people and events, memoirs, travelogues, and diaries can be as much a projection of the author's self as is the autobiography, the primary focus seems to be directed more toward historical or sociogeographical recounting than toward an examination of the narrating self. Telling of random deeds and events, they tend to treat life in a less continuous, more episodic manner. Time and again, they present the author in terms of external events. More than a personal story, they are a personal account of history. They are self-assertion more than self-revelation.

In most published autobiographies, the sense of self is subordinated to the preservation of the public image. The historian Ahmad Kasravi (1890–1946) and the poet 'Aref Qazvini (1882–1934), for instance, use their life narratives not for self-discovery but as tools for self-justification. Although they portray their lives with precision, the fear of publicly incurred misjudgment and a desire to set the record straight overshadow other concerns.

This distancing, a life turned into ethnography or sociopolitical description, hardens and reifies personal narratives. It does not allow much space to turn inward and reflect upon the self. V. S. Naipaul, in *Among the Believers: An Islamic Journey,* relays his frustrated attempt to get Ayatollah Sadeq Khalkhali to "show a little more than his official side. . . . I had been hoping to get him to talk about his life, I would have liked to enter his mind, to see the world as he saw it. . . . He could be probed into no narrative, no story of struggle or rise. He had simply lived; experience wasn't something he had reflected on. And, vain as he was ('I am very clever, very intelligent'), the questions about his past didn't interest him."[20]

And when it is not the official side or the self-selected, controlled, and socially acceptable image of the self that is portrayed, either the publication of an autobiography is postponed or it turns into a scandal, as did Jalal Al-e Ahmad's *Sangi bar Guri* [A Tombstone on a Tomb].[21] In this short autobiography (ninety-three pages altogether), Al-e Ahmad records with precision the story, the agonies, and the anxieties of his childlessness. His wife, Simin Daneshvar, has treated the same issue in some of her short stories, especially in "Mar-o Mard" [The Snake and the Man], under the guise and protection of a hidden, fictive identity.[22] *A Tombstone on a Tomb* is tantalizing in its distinctively personal, introspective form, in its directness, and in its refreshing treatment of taboo subjects. The writer, with the exuberance of a master storyteller, ventures where few Iranian men have been before him. The book, however, did not emerge into print during its author's lifetime. Published posthumously, it turned into a literary scandal; or in the words of *Keyhan-e Farhangi*'s reporter, "a conspiracy to distort the image of the honorable and rebellious Al-e Ahmad."[23] Amazingly enough, no one refutes the so-called facts, among them Al-e Ahmad's chauvinism or his illicit relations, depicted in the book. The arguments only revolve around whether it was wise to publish it at all. Not the details of Al-e Ahmad's life and character as he himself portrays them but rather making those details public seems to be the major objection of those who would have wished the book unpublished.

Silence about the self seems to protect and confer power. It establishes one's honor. By withholding personal information, one gains the upper hand and does not give away information that could be potentially misused. Sa'di, the highly revered didactic writer, dedicates one out of the eight chapters of his masterpiece, *Golestan* [The Rose Garden], to "the benefits of silence."[24] Jalal ed-Din Rumi is no less adamant in his advocacy of secrecy. In the story entitled "The King and the Slave-girl," he writes

> As long as you keep your secrets in your heart
> You achieve faster your heart desires.
>
> "He who keeps his secrets," said the Prophet
> "Quickly attains his real aims."
>
> Since the seed is hidden in the soil
> Its concealment causes the garden to thrive.
>
> Since they are hidden underground
> Gold and silver are transformed into mines.[25]

This kind of cultural context is not readily conducive to the development of personal life narratives and their generic uncovering of the self. As a matter of fact, another argument used to explain the paucity of autobiographies is exactly the fear that the information revealed in them can be used or, rather, misused against their authors. The vulnerability and defenselessness brought about by such an unnecessary disclosure of inner states and private matters jeopardize the author or others involved by giving away privileged information otherwise unavailable. When asked if he had considered writing an autobiography, the novelist Bozorg 'Alavi, imprisoned in 1937 for his alleged association with the Communist Tudeh party, censored and exiled for most of his life, told the interviewer:

Yes, he had thought about that, too, and even made notes. But an autobiography, in order to be meaningful, had to tell the whole truth. It needed to be written with candor and a feeling of freedom. One needed the license to say whatever was pertinent about oneself and one's past, which included other people. The time for that had not yet come. There were still people alive whose positions and welfare would be jeopardized, if his relationship with them were ever made public. Aside from which, even if one were able to write with a clear conscience, there would always be those who were ready to turn on one and declare that these were merely the words of a communist—that everything one wrote reflected the communist viewpoint. At his age, he had no intention of being party to any petty literary feud. He found such things childish. Under the circumstances, if an autobiography were truly called for, then much better to write it and have it published posthumously. After one's death, people would be more inclined to view one's life and works with greater objectivity.[26]

It is true that censorship has been a constant in most of the 1,100 years of Persian literature. Many writers and poets have claimed that they would have never been able to publish had they not evolved an ingenious method of encoding their messages. A manifestation of the strength of totalitarian regimes, religious fanaticism, and chaotic, ultimately repressive historical periods, this tradition of official censorship is important in any study of Persian literature. But censorship as an institution not only censors, it eventually creates voluntary censors. Censorship breeds self-censorship. It demands new realms, covers new grounds, and springs up in unpredictable spots. Deception turns into self-deception. As outer constraints are slowly internalized, evasion of censorship becomes not just an indispensable strategy for dealing with repression but also a handy way of dealing with the self. A life of concealment develops progressively in the misty atmosphere where all the channels of communication are rigidly held in control. Ingenious forms of protection and secrecy are devised as substitutes for the ordinary privileges of privacy.

The poem entitled "Dead End," by Ahmad Shamlu, best epitomizes how external censorship extends itself to the most intimate details of personal lives. Every drop of freedom seems to be squeezed out of this poem. Behind its plain language and its vivid style lie rich imagery and heavily veiled symbolism. Much violence is concentrated into few words, and with it the brutality portrayed becomes alarming, even macabre. The anxiety of a life of concealment lurks behind every line. Sheer, unredeemable pain and despair seem to be so intense that they permit the

poet neither the luxury of dreams nor the relief of hope. The struggle
to hide and to remain hidden becomes the only meaningful effort in
this otherwise sordid life.

> They sniff at your mouth
> Lest you'd said "I love you."
> They sniff at your heart.
>> It is a strange time, my love!
> And they whip love
> By the barricade.
>> Better to hide love in the closet.
>
> In this crooked dead end of cold
> They kindle fire
> Fueled with songs and poems.
> Don't risk thinking.
>> It is a strange time, my love!
> He who knocks on the door, at night
> Has come to snuff out the lamp.
>> Better to hide light in the closet.
>
> Those settled by the roads
> Are butchers
> With bloody axes and knives.
>> It is a strange time, my love!
> And they cut off smiles on the lips
> And melodies from the mouth.
>> Better to hide joy in the closet.
>
> Roasted canaries
> On the fire of lily and jasmine.
>> It is a strange time, my love!
> Satan, victorious and drunk
> Is feasting our mourning.
>> Better to hide God in the closet.[27]

Flames of burning books, jasmine, and lilies rise from this poem immersed in darkness and cold. Thugs and hatchet men — these decapitators
of light and love — are pledged to bring life to a dead end. Even time
is denied any forward movement, and the whole poem is plunged into

a perpetual present. In fact, the only motion is the intensification of terror. If in the first line, freedom of speech is annulled ("They sniff at your mouth"), soon inquisition of ideas and even feelings begins ("They sniff at your heart"). This rending of every humanizing emotion builds painfully through the poem. It finds its culmination in the necessity of hiding God in the closet.

The line of demarcation between the victim and the victor, between the tormented and the tormentor is very clear in this poem. On the one side are the executioners. In the slash of their knives, in the crack of their whips, in the thud of their chopping blocks, in the sting of their lashes, they prove their commitment to terror. On the other side are the executed. They are left with only one option. They have to hide all the love, art, joy, and faith that is left to them, which even in a bloody and mutilated state must be protected at all cost. The reader cannot help but shiver from this pernicious control that extends its tentacles in all directions and forces intimacy to take refuge in the closet.

External restrictions sustained over time eventually generate internal ones. Imaginary boundaries reinforce, perpetuate, or even substitute for the real ones. And although these private, sacred precincts protect, they also imprison. The sophisticated mechanisms that shield the inner self from exposure and intrusion also amputate and silence part of the self. A subtle silencing of the private self generates a certain artfulness in manufacturing responses to the outside world. The gap between *Daruni/ Biruni* [outside/inside] and *Zaheri/Bateni* [exoteric/esoteric] becomes so alarmingly large that sustaining an apparent match between the two becomes a formidable task to whoever has achieved it. *Zaher-o batenesh yekiyeh* [his/her outside matches the inside] becomes a flattering compliment, as if the normal state of being is to have a conscious, deliberate dichotomy between the two.

The onion-skin theory applies. External layers must be painstakingly discarded to reach the innermost layers. Language gets saturated with metaphors, allusions, overtones and undertones, reticences and double (if not multiple) meanings. Deliberate obscurities and ambiguities become part of daily intercourse. Just as it takes a trained individual to grasp the truth at the core of both religious and secular scriptures, it takes a special talent to decode daily intercourse and decipher innuendos.[28] Ceaseless concern with the hidden aspects of issues becomes, at times, obsessive.[29] Actions and ideas are not evaluated in terms of their inherent value and relevance but rather in terms of the presumption of their concealed dimensions. *Baten* and *Andaruni* [the inner] become a refuge, a sanctuary where real feelings and thoughts are safeguarded. But, progressively, the façade takes on a rigidity that overwhelms the suppressed part of the self. It turns into an impenetrable front and acquires a compulsory character. A certain role playing, a constant watchfulness are the inevitable outcome. The gesticulator becomes the gesture. United, they become indistinguishable, like identical twins.

Clearly, anyone living in a community needs to keep up appearances and to implement some degree of self-imposed censorship (Freud's superego, William James's social self, Jung's persona). Life in a glass house will probably never be; a complete reconciliation of inner and outer will prove impossible in principle and in fact. Privacy is a basic human need. "A concentration camp," in the words of Milan Kundera, "is a world in which people live crammed together constantly, night and day. Brutality and violence are merely secondary (and not in the least indispensable) characteristics. A concentration camp is the complete obliteration of privacy."[30] The issue at hand, here, is not the obliteration of privacy and the establishment of a concentration camp the size of life. The question is the extent of the disparity between what is considered private and public and the rewards or punishments for opening up.

One can keep a great disaccord between the inner and the outer, between the façade and the background. But a mask worn for too long becomes another face, a second nature. The façade becomes an integral part of the building. One can pretend to ignore or cover up one's feelings, but that does not alter the fact that they exist. In fact, the more thwarted the feelings, the stronger they get, gathering momentum to wage a surprise attack. They become a dangerously explosive force—a volcano at the point of eruption. That partly explains why, as the old saying goes, people "need locks on their lips." Before they leave the lips, words must be evaluated lest they betray the inner self.

Hefz-e aberu [to save face], *Hefz-e zaher* [to protect appearances], *Ba sili surat-o sorkh negah dashtan* [to keep the face red with a slap], and many more such proverbial sayings, still in use and practice today, perpetuate methods of dissimulation and mitigate against voluntary, unnecessary self-revelations. *Zaban-e sorkh,* [a red tongue], the fiery kind, the kind that is not under control and that divulges secrets, gives heads away. Wasn't Hallaj, the tenth-century Sufi martyr, executed for publicly announcing his views, loud and clear, for everyone to hear? Simply put, he was executed, it is argued, not because of what he said—other Sufis had said the same thing—but because of how he said it: publicly. Hafez (d. 1390) reminds himself and his readers of the dangers of indiscreet talking: "The friend who was hanged, said he / was incriminated because expose secrets did he."[31]

Investing in the necessity of secrecy and the pernicious presence of some form of terror and strangulation of basic human rights, there has developed a tendency among Iranians to blame external factors rather than internal ones. The tendency to talk obliquely and the unwillingness to be precise or to go on record are generally neglected while external factors are blamed and blown out of proportion. For instance, many argue that they prefer their autobiographies to be published posthumously in order not to jeopardize other people's position and welfare. But would all others involved also die with the autobiographer? Or is this postponement of publication a form of self-censorship?

Significantly, the Persian term *Sansur* [censorship], a borrowing from French, is narrowly interpreted in Iran. Persian dictionaries and encyclopedias define it in terms of governmental restrictions on publication. Yet socially as well as psychologically, censorship can repress communication on many other levels, not the least important of which is the personal. Many of the synonyms *Roget's International Thesaurus* offers for the word *censorship* imply the exercise of selection and rejection by oneself (on oneself) as much as by another; that is, suppression, repression, hush-up, deletion, omission, expurgation, inhibition, stifling, and suffocating.[32]

Acknowledging the part played by humility, discretion, and unfavorable living conditions, Simin Daneshvar offers more reasons for the self-imposed limitations on the direct revelation of the self:

> Generally speaking, an artist from the East is very humble and has little self-confidence. . . . Also, the writing of autobiographies cannot flourish in a conservative and possibly hypocritical society. . . . Our society fears sincerity and honesty. Recently, I read Simone de Beauvoir's autobiography. What a happy and cheerful life she had. She studied on time. She gratified her sexual needs on time. But then what about me—Simin Daneshvar—who had to witness thousands of unpleasant events. First, in a corner of [the city of] Shiraz, and later [in a house located] behind a cemetery in Tehran, I had to struggle for basic human needs. What is there to write about other than pain and sorrow?[33]

Seen within this context the rare attempts at autobiography found in contemporary Iran are the logical literary extensions of a culture that creates, expects, and values a sharply defined separation between the inner and the outer, the private and the public. They indicate strong forces of deindividualization, protection, and repression. Concealing, keeping the private private, is not just a matter of veiling and not just a woman's problem. It seems to be a relative constant of Persian experience. Perhaps the controversy on veiling can serve as a way of transposing this constant into the realm of contingent and time-bound historical/political constructs with the recognition that additional complications and complexities ensue from the sex-biased practice of veiling proper. In other words, women who have been deliberately, if not obsessively, kept away from the arena of public life and discourse have a still more restrained relation to public self-representation. Indeed, no traditional, veiled woman has ever published the details of her personal life, let alone an autobiography. In the resolutely nonsexual and impersonal writings of such women, the author remains almost inaccessible. The reader is kept at a strictly measured distance, learning very little of an intimate nature about the writer's personal life. Wanting to remain within the confines of her cultural context, such a woman assigns little value to the expression of personal experiences.

Hashemiyeh, a respected author of several books, was a highly learned scholar of religion who had reached the status of a *Mojtahed* [one who has achieved independent legal judgments in religious laws]. Interested in her life and her scholarship, Keshavarz-e Sadr, the compiler and editor of an anthology of women writers, "intended to write a detailed account of her life. Unfortunately, however, this humble lady avoided flaunting her scholarship or imparting any detail of her life. She disregarded my repeated requests for sharing any information on her professional biography."[34]

Even in interviews of female political figures of the Islamic Republic, women's traditional habit of self-effacement runs deep. Personal questions are generally evaded, and if answered at all, they are confined to familial relationships. In an interview, the political activist A'zam Talaqani was asked to talk about herself, her background, her education, her role in the revolution. Her answer to all those questions put together was a short "It is not important." But the interviewer insisted: "I have come from America where people give great importance not just to what is being said but to who is saying it. So you must dwell on the personal *[shakhsi]* aspects." Talaqani, with an antiautobiographical determination, still refused to concede, and her final answer was: "It does not matter. God knows our actions. He will decide, or people will write about them when we are gone. . . . If you must have this information, *Jamhuriya-Islami* newspaper has published a biographical sketch. You can look it up."[35]

Traditional veiled women have also refused to address the camera directly. On the whole, they have not shown much appreciation for photographs—those visual narratives.[36] If for one reason or another they had to take a picture, they diligently avoided imparting any feelings to it. If not taken candidly, their pictures are invariably without facial expression. "I had a particular problem with the elder women," writes Hamid Nafici, who was involved in archival documentation, "because they would object to being photographed without a veil, some even objected to being photographed altogether on religious or other grounds. . . . So the best I could do to resolve this contradiction with women was either to take candid pictures of them when they were not aware (and unveiled and unposed) or to take their pictures with veil on (and posed)."[37]

Only unveiled women have tried their hands at self-narrative, and the task has not been an easy one. In the first novel published by a woman, *Savushun,* the antiheroine, Miss Fotuhi, embodies this difficulty. She transgresses conventional female life-scripts.[38] Wanting voice and visibility, she unveils herself publicly before the compulsory unveiling act of 1936 and writes her life story. But her "nakedness," in both a literal and a literary sense, her appropriation of her body and of the pen, become her crimes. She is thrown into a mental asylum where both her body and her pen are kept under seal, censored, and suppressed. Self-representation turns into self-destruction, movement into immobility, song into silence, presence into absence. Having trespassed across the conventional sexual and textual boundaries, Miss Fotuhi is silenced, concealed, confined. Even trapped in a mental institution, however, she refuses to vanish into nothingness. She scribbles her untold tale and, ironically, gives her life-as-script to Zari, the conventional heroine who is her frequent visitor at the asylum. Zari is to place it in a safe-deposit box rented by Miss Fotuhi's brother. And so, ironically, even if fully written, her self-as-text, like herself, will eventually leave no trace behind. It will remain hidden in a locked box, its key in the hands of a man—the same man who has committed Miss Fotuhi to a mental asylum.

No one knows how many such women's autobiographies exist, securely buried: body and text in boxes, left to oblivion in silence and isolation like coffins. No one knows how many more women silently witnessed their urge to write their life stories die over and over again owing to unfavorable conditions. We do know, however, that women were ultimately irrepressible. They refused to surrender to full anonymity and found other channels for personal expression. They interwove the fabric of their lives in the warp and woof of beautiful carpet and tapestry. They revealed their talent in the looms of their stitchery and embroidery. They were perpetual storytellers, who imbued their tales, their lullabies, their songs, and their games with their personal lives. Their great grandmother, Shaherzad, had taught them that, as long as they could spin their tales, they wouldn't have their heads chopped off.

But I will not be talking about the unwritten, forgotten, locked-up, or disguised life-narratives. In all likelihood, most of them will not be unearthed and revived. They will remain unacknowledged identities, dead presences, veiled mysteries. The autobiographies I speak of here are the exceptionally few that escaped anonymity and were published.

Who are those women who dissociated themselves from the figures of the ideally mute, self-abnegating, self-denying women and subverted the system by writing autobiographies? Certainly none of the literary figures. As a matter of fact, even the most autobiographical among women writers have shown a pronounced aversion to giving even the scantiest biographical data on themselves. Forugh Farrokhzad, for instance, who systematically integrated a female self—her own—in her five collections of poetry, otherwise avoided talking about her personal life. When, during a radio interview, Iraj Gorgin asked her to talk about herself, she dismissed the question, saying: "Good heavens! Discussing this seems to me a rather boring and useless task. Well, clearly, anyone born has a birthday, is native to a certain city or a certain village, has studied in a certain school, and a handful of conventional and typical events have occurred in her life, such as falling in a pool during childhood, cheating in school, falling in love during adolescence, getting married, or some such things."[39]

Mahshid Amirshahi, whose adolescence is the stuff of most, if not all, of her short stories, a collection of which is titled *Be Sighe-ye Aval*

Shakhs-e Mofrad [First Person Singular], and whose personal experience of the Islamic revolution is the content of her novel-qua-political memoir, shows no less objection to talking directly about herself. In an introduction to a selection of her short stories published in 1972 and republished verbatim fifteen years later as the introduction to her first novel, *Dar Hazar* [At Home], she writes: "I don't believe my birthday, my birth certificate's number and place of issuance, my mother's name, and my father's occupation are interesting to anyone except officials of the office of registry. So would you kindly relieve me of the agony of writing these details as you will spare the readers of reading them? . . . To insist on knowing these details shows a lack of sensitivity."[40] But Amirshahi had earlier kept a diary, and her attempt at recording her personal life had caused her much trouble and agony, even fear. Years later, in one of her short autobiographical stories, "There and Then," she recalls how her diary was intruded upon by her father, abused, and used against her.

> For several years, fear was just another noun in a grammar book, a noun like intelligence. Or, it was a natural occurrence in science and geography books like an earthquake or volcanos. Fear didn't exist, and if it did, it was for others.
>
> But then fear sought me out again. It came upon me because of love. My father shook the notebook under my nose and said angrily, "What's this?"
>
> I said, "A diary. It is mine. Why did you read it anyway?"
>
> "It's none of your business," he said, and started reading the diary out loud, "I went to the movies with F., then we went out for ice cream." And he added, "Who do you think you are! Besides, who is F.? Aren't you ashamed of yourself?"
>
> The emotion that I felt was not shame, it was fear.[41]

Perhaps Farrokhzad and Amirshahi and many others like them were reacting, to a certain extent, to the obsessively sensationalistic interest of the critics (and even family members) in their lives, especially in their relationships with men. This interest replaced the serious attention that their works deserved and all too often led to their denunciation as decadent or too personal. The works of many women have been branded as merely autobiographical and devalued in the process for the primacy given to feelings and to an introspective, intimate kind of writing. This labeling has always carried negative connotations, designed to reinforce the notion that these women do not and cannot transcend the limits of the private. The works of many women have been slighted and excluded from literary histories and anthologies because the value structure of an almost exclusively male literary tradition has insisted that only certain kinds of experiences are worthy of serious consideration.[42] Women's personal lives have consistently lacked a part in this system. The following remarks by Faridoun Gilani in regards to Farrokhzad's early poetry—considered much more personal than her later work—express in a nutshell this kind of attitude: "It is only at the age of twenty-seven, after the publication of her first three collections, or rather from the age of twenty-seven that Forugh realizes she has to learn. Prior to then, her intellect lacked resources, her vision was limited. . . . To be accurate, her poetry was shallow, trivial, and enslaved to her highly immature feelings."[43]

Traditional criticism seems to have been more interested in its own version of women's lives than in their works. Compounding the critical neglect suffered by women writers, especially those in the classical tradition, has been a prurient fascination with their often colorful personalities rather than with their works. It is almost impossible to untangle myths from facts about them. These early women writers are more remembered for their lives than for their works. Although owing to the paucity of biographical data and a lack of larger sampling of their poetry, their lives have an enigmatic nature, they still share one predicament: their emergence as notorious figures. Mary Ellman aptly observes that "books by women are treated as though they themselves were women, and criticism embarks, at its happiest, upon an intellectual measuring of busts and hips."[44]

Rabe'e, living toward the end of the Samanid dynasty in the tenth century, is the first Iranian woman known to have written poetry. But what she is most remembered for is her tragic love affair. She was a beautiful princess, the daughter of Ka'b Qozdari. Though it inspired her with many delicate love poems, her love affair with her brother's slave, Bakhtash, brought her disrepute and finally death. Her brother, who through her poetry learned of Rabe'e's unconventional love affair, ordered her death. She was imprisoned in a bathhouse and her veins slashed. Rabe'e, allegedly dipping her fingers in her own blood and writing love poems on the bathhouse wall, has captured the romantic imagination of many. The value of her poems and her pioneering contributions to the development of Persian poetry have attracted a few. The romantic epic *Golestan-e Eram* (or *Bakhtash-Nameh*), by Reza Qoli Khan Hedayat, is inspired by that gloomy love affair.[45]

If Rabe'e is remembered most for this one love affair, Mahsati of Ganjeh (twelfth century) is famous for her numerous liaisons with various men, especially one with a young and cruel butcher. Jauhari of Bokhara, according to Jan Rypka, has turned Mahsati's love life into a work of fiction.[46] Of Mehron-nesa, we only know her teasing of an old husband and her love affair with the young and prosperous Shahrokh Mirza.

This rather obsessive interest in the sensational aspects of women's lives overshadows the critical attention due their works. Perhaps the refusal or reluctance of women writers to impart factual information about themselves is, among other things, an attempt to focus attention on their writing rather than on the writer. In fact, both Farrokhzad and Amirshahi, after refusing to talk about themselves, proceeded immediately to draw attention to the inherent value of their works.

In any case, the emergence of women's autobiographies in Iran can be traced to no earlier than the mid-twentieth century, when Banu Mahvash, a singer/dancer, and Maleke-ye E'tezadi, a political activist, published their highly unconventional life stories. Although *Taj-os Saltaneh's Memoir*, written in 1924, precedes both these autobiographies, it was not published until 1982.

However limited in number, women's autobiographies constitute a highly heterogeneous body of works. From the political activist Ashraf Dehqani to Princess Ashraf Pahlavi, from the Marxist revolutionary Marziyeh Osku'i to Empress Soraya Bakhtiar, Mohammad Reza Shah Pahlavi's second wife, their works include political allegiances from royalist to communist, from rightist to leftist, from reformist to revolutionary. Within the broad framework of religious ideology, they are no less divergent. At one extreme are the women fully committed to secularization. At another extreme, the traditionalist Parvin Nowbakht sees salvation only in the reinstitution of Islamic values and an Islamic worldview. The autobiographers are as diverse in their backgrounds as in their views. From Empress Farah Pahlavi to Forugh Shahab to Shusha Guppy they represent different social and economic statuses.[47]

Underneath these dissimilarities, however, lurk fascinating similarities. Most of these autobiographers were famous, if not notorious, before their embarking upon their life-narrative projects. For one reason or another, their lives had already been uncovered, exposed, publicly talked about. Significantly, the writing of autobiographies has been popular among women of the Pahlavi court: the memoirs of Princess Shams Pahlavi published in installments in *Etela'at Mahiyaneh*, *The Autobiography of H.I.H. Princess Soraya*, Empress Farah Diba's *Mes Mille et un Jours*, and Princess Ashraf Pahlavi's *Faces in the Mirror* followed by *Never Resigned*. All except the first one were written originally in languages other than Persian and published outside of Iran.

Most of these life-scripts have a sense of self deeply rooted in the public domain, representing what Bakhtin calls rhetorical autobiography.[48] They are devoted mainly to the defense of a political career, a religious cause, a notorious life. Resembling beefed-up curriculum vitae, they are usually purposive, characterized by one major preoccupation or another. Although their time frame is often stretched by means of free association, flashback, and flash-forward to cover a whole life, they have the manifest intent of recording the unfolding of a specific event or a particular stretch of time. The very act of writing these personal narratives is presented at times as a sort of duty, a mission sometimes divinely planned, sometimes politically or socially mandated. Parvin Nowbakht explains why she finally decided to write *Marivan Lake, at Six O'clock:* "Why do I write? Why do I write these memoirs? Why do I pollute the dearest memories of my life's most precious moments with the mediocrity of words? Why should these memories reach the ears of others? . . . Well, I write only because you [her husband] ordered me to."[49]

It is only by disappearing as author and becoming a medium for obeying her husband's command that Nowbakht is able to write her story at all. She is a chosen vessel bearing her husband's words, a husband who, although martyred, converses with her through dreams and intimate communing. Nowbakht thus refuses to assume the traditional responsibility of an autobiographer. She deliberately and consistently erases her self from the text. *Marivan Lake, at Six O'clock* is really an impersonal narrative that strives to record the martyrdom of a husband.

Of the concerns that recur frequently in these works, the most common is the desire to destroy a false image. Their primary purpose proves time and again to be the rectification of misperceptions regarding the author, setting the record straight once and for all. Through control of what the reader should know about the author, they present and cultivate a more desired public image. As cultural efforts at self-vindication, such autobiographies seem to be addressed to an invisible judge and jury. *Faces in the Mirror* is a case in point.

Called a Dragon Lady, the Black Panther, the Man with a Skirt, Princess Ashraf Pahlavi uses her autobiography as a means for "considering these charges candidly and truthfully." As the daughter of Reza Shah Pahlavi, as the twin sister of Mohammad Reza Shah Pahlavi, and especially as an influential political activist, nationally and internationally known, Princess Ashraf was feared, admired, hated, but never neglected. She was actually a primary source for juicy rumors and a main target of criticism for an amazingly large array of Iranians: the "bourgeois, the Left, or the clergy."[50] Her life or, rather, stories about her life are plentiful. Exaggerated, bordering on the fantastic, they are an amazing mixture of fact and fiction put together. In her own words:

Two decades ago French journalists named me "La Panthère Noire" (The Black Panther), and I must admit that I rather like that name, and that, in some respects, it suits me. Like the panther, my nature is turbulent, rebellious, self-confident. Often, it is only through strenuous effort that I maintain my reserve and my composure in public. But in truth, I sometimes wish I were armed with the panther's claws so that I might attack the enemies of my country. I know that these enemies — and particularly in the light of recent events — have characterized me as ruthless and unforgiving; almost a reincarnation of the devil himself. My detractors have accused me of being a smuggler, a spy, a Mafia associate (once even a drug dealer), and an agent of all intelligence and counterintelligence agencies in the world.

It is in part such allegations that have also led me to write this book — not as a way of defending myself, but as a way of considering these charges candidly and truthfully, and as a way of setting out the political events in my country, as well as the events of my personal life.[51]

Also typical of all these works is a firm belief in the author's privileged knowledge of herself, of her "real," unified self. Most of them strive to reveal their author's true identity buried beneath thick layers of misconceptions and false accusations. They show a totally different private self beneath the social one. It is comfortably taken for granted that the core and the shell, the inner and the outer, the essence and the appearance do not and need not correspond. Self-analysis is not the favored objective of the overwhelming majority of these works. Although they purport to be vehicles to allow the authors to speak for themselves, most of them actually incorporate multiple voices, especially that of a biographer. Because their approach to the author's own life is not particularized, the distinction between biography and autobiography is at times blurred. In fact, some of these works were allegedly written by ghost writers. Just as biography is somehow limited by the writer's lack of access to the private life of the subject, so, too, this kind of book keeps its reader at a certain distance. Preoccupation with rectification of the public image occupies such a space that the self recedes to the background.

Even Shusha Guppy, who left Iran at an early age never to return and came to be celebrated internationally as a singer of folk songs and as a journalist, is, in the words of Taqi Modarressi, "strangely absent" from her beautifully written, deeply moving book.[52] Although Guppy proves herself to be a master storyteller and pays a romantic homage and a poetic tribute to a country and a childhood she has left behind, she basically effaces herself from *The Blindfold Horse, Memories of a Persian Childhood.* Guppy's account of her childhood — exotic and nostalgic — can also be seen as a distancing device. It allows her to look at her own life from a safe distance, both geographically and emotionally, an ethnographic distance. When she enters the narrative it is mainly as the seer rather than the seen, the narrator rather than the narrated, the tourist rather than the toured. To borrow her own metaphor, her childhood becomes yet another image in her version of a magical and verbal *Shahre Farang.*

But, of all the hawkers, the most popular was the *Shahre Farang* (a City in Europe) man. He pushed his big black box on a wheelbarrow shouting:

"Come and see the *Shahre Farang!* Travel with me to the land of the Farangi and see its marvels! . . ."

Children rushed from all directions and offered the *Shahre Farang* man their coins.

"Easy now! Four at a time!"

The first four tiny spectators would crouch and glue their eyes to the little windows that opened on the magical world within, their hands cupped around the rims better to shut out light and reality. Presently the man would set his machine in motion turning a handle at the back, and a marvellous tapestry would unfold: Versailles, the Tuileries, Buckingham Palace, Windsor Castle. . . . Peacocks roamed amid luxuriant gardens, swans glided over glassy ponds, young lovers, princes and princesses one and all, resplendent in their fineries, strolled arm in arm towards bowers and woods. And, all the while, the man chanted a semi-rhymed commentary in a mesmeric voice. But as you were completely transported into the exotic magical world he conjured, the image froze:

"End of your pennies!" he said cruelly. "Next lot!"[53]

Among the autobiographies considered here, *Taj-os Saltaneh's Memoir* is an exception.[54] It is a striking, original venture in self-reflexivity and self-revelation that goes far beyond the conventional. Although it lacks any outstanding literary merit, it bears on central issues concerning women in contemporary Iran. In this book, a culturally defined, silent woman becomes a self-defined, articulate author producing a narrative characterized and unified by an integrated conception of her individuality. In her almost faithless world, well on its way to becoming secularized, Taj-os Saltaneh assumes the task of narrating her own history, which she considers "the best preoccupation in the world." She is convinced her narrative subject—herself—holds sufficient interest and importance for herself as well as for her readers. Defending her self-scrutiny and self-interest to her teacher and cousin, who is not convinced of the worth of such an undertaking, she says: "Ah! My dear teacher and cousin! Do you believe that I should occupy myself with any other kind of history, while my own past and present is a sad and amazing history? Is reviewing one's own history not the best preoccupation in the world?"[55]

Taj-os Saltaneh's Memoir is a valuable cultural and historical document because it provides an intimate glimpse into a neglected topic — the everyday life of a woman. The author, born in 1883 and the daughter of Nasser al-Din Shah Qajar, was highly educated for her time. She was well versed in Western literature, played music (piano and tar), and painted. She was thought to be exceptionally beautiful, with a beauty that, according to some of her contemporaries, not only "whetted the appetite of any man"[56] but, in the words of one of her several admirers, the poet 'Aref Qazvini, even captured her own heart: "Ever since she beheld her face in the mirror / She has been captivated by her own beauty."[57]

Taj-os Saltaneh not only unveiled herself publicly before the 1936 unveiling act but, by writing an autobiography, committed yet another public unveiling of her private life. She knew she was trespassing beyond the accepted paradigms of female self-representation: "My relatives will criticize my freedom of pen. . . . However, with conscience as my guide, I will write of my whole family history."[58] And write of her whole family she did, and much more. She openly challenged some of the most cherished ideals of her society and took men to task:

> Ah my teacher! Why you, an educated man, who fully realizes the good and bad of veiling, don't hold the hands of the women in your family and tribe, and take them out in public. For how long are you to remain their servant and porter or, in some fancy words, the master and owner of these poor wretches?

> Obviously, these loud words will fall on deaf ears. Even if through a thousand reasons I prove the ills of veiling to you, because you are Iranian, ill-tempered, and always concerned with superficialities, you'll say: "So and so [Taj-os Saltaneh] writes all these and opposes common beliefs because she is beautiful, bored with home, or wants to stroll freely in public." You might even curse me in your heart and claim that I argue for illegitimate causes for women.[59]

Cursed she was and notorious, too. Her views, which could not be accepted by those around her, were met with apathy and hostility. The pain of enduring an unresponsive, often hostile, social setting, however, was compounded by Taj-os Saltaneh's own conflicting aspirations. She had adopted new values without quite rejecting the old ones. Marginal to both value systems, she suffered not only from unfocused rage but from guilt as well. The self-image Taj-os Saltaneh projects in her autobiography is a tangle of contradictions. At times she poses as a committed exponent of feminist ideas. At others, she is an emotionally damaged, guilt-ridden woman who uses every occasion to justify her violation of cultural expectations. She feels guilty of being different, guilty of being too beautiful, of being desired, of desiring, of not being motherly enough, of being too individualistic, guilty everywhere and at every turn. Hers is the tale of a traumatized imagination.

Taj-os Saltaneh's deviant behavior soon became a threat to the society at large as well as to herself. According to Bamdad: "This beautiful woman spent the last years of her life on the bed of sickness, suffering intense and almost unbearable pain, but thanking God and trusting that this penance for her sins in the lower world would save her in the world above."[60] Considered guilty by her society (and even posthumously by her admirers such as Bamdad), the guilt-ridden Taj-os Saltaneh attempted suicide three times and her life-narrative waited almost six decades before finally being published in 1982.

Taj-os Saltaneh's Memoir as well as the other women's autobiographies are located well outside the conventions of acceptable exposure of a woman's life and voice. Transgressive in more ways than one, they unveil the hitherto private, the once taboo. With a distinctively feminine voice, they tell a tale—their own tale.

The history of women's autobiography writing in Iran shows interesting differences compared to the development of the genre in the West and to Iranian men's autobiographies in general. It is not a latter-day development out of religious autobiographies. In fact, it proves to be a development away from religion, rushing toward secularization. Unlike men's autobiographies and lacking their even, often unemotional language, women's autobiographies focus on relationships and interrelatedness. If in the first-person narratives related by male authors, women are at best marginalized, in female-centered discourses, the self is represented in its relations with men. The unfolding of the narrator's consciousness usually takes place through relationships with a chosen masculine other. Marziyeh Osku'i discovers and reveals herself in relation to the masses, the faceless crowd, personified as a lover.[61] Parvin Nowbakht, with no less intensity, focuses on a spiritual community at the center of which is her martyred husband. In spite of a distinctive personality present throughout her *Faces in a Mirror,* Princess Ashraf Pahlavi seems ceaselessly to need a man through whom to define herself.

Paradoxically, this man is her twin brother, Mohammad Reza Shah Pahlavi, who offered her as a sacrificial lamb on the altar of revolutionary fervor by denouncing her and exiling her first in 1951 and again in 1978.

But even if some of these autobiographies follow in their delineation of relationships a conventional pattern, even if they are ambivalent about self-exposure and self-attention, still the choice of an autobiographic format attests to the singularity of the enterprise. It bears the individual and individualized imprint of a female voice. By textualizing personal experience, by saying "I" in a written and public text, this choice shows a reverence for and fascination with the individual. It bespeaks a growing need for a literature of a woman-self in which woman becomes both the object and the subject of scrutiny. In short, whether the self is uncovered, dis-covered, or re-covered in these life-narratives, they all testify to a frantic search by women for autonomy and public self-expression.

PART FOUR

Voices Through the Veil

10

The Birth of Neotraditional Feminism

*O*f the beginning of Iranian women's literary tradition coincides with their attempts to unveil, then how have the mandatory veiling and rules of modesty *[Hejab]* of recent years affected women writers? The answer seems paradoxical. Despite compulsory veiling, or perhaps partly as a reaction to it and its corollary side effects, women's literature flourishes in a proliferation of books, articles, and journals by and about women inside and outside the country. Despite an acute shortage of paper and despite various forms of censorship, the number of books published and sold in the last decade far exceeds prerevolutionary levels. Between the winters of 1983 and 1985, 126 books by or about women were published in Iran. In the course of twelve months, more than 500 such articles were written.[1] If compulsory veiling was meant to segregate and silence women, then it has not been successful. Women's unprecedented visibility in literature is only one eloquent testimony to this failure.

Certainly, it would be wrong to assume that veiling or changes affecting women's personal freedom bring about immediate changes of the same magnitude in their literature. The attempt of the Islamic Republic to replace the "Pahlavi-produced, westernized"[2] woman with an Islamic ideal of womanhood—in literature or in life—will, if possible at all, need more than just a few years to come to fruition. The effort to supplant the previous "poisoned" and "corrupt"[3] literature with one that promotes the Islamic ideal of femininity also requires more than just the few years that have elapsed.

Although the Islamic Republic has not as yet openly expressed an official view on the role and portrayal of women in literature, it has

231

taken a clear position on the participation and representations of women on the movie screen. According to film and video regulations, observes Hamid Nafici:

> Muslim women must be shown to be chaste and to have an important role in society as well as in raising God-fearing and responsible children. In addition, women must not be treated like a commodity or used to arouse sexual desires. These general and ambiguous guidelines have had a profound effect on the use and portrayal of women in cinema. The most significant is the avoidance of stories involving women altogether, thus evading entanglement with censors. If women are portrayed at all, a whole new grammar of film is applied, including these features: women actors are given static parts or are shot in such a way as to avoid showing their bodies. Thus, they are filmed in longshot, with fewer close ups and facial expressions. In addition, eye contact and touching between men and women are discouraged.[4]

Yet in spite of the exacting rules about what can and cannot be shown on the screen, women's active participation in Iranian cinema has come a long way since the revolution. In the last few years, women have taken key roles in several movies. "In postrevolutionary cinema there have emerged in a single decade more women directors of feature films than in all the eight decades preceding the revolution."[5]

The unwritten yet prevailing attitude toward women's literature also stresses codes of modesty and emphasizes the need to exercise Islamic morality. Literature has consistently held a privileged position for the Islamic Republic. Considering "the pen to be mightier than the sword" or than "all of Reza Khan's [Reza Shah Pahlavi] bayonets,"[6] the post-revolutionary government has refused to view literature as a mere source of aesthetic enjoyment. On the contrary, it has regarded literature as an effective means of politicizing, educating, and inspiring. In meeting with representatives of the Writers Association of Iran two weeks after the revolution, Ayatollah Khomeini addressed his audience as "gentlemen" (though it included the prominent woman writer Simin Daneshvar) and demanded that they educate their constituencies as the clerics do. "What I request from the writers is that they be committed as we clerics are. You gentlemen writers must be committed. Now, you should use your pen for the welfare of this people and write for the welfare of this society."[7] In the words of then President Khamene'i at the Congress of Poetry, Literature, and Art in 1982: "If a revolution and a culture does not utilize art to establish and express itself, that revolution will fail to take root and mature."[8]

Living during a time that demands that its writers reexamine, reevaluate, and redefine not only the nature of artistic activity but the very essence of art, women writers have managed to take a visibly more active part in the Iranian literary mainstream. The increasing number of books and articles have turned women's issues into a dominant discourse. Inside Iran, secularly oriented women resist and challenge restrictive laws imposed in the name of Islam. Religiously oriented women discuss issues from within the Islamic tradition itself, and the society at large seems to accept these changes with more ease and openness. Women's issues are no longer considered automatically as middle-class or bourgeois concerns. There is, in fact, a coming together of different groups discussing radical issues within the strict confines of Islam. Women challenge androcentric ideology through Qor'anic passages. Boundaries previously set by religion are being crossed without necessarily causing offense. This desegregation of traditional women, this new perception of their roles, status, and aspirations, have created a highly charged atmosphere. The influence of this neotraditionalism regarding women has spread beyond the borders of cities and of the readily identifiable social classes.

In exile, prominent women writers have continued to write even more prolifically than before. After years of silence, Mahshid Amirshahi has published *Dar Hazar* [At Home], and she is now finishing another autobiographical novel, *Dar Safar* [Away from Home]. Goli Tarraqi wrote the short story "Bozorg Banu-ye Ruh-e Man" [The Grand Lady of My Soul] and is putting the final touches on the long novel *Khaterat-e Aqaye Alef* [The Memoirs of Mr. Alef]. Partow Nuri-'Ala has published the poetry collection *Az Cheshm-e Bad* [Wind's Eye View] and *Dow Naqd* [Two Criticisms]. While giving impetus to established literary figures, the revolution has also created a rush of new writers with widely divergent social and economic backgrounds. Younger women in exile have found a more readily available platform for expression and publication in such postrevolutionary women's journals as *Nimeye Digar* [The Other Half], *Zan* [Woman], *Peyk-e Ashena* [Friendly Messenger], *Forugh* [Forugh], *Zan-e Irani* [Iranian Woman], and *Panjareh* [Window].

Most postrevolutionary women's writings are acts of definition and self-definition, both personal and social, autobiographical and political. Although it is true that from its inception women's writing has been political, in the last ten years it has become politicized more than ever before. One of the most exciting developments has been a widening of thematic scope and a simultaneous concentration on resistance against repression of any sort. Women are raising their voices, telling their tales. Even those who portray themselves as victims of society—conforming, enduring, and suffering—are gaining a significant victory in being able to plead their own cases and make their stories heard in their own words. They are survivors, the ultimate rebels, irrepressible, vocal, and articulate.

A sense of sisterhood and of identification between the writer and other women dominates this literature. A more intense sense of political consciousness and a more ardent involvement with the issues of the day thematically differentiate these writings from earlier ones. Women's limitations and suffering are not seen as merely personal, private. They are not depicted as unavoidable. Rather, they are portrayed as endemic to social structures that can and ought to be altered. Anger and revolt emerge as major themes.

Iranian women, whether veiled or not, at home or in exile, are writing more than ever before. They are telling their stories, describing their reality, articulating the previously unarticulated. Concerned with modernity, the arrival of the twenty-first century, the unavoidability of change, they are reappraising values, worldviews, and spaces, literary or otherwise. Instead of merely reacting to notions of modernity or tradition, some women writers have been trying to reconcile the two. The poetry of Simin Behbahani is perhaps the most eloquent expression of this synthesis and revitalization of the old and the new. Her poetry neither affirms nor negates the Iranian or the Western tradition. Rather, it proves the instability upon which the dialectic between the two traditions is played. Here the discourses of "modernity" and "tradition" no longer compete with, but complement, each other. They transform, restructure, and reconstruct each other. Against the background of painful back-and-forth shuttling between intense identification with and total rejection of tradition, against the inconsistencies of her time, this poetry bears eloquent witness to the possibility of both fluidity and permanence.

I do not mean to imply that the issue of modernity as a concept or a vision is resolved in this body of writing. Modernity has been and continues to be a central epistemological, aesthetic, and ethical problem of contemporary Iranian literature (and history). What I see as refreshingly liberating in Behbahani's writing, especially in her last two collections, is the fact that it neither advocates a return to "pure" ethnic origins nor does it accept the exclusiveness of Western models of individualism, democracy, objectivity, women's rights, gender relations, and so forth. I would like to end my book on a note of hope and promise with emphasis on the neotraditionalism in Behbahani's poetry.

～～～～～

Simin Behbahani was born in Tehran in 1927. She grew up there and was betrothed, before finishing high school, to Mr. Behbahani. The marriage was not a successful one. After sixteen years and three children, it ended in divorce. Years later, Behbahani married Manuchehr Kushiar.[9] In a productive career spanning more than four decades, Behbahani has produced seven poetry collections and a recent autobiography/memoir entitled *An Mard, Mard Hamraham* [That Man, My Male-Companion]. Her first book, *Tar-e Shekasteh* [Broken String], was published in 1951 when the poet was barely twenty-four. Between 1956 and 1983, six other books of her poems were published. This is a prodigious output considering that Behbahani was a full-time high school teacher for twenty-nine years, a housewife, and a mother of three children.

Unlike Forugh Farrokhzad, her contemporary modernist poet, Behbahani has been virtually neglected by the literary establishment. Although her work has compelled the attention and admiration of an ever-growing number of readers, few have written about it. Not a single book has been devoted to the study of Behbahani's life or poetry. For several decades, she has been missed or dismissed in literary books and anthologies — inside or outside the country. None of her poems, let alone any of her poetry collections, have been translated into English. It is only in the last few years that the trend is finally reversing itself, and Behbahani is being given some overdue recognition. Like most other women writers discussed in this book, against difficult odds of neglect, slight, economic hardship, divided loyalties, Behbahani has earned her prominence by the strength of her personality, her talent, and her perseverance.

As one reads through the seven books of Behbahani's collected verse, one sees that her poetry includes a wide variety of experiments with forms and ultimately becomes the transformation of a conventional and mainly masculine poetic form. What emerges as one of the greatest strengths of her work is the creative use she makes of *Ghazal* [a sort of ode made of a few (usually between seven and twelve) monorhyming couplets]. In an age characterized by violent breaks with or by total absorption in the past, Behbahani has consistently challenged reactionary views of tradition. Working with inherited verse forms, she has not only become a master and innovator of devices and techniques but has also found a complex and distinctive voice. Her neotraditionalism stands out against the dominant spirit of her time: the desperate search by self-consciously modernist poets for new forms that would enable them to break with tradition. And this neotraditionalism extends beyond her verse forms. For her themes, too, Behbahani digs deep into her culture and finds familiar motifs to revitalize and to be revitalized in her poetry. Her series of sixteen poems dedicated to *Kowlis* [Gypsies] is such a reappropriation and reappraisal of a familiar figure.

The Persian word *Kowli,* translated roughly as "Gypsy," is dazzlingly rich in connotations in Iranian popular belief. Behbahani's poetry fully exploits that wealth. A Gypsy—always a woman in her poetry—is a mutant. Ambiguous and unclassifiable, she has an amorphous social status. She has no home of her own, is in constant wandering, migration. She is socially and culturally marginal but refuses to be domesticated. Not recognized in her capacities as daughter, wife, mother, she has no family-bound existence. She has a reputation for aggressive nonconformity. Presented as victim—homeless, exiled—she is also endowed with magical powers. She can turn bodies into texts and read palms; she tells fortunes; she intuits the past and divines the future. She is resilient, a survivor.

A Gypsy is mobile, and her mobility affords her visibility. She is not confined in the home. Unmindful of rules of modesty, she has a public presence. To appreciate the significance of her freedom to roam at will, one should look at it against the backdrop of the normative immobility of women in Middle Eastern societies. The privilege of mobility holds such a special value for a woman in a sexually segregated society that Fatima Mernissi, in her treatise titled *Women in Moslem Paradise,* equates it with a paradisiacal right. "One thing I discovered while scrutinizing my place in Paradise is that one ought to insist on the right to move freely in and out of it if one so desires. More important than Paradise is the freedom to move around without conditions; without qualifications; without permission. More important probably than the right to enter Paradise, is the right to leave it for no reason other than a totally arbitrary, whimsical desire to discover other horizons."[10]

Another powerful challenge presented by the figure of Gypsy is her public voice. Her name is, in fact, somehow negatively, associated with voiced existence. Ironically, in a preface written to a collection of her selected poems, Behbahani, reminiscing about a childhood ear infection, writes: "The doctor interpreted my infantile screaming as *Kowligari* [Gypsy-like] and told my mother, 'this girl will avenge you.'"[11] This short sentence shows in a nutshell a Gypsy's ambivalent position. Although condemned, she is also admired; abased, she is also exalted. If she is, as so many legends about her suggest, unruly and loud, she can also demand her rights and those of others.

As a social type, a Gypsy transgresses proprieties and boundaries. Her repeated journeys, literally from one village, city, even country, to another, and figuratively from one universe of definitions and meanings of femininity to another, defy laws of seclusion and segregation. The figure of the Gypsy unavoidably challenges the narrow definitions of womanhood in Iran. Indeed, some of her defining attributes are those commonly reserved for men. She is a potent cultural figure. She is the ideal and the counterideal. She combines many intense and contradictory feelings about womanhood.

Behbahani recognizes the subversive potentials of the figure of the Gypsy. Instead of importing a model or inventing a new heroine, she appropriates what is already there. This reliance on the culturally familiar has proved to be a fruitful strategy. In the last few decades, any defiance of conventions, flaunting of family authority, and challenge to patriarchal authority, have automatically been seen and interpreted as a desire to Westernize. Feminism, a word for which there is no Persian equivalent to this day, as a movement and as a perspective has been readily labeled and dismissed as Western, an imitation of Western ways, a surrender to foreign powers. If Babism [a religious faith proclaimed in Iran] was used in the mid-nineteenth and early twentieth century by antifeminists to justify their condemnation of those who fought for women's rights, the target of anger later switched to the West. Progressively, the issue of woman's emancipation became a major grievance of nationalistic reactions to foreign powers and their local representatives. A secular Iranian feminist thus confronts formidable problems. On the one hand, she has to challenge historically engrained forms of gender domination. On the other hand, she has to disentangle her every move from what is labeled Western imperialism, or the betrayal of one's indigenous culture to alien infiltration and domination. The Iranian feminist has also been blamed, time and again, for not representing Iranian women or having their best interest at heart. Although in the face of enormous class differences, ethnic variables, and educational gaps no one can claim to represent the "Iranian woman," still feminists have been criticized for their focus on "bourgeois" issues affecting "bourgeois" women. Their alleged failure to address the needs and aspirations of tribal, rural, and lower-class women has been a major source of grievance and a readily available platform to undervalue and even delegitimize their efforts.

The poetry of Simin Behbahani, despite the radical connotations of her feminism, has been spared such damaging categorization. Although it is impossible to account for this attitude in terms of any simple or obvious cause, and although Behbahani has never been the center of hot literary debate, it is still significant that her relentless advocacy of an autonomous, unconventional female identity, such as that embodied in the figure of the Gypsy, has never been condemned. Perhaps Behbahani's advocacy of change through the familiar idioms of her own culture has been the saving grace. In her uses of the figure of the Gypsy, Behbahani casts a familiar figure in a heroic mold, questions received interpretations of her life, and promotes radical changes. She revives and then revises mythologies that govern patriarchal thinking. By reinterpreting the figure of the Gypsy, Behbahani asserts the Gypsy's power rather than her victimhood and turns her into a triumphant image of female autonomy.

The following poem, Gypsy poem number 13, forms an eloquent endpiece to this book. It advocates and celebrates the transcendence of three central cultural fears: woman's visibility, woman's mobility, and woman's voice.

> Sing, O, Gypsy, in homage to being, sing
> To register your presence in people's ears, sing.
>
> Eyes and throats burn from the smoke that trails monsters
> Scream if you can, of the terror of this night. Sing.

The secret of the monster's life hides in the stomach of a fish
That swims in waters to which you cannot reach.

Every maiden holds the head of a monster on her lap
Like a lump of coal in silver wrapped.

The rapacious monsters have plundered from the pretty maidens
The silk of their cheeks, the agate of their lips.

O, Gypsy, with the yearning for liberty, stamp your feet,
To receive an answer, send a message with their beat.

There is a purpose to your existence in the scheme of things
Draw a spark, make a fire, stamp your feet.

Ages dark have crushed your body, warping it inwards,
Do not remain a mere trace on a rock, rise up, and sing.

O, Gypsy, to stay alive you must slay silence!
I mean, to pay homage to being, you must sing.[12]

Notes
Works Cited
Index

Notes

(Subsequent citations of transliterated titles are given in English.)

Preface

1. Farzaneh Milani, "Grandmother and Jasmine," *Omid* 1, no. 2 (Nov.–Dec. 1987): 91. I have benefited from Kaveh Safa, Afsaneh Najmabadi, Bahiyeh Nakhjavani, and Geoffrey Gardner's translations of "Grandmother and Jasmine." I am most grateful to them.

2. Fazlollah Garakani, *Tohmat-e Sha'eri* [Accused of Being a Poet] (Tehran: Alborz, 1977).

3. Forugh Farrokhzad, *Iman Biavarim be Aghaz-e Fasl-e Sard* [Let Us Believe in the Dawning of a Cold Season] (Tehran: Morvarid, 1974), 44.

1. A Walled Society

1. The conspicuous absence of women is confined neither to arts nor to Iran. "The majority of women in the ancient Orient have left no trace in the historical records. They remained nameless and unnamed. Exceptions that escaped anonymity are mostly of a notorious kind. To the qualities that guaranteed a number of these women a place in history belong love of intrigue, artful and treacherous seductiveness, cruelty and even murderousness" (Helen Sancisi-Weerdenburg Groningen, "Exit Atossa: Images of Women in Greek Historiography on Persia," in *Images of Women in Antiquity,* ed. Averil Cameron and Amelie Kuhrt [Detroit: Wayne State Univ. Press, 1983], 20–33).

2. Ibid., 22.

3. I do not mean to privilege novels written over stories told; I do not necessarily prefer poems to lullabies; I don't believe creativity is the prerogative of an elite — literate and literary. On the contrary, I see the utmost of creativity in the works of many illiterate, nonliterary persons. This often undocumented artistic tradition cannot be underestimated and the creative variations among women minimized, neglected.

241

I will not be talking, however, about this wealth of multimedia artistic expression. Rather, my primary concern is one specific medium: written literature.

4. There is no conveniently typical or general Iranian woman who could represent the experiences of Iranian women. Iran has undergone, and is currently undergoing, rapid and dramatic changes. It is far from being a homogeneous society. Local variations, negotiations of, and adaptations to new national and international pressures mitigate and, at times, contradict any general outline. Socioeconomic variables, ethnic backgrounds, and religious inclinations each have their impact. In addition, great disparities between urban, rural, and tribal populations, upper and lower classes, and the educated and the illiterate preclude any typical characterization. Nonetheless, even without homogeneity or universality, one can speak of some basic patterns and characteristics that can be discerned beneath local variations.

5. Ayatollah Ruhollah Khomeini, "Veils of Darkness, Veils of Light," in *Islam and Revolution,* trans. Hamid Algar (London: KPI, 1985), 396.

6. Bijan Gheiby, *"Chador* in Early Literary Sources," in *Encyclopaedia Iranica,* ed. Ehsan Yarshater (London: Routledge & Kegan Paul), fasc. 6:609.

7. Ibid.

8. Participation in a vast range of economic activities forces rural and tribal women into wearing functionally more appropriate, physically less-confining clothing. Their observation of certain rituals, however, such as covering the hair, the lower lip, etc., when in the presence of forbidden men, is their pragmatically necessary form of compromised veiling. When these women migrate to towns, they invariably adopt the practice of fully veiling themselves. Their previous local clothing proves to be unaccommodating in the new environment; and more importantly, perhaps, the city form of veiling can be considered a sign of their upward mobility and the expression of their new status.

9. For an interesting account of Huda Shaarawi's life, see Huda Shaarawi, *Harem Years, The Memoirs of an Egyptian Feminist,* trans. and ed. Margot Badran (New York: Feminist, 1987).

10. Sarah Graham-Brown, *Images of Women* (London: Quartet, 1988), 141.

11. It is perhaps a cliché but nonetheless a truism that until recently Iranian women were captives of distorted images. If at home they were confined within the tight mold that tradition imposed upon them, in the West they were reduced to dimensionless characters, labeled, oversimplified, stereotyped. In harems, behind walls and veils, actively involved in revolutionary movements, they have been a mystery to the West. Occasionally, when the eyes of Western cameras witness their vital spirit, the media and their audience are amazed. But as soon as the cameras and the photographers return home, they are pushed back—once again—behind the thick veil of a distorted, yet more familiar, image. Once again, they become voiceless, powerless, and dimensionless, as exotic as their image of passivity in secluded gardens, as opaque as the opacity of the veil that covers them physically. Actually, the veil has been an enigma. Most Westerners have expressed total bewilderment at the institution of veiling. By distancing, defamiliarizing, and exoticizing the Iranian (or Middle Eastern) woman through her veil, there has been a tendency to view her as both sexually exotic and culturally oppressed by her seclusion and segregation.

12. The negative charges associated with these presumably feminine powers can also be questioned and challenged. For an interesting redefinition of *gossip*, for instance, see Patricia Meyer Spacks, *Gossip* (Chicago: Univ. of Chicago Press, 1986). In her preface, Spacks writes: "My mission began to define itself as a rescue operation: to restore positive meaning to a word that had once held it, and to celebrate a set of values and assumptions particularly associated with women, as well as with gossip."

13. For a full and fascinating study of the powerful symbolic charge of the extremes of high and low in a culture, see Peter Stallybrass and Allon White, *The Politics and Poetics of Transgression* (London: Methuen, 1986).

14. Shams ed-Din Mohammad Hafez, *Divan* [Collection of Poems], ed. Parviz Natel Khanlari (Tehran: Kharazmi, 1980), 684.

15. Quoted in Talat Halman, "Jalal al-Din Rumi: Passions of the Mystic Mind," in *Persian Literature*, ed. Ehsan Yarshater (New York: Bibliotheca Persica, 1988), 200.

16. For an interesting article on "Women and the Semiotics of Veiling and Vision in Cinema," see Hamid Nafici's forthcoming article in *American Journal of Semiotics*.

17. For footbinding in China, see Howard S. Levy, *Chinese Footbinding* (New York: Walton Rawls, 1966); Feelie Lee, "Bound and Unbound Feet" (Ph.D. diss., Wright Institute, 1982); Mary Daly, *Gyn/Ecology* (Boston: Beacon, 1978); William A. Rossi, *The Sex Life of the Foot and Shoe* (Ware, England: Wordsworth, 1989). For some similarities and dissimilarities between veiling and footbinding, see Farzaneh Milani, "Woman's Body as Sign and Symbol: On Veiling and Footbinding," *Iran Nameh* 8, no. 2 (1990): 246–60.

18. See Carol Karlsen, *The Devil in the Shape of a Woman* (New York: Vintage, 1987); Selma R. Williams and Pamela J. Williams, *Riding the Nightmare* (New York: Atheneum, 1978); H. R. Trevor-Roper, *The European Witch-Craze* (New York: Harper Torchbooks, 1967); Barbara Ehrenreich and Deirdre English, *Witches, Midwives, and Nurses* (New York: Feminist, 1973); Erica Jong, *Witches* (New York: Abrams, 1981).

19. For a moving personal account of clitoridectomy, see Nawal el Saadawi, *The Hidden Face of Eve* (Boston: Beacon, 1981).

20. I am most grateful to Janet Beizer for sharing with me her several insights into hysteria and the unpublished materials for her forthcoming book, *Ventriloquized Bodies: The Narrative Uses of Hysteria*.

21. See Kim Chernin, *The Obsession, Reflections on the Tyranny of Slenderness* (New York: Harper & Row, 1981); Susie Orbach, *Hunger Strike* (New York: Avon, 1986).

22. See Peggy Reeves Sanday, *Fraternity Gang Rape: Sex, Brotherhood, and Privilege on Campus* (New York: New York Univ. Press, 1990).

23. Fatima Mernissi, *Beyond the Veil*, rev. ed. (Bloomington: Indiana Univ. Press, 1987), ix.

24. Farrokhzad, *Dawning of a Cold Season*, 76.

25. Edward W. Said, *Orientalism* (New York: Vintage, 1979), 291.

26. Mahshid Amirshahi, "Introduction," in a forthcoming collection of short stories by Iranian women writers, compiled and edited by John Green.

27. Iraj Gorgin, "An interview with Forugh Farrokhzad," in *Arash*, ed. Syrus Tahbaz (Tehran: Darakhshan, 1966), 33.

28. Simin Behbahani, "We Have Run and We Are Still Running," *Doniya-ye Sokhan*, no. 13 (Nov. 1987): 61.

29. Tahereh Saffarzadeh, *Mardan-e Monhani* [Curbed Men] (Shiraz, Iran: Navid, 1987), 91.

30. Shahrnush Parsipur, "Why Do You Write?" *Doniya-ye Sokhan*, no. 17 (Mar. 1988): 10.

31. Elaine Showalter, "The Feminist Critical Revolution," in *The New Feminist Criticism,* ed. Elaine Showalter (New York: Pantheon, 1985), 4.

32. Iranian women, it seems, have been concealed in a cloak of anonymity in the West even though stereotypical assumptions about them abound. This veiling has been extended to their literature as well. This critical negligence can be witnessed in their conspicuous absence from world anthologies in general and anthologies of world literature by women in particular. For instance, the "first landmark collection," which surveys "women writers in the modern historical period from an international perspective," in its 1,267 pages does not so much as mention the Iranian women writers. See Marian Arkin and Barbara Shollar, eds., *Longman Anthology of World Literature by Women, 1875–1975* (New York: Longman, 1989).

33. Forugh Farrokhzad, *Tavalodi Digar* [Another Birth] (1964; reprint, Tehran: Morvarid, 1972), 159.

2. The Concept of Veiling

1. Barbara G. Walker, *The Woman's Dictionary of Symbols and Sacred Objects* (San Francisco: Harper & Row, 1988), 161.

2. See Reza Barahani, *Tarikh-e Mozakar* [Masculine History] (Tehran: Elmi, n.d.).

3. Leaving the theories of origin for what they are and believing that the complex phenomenon of veiling has neither one origin nor one function, I will cite only a few examples to show the disagreement among Iranians concerning the beginning of the veiling practice. I will confine myself to contemporary texts. The prominent writer Sadeq Hedayat (1903–1951), criticized most vehemently the role of Islam in the oppression of women. Extolling women's exalted position before Islam, he referred to pre-Islamic Iranian empresses and reminded the reader that "we did not have the habit of burying our girls alive" (*Parvin, Dokhtar-e Sassan* [Parvin, the Daughter of Sassan] [Tehran: Amir Kabir, 1963], 13).

Hedayat's work contains many such examples of barbed sarcasm and bitter antagonism toward Islam with reference to women. A few lines from the preface to *Neyrangestan* (Persian Folklore) perhaps best sum up his attitude: "Every aspect of life and thought, including woman's condition, changed after Islam. Enslaved by man, woman was confined to the home. Polygamy, injection of fatalistic attitude, mourning, sorrow and grief led people to seek solace in magic, witchcraft, prayer, and jinnis" (*Neyrangestan* [Tehran: Parastu, 1965], 18). Hedayat's antagonism reached the magnitude of a blanket condemnation, and to Islam he attributed not only the suffering and corruption of his characters but also the practice of veiling. See *Neveshteha-ye Parakandeh* [The Scattered Writings] (Tehran: Amir Kabir, 1965), 414.

Badr ol-Moluk Bamdad writes: "The practice of secluding the female half of the community spread to Iran as a result of political factors and worldwide tendencies, such as the Arab and Mongol invasions" (*From Darkness into Light: Women's Emancipation in Iran*, trans. F. R. C. Bagley [Hicksville, N.Y.: Exposition-University, 1977], 7). Guity Nashat, on the other hand, believes that "by the seventh century A.D., respectable women in the Byzantine and Sassanian empires were secluded, and they appeared in public veiled" ("Women in the Middle East," in *Restoring Women to History* [Bloomington, Ind.: Organization of American Historians, 1988], 21). Jalil Ziyapur maintains that in pre-Islamic Iran women used *Chador* "because some designs on plates show them veiled" (*Pushak-e Zanan dar Iran* [Women's Clothing in Iran] [Tehran: Vezarat-e Farhang va Honar, 1968], 114).

Westerners have been no less divergent in their views on the origin of veiling. Some consider Iranians as the early practitioners of the veil. Others "blame" the Turks for their seclusion of women. Still others trace veiling to the Byzantine Empire or even Judaism. Barbara Freyer Stowasser writes: "Seclusion and veiling, however — both presumably of Persian and possibly Byzantine origin — were legitimized by exegetes who interpreted the vague and general Koranic provisions to sanction them" ("The Status of Women in Early Islam," in *Muslim Women*, ed. Freda Hussain [London: Croom Helm, 1984], 25). Saadawi believes that "the veil was a product of Judaism long before Islam came into being. It was drawn from the Old Testament where women were abjured to cover their heads when praying to Jehovah, whereas men could remain bareheaded because they had been created in the image of God" (*The Hidden Face of Eve*, 5).

4. All references to the Qor'an are from *Holy Qur'an*, trans. M. H. Shakir (New York: Tahrike Tarsile Qur'an, 1985).

5. As quoted in Jamal A. Badawi, "Dress Rules for Muslim Women," *The Muslim World League Journal* 9, no. 2 (Dec. 1981).

6. *Mahram* relationships are formed either consanguineously or affinally. The former category includes one's immediate family, paternal ancestors, maternal and paternal siblings, and siblings' children. The latter includes paternal ancestors and one's spouse(s), spouses of children, and their children.

7. Gh. Hadad Adel, "Clothing and the Secret of the Self," *Mahjubah* 3, nos. 4, 5, 6 (Aug.–Oct. 1983): 62.

8. As quoted in Mernissi, *Beyond the Veil*, 141.

9. Sheykh Zabihollah Mahalati, *Kashf-ol Ghorur ya Mafased-ol Sofur* [Learning about Vanity or the Evils of Unveiling] (Tehran: Askari, 1959), 9. I am grateful to Mohammad Tavakoli for sharing this book with me.

10. Women's gazes are also subject to control. For instance, it is a popular belief that a baby will resemble the person at whom the mother happens to look when the baby first moves. Although it might be argued that this curious explanation can at least partially account for inexplicable resemblances, it nonetheless conveys the shared belief in the potency of eyes and the dangers of wandering gazes.

11. As quoted in Afsaneh Najmabadi, "Hazards of Modernity and Morality," unpublished article.

12. Bamdad, *From Darkness into Light*, 98.

13. Ibid., 100.

14. As quoted in Michael Fischer, "On Changing the Concept and Position of Persian Women," in *Women in the Muslim World*, ed. Lois Beck and Nikki Keddie (Cambridge, Mass.: Harvard Univ. Press, 1978), 190.

15. Gertrude Bell, *Poems from the Divan of Hafez*, as quoted in Hassan Javadi, *Obeyd-e Zakani* (Piedmont, Calif.: Jahan, 1985), 11.

16. W. Morgan Shuster, *The Strangling of Persia* (New York: Century, 1912), 198.

17. Sheykh Mohammad Nabil Zarandi, *The Dawn-breakers*, trans. and ed. Shoghi Effendi (Wilmette, Ill.: Baha'i Publishing Trust, 1932), 550.

18. For an interesting and pioneering study of women's movements in Iran, see Eliz Sanasarian, *The Women's Rights Movements in Iran* (New York: Praeger, 1982).

19. Mirzade-ye 'Eshqi, *Koliyat-e Mosavar-e 'Eshqi* [Illustrated Works of 'Eshqi], ed. 'Ali Akbar Moshir-Salimi (Tehran: Sepehr, 1978), 218.

20. Iraj Mirza, *Iraj Mirza*, ed. Mohammad Ja'far Mahjub (Tehran: Andisheh, 1974), 177.

21. Mangol Bayat-Philipp, "Women and Revolution in Iran, 1905–1911," in *Women in the Muslim World*, 301.

22. See Yahya Arianpur, *Az Saba ta Nima* [From Saba to Nima], vol. 2 (Tehran: Jibi, 1976).

23. For a biographical sketch of Qa'em Maqam and her poetry, see *Zaleh* [Zaleh], ed. Pezhman Bakhtiyari (Tehran: Khajeh, n.d.); for Zand-Dokht's life and poetry, see *Zand-Dokht* [Zand-Dokht], ed. Tal'at Bassari (Tehran: Zohuri, 1967).

24. Keshavarz-e Sadr, *Az Rabe'e ta Parvin* [From Rabe'e to Parvin] (Tehran: Kavian, 1956), 149.

25. Roger M. Savory, "Social Development in Iran During the Pahlavi Era," in *Iran under the Pahlavis*, ed. George Lenczowski (Stanford: Hoover Institution Press, 1978), 97.

26. Ashraf Pahlavi, *Faces in the Mirror* (Englewood Cliffs, N.J.: Prentice-Hall, 1980), 24.

27. Savory, *Iran under the Pahlavis*, 98.

28. Bamdad, *From Darkness into Light*, 96.

29. Savory, *Iran under the Pahlavis*, 98.

30. After the institution of the Islamic Republic, the birthday of Hazrat-e Fatemeh, the daughter of the Prophet Mohammad, is celebrated as Women's Day.

31. Bamdad, *From Darkness into Light*, 96.

32. In his novel *Cheshmhayash* [Her Eyes] (Tehran: Amir Kabir, 1978), Bozorg 'Alavi, like many others, sympathizes with the pain and agony inflicted upon a woman who is forcibly unveiled. "The woman is embarrassed. She is ashamed to appear like this even in front of her own husband. One would think she were being dragged through thorns, suffering their lacerations all over her unveiled body. She anticipates more pain and agony" (44).

33. Jalal Al-e Ahmad's short story entitled "Jashn-e Farkhondeh" [The Auspicious Celebration] portrays how a religious man subverts the government's ordinance that requires him to appear at a party accompanied by his unveiled wife. Relying on the institution of temporary marriage, which allows him to marry a woman for a limited time, he contractually marries the daughter of a friend for the two hours during which he has to attend the party. Meanwhile, his veiled wife remains home, unaffected by the royal decree (*Panj Dastan* [Five Stories] [Tehran: Ramin, 1977]). For a detailed and pioneering study of temporary marriage, see Shahla Haeri, *Law of Desire: Temporary Marriage in Shi'i Iran* (Syracuse: Syracuse Univ. Press, 1989).

34. *Sima-ye Zan dar Kalam-e Emam Khomeini* [Images of Women in the Words of Emam Khomeini] (Tehran: Sazeman-e Chap va Entesharat, 1987), 43.

35. Gholam Hossein Sa'edi, *Ahl-e Hava* [People of the Wind] (Tehran: Tehran Univ. Press, 1966), 15.

36. Pahlavi, *Faces in the Mirror,* 25.

37. Sina Vahed, *Qiyam-e Gohar Shad* [Gohar Shad Uprising] (Tehran: Vezarat-e Ershad-e Eslami, 1982), 50. Details of the Gohar Shad uprising are varied and conflicting in different sources. In Roy Mottahedeh's *Mantle of the Prophet* (New York: Simon & Schuster, 1985), 'Ali Hashemi recounts the uprising thus: "In mid-July of 1935, angry crowds thronged into the courtyard of the shrine in Mashad, the burial place of Imam Reza, the brother of the Fatemeh who is enshrined in Qom, and for the Shiah the holiest spot in Iran. They came to hear preachers attack the policies of Reza Shah. When they did not disperse, Reza Shah's troops mounted machine guns on the roofs overlooking the courtyard and opened fire. Over one hundred people were killed. Three hundred soldiers who had refused to fire were shot" (60).

38. Savory, *Iran under the Pahlavis,* 123.

39. During the prerevolutionary period, along with casinos and nightclubs the post of minister of state for women's affairs disappeared. In its stead, a Ministry of Religious Affairs was set up.

40. This renewed interest in veiling is not confined to Iran. Many revivalistic movements, shaking the very foundation of Middle Eastern nations, focus on the issue of women's veiling as well.

41. There are no reliable statistics on the actual number of unveiled women in prerevolutionary Iran. In his interview with Oriana Fallaci, Ayatollah Khomeini claimed that if all those who wanted the veil were to express their feelings, "thirty-three million out of thirty-five million would support the veil." (*Images of Women,* 50.)

42. William Shawcross, *The Shah's Last Ride,* (New York: Simon & Schuster, 1988), 50.

43. As quoted in *In the Shadow of Islam,* compiled by Azar Tabari and Nahid Yeganeh (London: Zed, 1982), 126.

44. According to Zahra Rahnavard: "In the East, particularly in our country and since the era of Islam, woman has been the source of dignity for the nation. Therefore if this source was disrespected, then the nation's spirit is broken. In the wars, one of the first acts by the conquering nations is to rape the womenfolk of the de-

feated. . . . The colonizers with their programme of forced unveiling pursued the same programme of rape and plunder of our nation except that it was in a twentieth-century language" (as quoted in *Women of Iran, the Conflict with Fundamentalist Islam,* ed. Farah Azari [London: Ithaca, 1983], 216).

45. Ayatollah Khomeini, quoted by Nesta Ramazani, "Behind the Veil: Status of Women in Revolutionary Iran," *Journal of South Asian and Middle Eastern Studies* 4, no. 2 (Winter 1980), 30.

46. Even harems and polygamy are presented as protective of women. In *Women's Rights in Islam,* Ayatollah Morteza Mottahari, a leading member of the clergy and a university professor assassinated in 1979, writes: "If the hero of *One Thousand and One Nights* were to come alive again and experience the multitude of possibilities of Western sensual life, provided free of charge, he would have never bothered with costly harems. While thanking the Westerners who have saved him from the agonies of maintaining a harem, he would immediately call for the abolition of expensive institutions such as polygamy and temporary marriage which create too many obligations and responsibilities for men vis-à-vis women" (*Women's Rights in Islam* [Qom, Iran: Sadra, 1978], 47).

47. 'Abdul Karim Biazar Shirazi, *The Oppression of Women Throughout History,* trans. Laleh Bakhtiar (Tehran: Ba'that, 1986), 86.

48. Dariush Shayegan, *Asiya dar Barabar Gharb* [Asia Confronting the West] (Tehran: Amir Kabir, 1977), 29.

49. Ayatollah Morteza Mottahari, *Mas'ale-ye Hejab* [The Issue of Veiling] (Tehran: Enteshar, 1983), 56.

50. An episode from the frame story of *The Thousand Nights and a Night* clearly indicates the fear of women's active, ultimately uncontrollable, sexuality. In this story, female sexual energies filter through the coffinlike box in which a monster husband has enclosed his wife. The monster hides the woman he loves in a casket securely enclosed in a coffer, locked with "seven padlocks of steel" (10). But as soon as he unlocks the casket to lay "his head upon the lady's thighs" and sleep, he gets betrayed. The white-skinned beauty softly lifts him off her lap and signals to the two closest available men (who, out of fear of the monster, had climbed to the top of the nearest tree) to come down and make love to her. Threatened by her, they "did by her what she bade them do; and, when they had dismounted from her, she said, "well done! She then took from her pocket a purse and drew out a knotted string, whereupon were strung five hundred and seventy seal rings . . . signets of five hundred and seventy men who have futtered me upon the horns of this foul, this foolish, this filthy Ifrit" (*The Thousand Nights and a Night,* trans. Richard F. Burton [London: Burton Club, 1886], 12). If a giant, whose legs when stretched out extended down to the sea, can be so easily deceived five hundred and seventy times by a woman enclosed in a coffer, the lot of nongigantic men should need no elaboration.

51. That is why small girls and postmenopausal women are allowed to mix more freely with men. Restrictions increased with puberty somehow subside when the woman is no longer assumed to be a sexual being, i. e., with the onset of menopause. For an interesting and thought-provoking argument of women's powerful sexuality

in Islam, see the Moroccan sociologist Mernissi's *Beyond the Veil* and Fatna A. Sabbah's *Woman in the Muslim Unconscious,* trans. Mary Jo Lakeland (New York: Pergamon, 1984).

52. Reza Barahani, *The Crowned Cannibals* (New York: Vintage, 1977), 62.

53. *Zan-e Ruz* [Today's Woman] editorial, Apr. 7, 1984.

54. Iranian women's delegation to the U.N. Decade for Women Conference at Copenhagen, July 1980, quoted in Tabari and Yeganeh, *In the Shadow of Islam,* 193.

55. *Images of Women,* 144.

56. Sousan Azadi's account of veiled women water-skiing after the compulsory veiling act is far from the image of the secluded woman. "When water-skiing, women were forced to wear hejabs and full-body wet suits. With that rule in effect, there was an immediate shortage of wet suits and those women unlucky enough to be able to get only short-legged wet suits had to wear long trousers over them. Even in our fear, we had to laugh at the sight of a woman flying over the water, covered from head to toe, the hejab flapping in the wind. When she had the misfortune to fall in the water, she did not know what to retrieve first: her skis or her hejab" [with Angela Ferrante, *Out of Iran,* (London: Futura, 1987), 133].

57. Quoted in Tabari and Yeganeh, *In the Shadow of Islam,* 194.

58. Azadi, *Out of Iran,* 223.

59. Shusha Guppy, *The Blindfold Horse, Memories of a Persian Childhood* (London: Heinemann, 1988), 123.

60. *Stories by Iranian Women since the Revolution* trans. Soraya Sullivan (Austin: Univ. of Texas Press, 1991), 134.

3. The Perils of Writing

1. It should be noted that Islam discourages the making of figures—male or female. Even in those paintings that do not exclude the human figure, "it has, on the whole, only a secondary significance. In addition one finds, too, that the human figure is usually highly stylized or rendered in such a way that its features have the aspect of caricatures, while in still other cases painted figures are given in a disembodied, flat manner, which makes them appear to be without corporeal substance" (Richard Ettinghausen, "The Immanent Features of Persian Art," in *Highlights of Persian Art,* ed. R. Ettinghausen and E. Yarshater [Boulder, Colo.: Westview Press, 1979], xv).

2. *Layla and Majnun* is undoubtedly one of the most popular Middle Eastern love stories. Different versions of this legend abound in the Middle East and appear again and again in poems and songs, in older tales and modern movies. "Many later poets have imitated Nizami's work," writes R. Gelpke in a postscript to his translation of *Layla and Majnun,* "even if they could not equal and certainly not surpass it; Persians, Turks, Indians, to name only the most important ones. The Persian scholar Hekmat has listed not less than forty Persian and thirteen Turkish versions and the Nizami editor Dastgerdi states that he has actually found more than 100." (Nizami of Ganja, *Layla and Majnun,* trans. R. Gelpke [Boulder, Colo.: Shambala, 1978], 200).

3. Mottahedeh, *Mantle of the Prophet,* 10.

4. Jalal Al-e Ahmad, *Sangi bar Guri* [A Tombstone on a Tomb] (Tehran: Ravaq, 1981) (hereafter, *Tombstone on a Tomb*).

5. Simin Daneshvar, *Ghorub-e Jalal* [Jalal's Sunset] (Tehran: Ravaq, 1981).

6. Abi Hamid Ghazali, *Al-Tibar Al-Masbuk fi Nasihat al-Muluk* [Advice to Kings], as quoted in Nashat's "Women in the Middle East," 41.

7. Ayatollah Ruhollah Khomeini, *Resaleh-ye Novin* [New Treatise], trans. 'Abdul Karim Biazar-e Shirazi (Tehran: Ketab, 1982), 69.

8. *Kalileh-o-Demneh* [Kalileh and Demneh], trans. Hassan Tehranchian (New York: Harmony, 1985), 38.

9. Shahrnush Parsipur, *Zanan Bedun-e Mardan* [Women Without Men] (Tehran: Noqreh, 1989), 50.

10. Sadeq Hedayat, *Buf-e Kur* [The Blind Owl] (1941; reprint, Tehran: Amir Kabir, 1972). For an English translation of *The Blind Owl,* see D. P. Costello (London: John Calder, 1957; New York: Grove, 1957). Roger Lescot has translated this novel in French: *La Chouette Aveugle* (Paris: José Corti, 1953).

11. Sadeq Hedayat, *Sayeh Roshan* [Chiaroscuro] (1933; reprint, Tehran: Parastu, 1964), 84. Ahmad Karimi-Hakkak has translated this short story in English. For this and other translated short stories of Hedayat, see Ehsan Yarshater, ed. *Sadeq Hedayat: An Anthology* (Boulder, Colo.: Westview, 1979).

12. Mosleh ed-Din Sa'di, *Bustan* [The Orchard] (completed in the thirteenth century; reprint, Tehran: Kharazmi, 1989) and *Golestan* [The Rose Garden] (reprint, Tehran: Kharazmi, 1989). Both works have been repeatedly translated into English and other languages.

13. Nizami, *Layla and Majnun,* 53.

14. Ibid., 145.

15. As quoted in Michael C. Hillmann, *A Lonely Woman* (Washington, D.C.: Three Continents and Mage, 1987), 31.

16. Forugh Farrokhzad, *Bride of Acacias,* trans. Amin Banani and Jascha Kessler (New York: Caravan, 1982), 132.

17. Salman Rushdie, *Shame* (New York: Vintage, 1983), 34.

18. Hakim Abol-Qasem Ferdowsi, *Shah Nameh* [The Book of Kings] (completed ca. A.D. 1000; reprint, Tehran: Amir Kabir, 1966), 535. There are various translations of selective passages of this epic in English.

19. "From Michael Jackson to . . . ," *Sureh* 2, no. 4 (1990): 5.

20. "Cultural Recklessness," *Bayan,* no. 2 (1990): 25.

21. Forugh Farrokhzad, *Asir* [Captive] (1955; reprint, Tehran: Amir Kabir, 1974), 74 (hereafter *Captive*).

22. Farrokhzad, *Another Birth,* 156.

23. As quoted in 'Ali Akbar Dehkhoda, *Amsal-o-Hekam* [Maxims] (Tehran: Amir Kabir, 1982) 2:921. "Al-Hamd" is a Qor'anic chapter. *Vis-o-Ramin* is a romantic epic by the eleventh-century poet Fakhr ed-Din Gorgani. The latter has been translated into English by G. Morrison, Persian Heritage Series no. 14 (New York: Columbia Univ. Press, 1972).

24. Virginia Woolf, *A Room of One's Own* (1929; reprint, New York: Harcourt, Brace & World, 1957).

25. Keshavarz-e Sadr, *From Rabe'e to Parvin.*

26. It should be borne in mind that the male members of the Qajar dynasty did not hesitate to try their hands at poetry either. As Edward G. Browne points out, "The *Gulshan-i-Mahmud* contains notices of forty-eight of Fath-Ali-Shah's sons who wrote poetry, and at a later date the Royal family supplied Persia with another verse-making autocrat in Nasirad-Din Shah (A.D. 1848–1896)" (*A Literary History of Persia,* vol. 4, *Modern Times 1500–1924* [Cambridge: Univ. Press, 1930], 298).

27. Sanasarian, *Women's Rights Movements in Iran,* 14. In *Zanan-e Ruznameh Negar va Andishmand-e Iran* [Women Reporters and Thinkers of Iran] (Tehran: Mazgraphic, 1972), Pari Sheykh-ol Eslami writes: "During the reign of the Qajar Dynasty women were taught how to read. They were, however, strictly prohibited from writing or becoming writers. This was perhaps to stop women from writing love letters or some such matters to men. Yet, in spite all of this, there were some educated and learned women in the harems" (84).

28. Data concerning women's literacy in the early twentieth century are scarce. In 1944, however, compulsory education was finally enacted although not effectively enforced until 1955. The upsurge of girls' schools and the full support they received from the Pahlavi regime increased the literacy rates among women enormously. "By 1978 about 38 percent of the students in Iranian universities and almost half of the 50,000 students studying abroad were women" (Sanasarian, *Women's Rights Movements in Iran,* 107). The Islamic Republic, too, aware of the importance of education in islamizing, politicizing, and socializing women, is encouraging education and making every effort to train its ideal woman through education.

29. For an interesting analysis of women's access to education in the Islamic Republic of Iran, see Sahar Qahreman, "The Islamic Government Policy Towards Women's Access to Higher Education in Iran," *Nimeye Digar,* no. 7 (Summer 1988): 16–32.

30. Mottahedeh, *Mantle of the Prophet,* 89.

31. Bamdad, *From Darkness into Light,* 47.

32. Ibid., 42.

33. Sanasarian, *Women's Rights Movement in Iran,* 39.

34. Mahnaz Afkhami, "Iran: A Future in the Past — the 'Prerevolutionary' Women's Movement," in *Sisterhood Is Global,* ed. Robin Morgan (New York: Anchor, 1984), 330.

35. Salman Rushdie, *Is Nothing Sacred?* The Herbert Read Memorial Lecture (n.p.: Granta, 1990), 12.

36. A large number of women seem to have written poetry. Many never published, and those who did usually lacked the reputation as well as the bulk of poems of their male peers. Anthologies of women poets are filled with the works of such women.

37. Only a few Persian women poets have managed to emerge from obscurity. Except for Rabe'e, Mahsati, and a few other isolated figures, classical Persian literature is dominated by men. Women, at best, are presented in the margins of literary culture, and the writings of many expressive, sensitive souls have fallen into oblivion.

Major studies of poetry deal almost exclusively with the work of men, and the gap in quality and quantity between the critical attention devoted to male poets and that accorded to female poets is alarming. Keshavarz-e Sadr, in *From Rabe'e to Parvin*, remarks astutely that: "Historians have written about male poets to some extent. Unfortunately, however, they have neglected the works and biographies of female poets. That is why the number of known women poets must be quite different from the actual number of those who wrote poetry. It is indeed this very nonchalance and indifference that complicates the study of the life and poetry of women poets" (31).

38. Miss Fotuhi confronts apathy, neglect, and aggression not only from the more conservative sector of the society but also from the most radical. Actually, no one is more violent toward her than her own brother. Ironically, Mr. Fotuhi is a political activist with utopic zeal. He is the idol of all his students, an embodiment of egalitarian demands for his people. Within the confines of his own home, however, Mr. Fotuhi is the personification of authoritarianism, an agent of emotional and intellectual repression. Insensitive to what his sister is struggling for, he has neither the interest nor the time to help her. His sole commitment is to some political abstraction. This commitment is so idealistic, so unquestioned, so escapist in nature that no room is left for his own sister. Mr. Fotuhi wants to help the whole country but does not want to help her. He confines her to the asylum, keeps her there, and rarely, if ever, visits her.

39. Simin Daneshvar, *Savushun* (Tehran: Kharazmi, 1969), 107.

40. Badr ol-Moluk Bamdad, in her book on women's emancipation in Iran, refers to one Shams ol-Haya Mansuri, who in the early years of the present century volunteered, along with five other colleagues, in the education service in the city of Shiraz. Deeply involved in women's issues, they all decided to discard black veils in favor of light-colored ones. The first day they ventured out, "they had scarcely walked any distance before such a terrific hubbub blew up that they had to run separately for refuge in nearby houses. They suffered injuries to their heads and hands and were obliged to give up their innovation" (*From Darkness into Light*, 85). Although not much is known about the lives of these five women, Miss Fotuhi, who does not give up the "innovation," ends up paying dearly for her rebelliousness.

41. One could also argue with Sandra Gilbert and Susan Gubar that "the madwoman in literature by women is not merely, as she might be in male literature, an antagonist or foil to the heroine. Rather, she is usually in some sense the author's double, an image of her own anxiety and rage. Indeed, much of the poetry and fiction written by women conjures up this mad creature so that female authors can come to terms with their own uniquely female feelings of fragmentation, their own keen sense of the discrepancies between what they are and what they are supposed to be" (*The Madwoman in the Attic* [New Haven: Yale Univ. Press, 1979], 78).

42. Bassari, *Zand-Dokht*, 25.

43. Hillmann, *A Lonely Woman*, 42.

44. Mahshid Amirshahi, *Ba'd az Ruz-e Akhar* [After the Last Day] (1969; reprint, Tehran: Amir Kabir, 1976), 20.

45. In the West, there has been much talk about the anxiety of authorship and readership endemic to literature by women. In Iran, another anxiety, the dependency

on an all-male critical establishment, must be added to this list. The crux of this difficulty is that women writers have been primarily dependent on men for recognition and criticism. They are thus triply dependent upon the dominant group definition of womanhood. Although in 1955 a woman, Nur ol-Hoda Manganeh, edited and published *Bibi* [Lady], a monthly magazine dedicated mainly to literary criticism, to this day women's role as literary critic remains almost negligible.

46. Suzanne Juhasz, *Naked and Fiery Forms, Modern American Poetry by Women: A New Tradition* (New York: Harper & Row, 1976), 2.

47. Bamdad, *From Darkness into Light*, 33.

48. I do not mean to suggest that physical and artistic creation are antithetical. All I am saying is that childbearing and child rearing have thus far reduced enormously the amount of time, energy, and mental concentration a woman can use for her artistic aspirations. In her delightful book, *How to Suppress Women's Writing*, Joanna Russ expresses this conflict through one woman's sardonic remark: "I was able to snatch a few precious days in the month of January in which to write undisturbed. But . . . when shall I ever be so fortunate again as to break a foot?" (Austin: Univ. of Texas Press, 1983), 140.

49. Tillie Olsen, *Silences* (New York: Delacorte/Seymour Lawrence, 1978), 16.

50. Ibid., 13.

51. Virginia Woolf, *The Death of the Moth and Other Essays* (1942; reprint, New York: Harcourt Brace Jovanovich, 1974), 237.

52. Amir Esma'ili and Abol-Qasem Sedarat, eds., *Javedaneh, Forugh Farrokhzad* [Immortal, Forugh Farrokhzad] (Tehran: Marjan, 1972), 17.

53. Farrokhzad, *Captive*, 34.

54. Ibid., 135.

55. Forugh Farrokhzad, *Divar* [Wall] (1956; reprint, Tehran; Amir Kabir, 1971), 44 (hereafter *Wall*).

56. Farrokhzad, *Bride of Acacias*, 67.

57. If in "Green Delusion" Forugh considers herself half an entity: "In my half-grown heart the void grew / and no other half joined to this half," she views married women as "whole." "Give me sanctuary, o you simple whole women."

58. Erica Jong, *Fear of Flying* (New York: New American Library, 1974), 157.

59. Farzaneh Milani, "Pay-e Sohbat-e Simin Daneshvar" [An Audience with Simin Daneshvar], *Alefba*, no. 4, n.s. (Fall 1983), 155.

60. Farrokhzad, *Dawning of a Cold Season*, 47.

4. Becoming a Presence: Tahereh Qorratol'Ayn

1. Martha L. Root, *Tahirih the Pure* (1938; reprint, Los Angeles: Kalimat, 1981), 102.

2. Ibid.

3. 'Ali Quli Mirza E'tezadol-Saltaneh, *Fetne-ye Bab* [Bab's Conspiracy], 2d ed., annot. 'Abdol-Hossein Nava'i (Tehran: Babak, 1965), 168.

4. 'Ali Akbar Moshir-Salimi, *Zanan-e Sokhanvar* [Eloquent Women], vol. 2 (Tehran: 'Elmi, 1956), 2:72.

5. Ahmad Kasravi, *Baha'igari* [Baha'ism] (Tehran: Mard-e Emruz, 1956), 81.

6. According to Abbas Amanat, *Resurrection and Renewal* (Ithaca, N.Y.: Cornell Univ. Press, 1989), bitter reproaches "eventually forced him [Molla Saleh, Tahereh's father] to emigrate from Qazvin and retire in the 'Atabat [in Iraq], where he died in 1283/1866" (322). As for the three children, Martha Root writes in *Tahirih the Pure* that in an interview with Tahereh's grandson, she was told the two sons "ran away from home because their father was not good to them; one son went to Najaf [a city in Iraq] and the other went to live near Tehran; the girl died not long after the passing of her mother" (51).

7. Edward G. Browne, *Traveller's Narrative* (Cambridge: Cambridge Univ. Press, 1981), 309.

8. The introduction to *Bahaism: Its Origins and Its Role* (The Hague: Nashr-e Farhang-e Eslami: n.d.), n.p.

9. Mirza Mohammad Taqi Sepehr, *Nassekh-ol Tavarikh-e Qajari-ye,* ed. and annot. Jahangir Qa'em Maqami (Tehran: Amir Kabir, 1958), 3:48.

10. Sepehr, *Nassekh-ol Tavarikh-e Qajari-ye,* as quoted in Amanat, *Resurrection and Renewal,* 321.

11. Ibid., 48.

12. Mohammad Ebrahim Bastani-ye Parizi, *Haft Sang* [Seven Stones] (Tehran: Danesh, 1967), 357n. 3.

13. Root, *Tahirih the Pure,* 51.

14. Bamdad, *From Darkness into Light,* 20.

15. Amanat, *Resurrection and Renewal,* 297.

16. Ibid.

17. Ibid., 309.

18. H. M. Balyuzi, *The Bab* (Oxford: George Ronald, 1974), 164.

19. Amanat, *Resurrection and Renewal,* 314.

20. 'Abbas 'Abdul Baha', *Memorials of the Faithful* (Wilmette, Ill.: Baha'i Publishing Trust, 1971), 201.

21. According to Browne in *A Traveller's Narrative,* 314, Subh-e Azal maintained that "when carried away by her eloquence," Tahereh would allow her veil "to slip down her face, but she would always replace it after a few moments."

22. Sepehr, *Nasekh-ol Tavarikh-e Qajari-ye,* 60.

23. Shoghi Effendi, *God Passes By* (Wilmette, Ill.: Baha'i Publishing Committee, 1944), 32.

24. Ibid., 32.

25. Lady Mary Sheil, *Glimpses of Life and Manners in Persia* (1856; reprint, New York: Arno, 1973), 85.

26. E'tezadol-Saltaneh, *Fetne-ye Bab,* 185. Epicurus is the ancient philosopher (341–271 B.C.) thought to have condoned complete pursuit of sensual gratification.

27. Browne, *A Traveller's Narrative,* 313.

28. Hesam Noqaba'i, Tahereh (n.p.: 1983), 156.

29. Moojan Momen, ed., *The Babi and Baha'i Religions, 1844–1944* (Oxford: George Ronald, 1981), 133.

30. Lowell Johnson, *Tahirih* (Johannesburg: National Spiritual Assembly of the Baha'is of South and West Africa, 1982), 35.

31. Dimitri Marianoff and Marzieh Gail, "Thralls of Yearning Love," *World Order* (Summer 1972): 41.

32. Amanat, *Resurrection and Renewal*, 322.

33. Parsipur, "Why Do You Write?" 10.

34. Moojan Momen, ed., *Selections from E. G. Browne on the Babi and Baha'i Religions* (Oxford: George Ronald, 1987), 241.

35. Mo'in ed-Din Mehrabi, *Qorratol'Ayn* (Cologne: Ruyesh, 1989), 148.

36. Noqaba'i, *Tahereh*, 161.

37. Mehrabi, *Qorratol'Ayn*, 149.

38. In *From Darkness into Light*, Bamdad claims that one of Tahereh's close associates, the wife of "Seyyed Kazem Rashti, had invited a number of enlightened ladies to her house to discuss the disastrous condition of the country and the deplorable status of its women." This meeting led to the foundation of "an organized body called the National Ladies Society" (34).

39. Quoted in Williams and Williams, *Riding the Nightmare*, 41.

40. L'Estrange Ewen, *Witch Hunting and Witch Trials* (London: Stephen Austin and Sons, 1929), 68.

41. Balyuzi, *The Bab*, 164.

42. 'Abdul Baha', *Memorials of the Faithful*, 202.

43. Quoted in Mangol Bayat, *Mysticism and Dissent: Socioreligious Thought in Qajar Iran* (Syracuse: Syracuse Univ. Press, 1982), 116.

44. Baharieh Rouhani Ma'ani maintains that "the painful plight of many early Babi and Baha'i women has escaped even the keen eye and the critical pen of Baha'i historians, whose attitudes were so conditioned by the customary practices and unjust traditions of the time that they did not notice the struggles of most of the early women believers; or if they did, these appeared so insignificant to them that they did not warrant professional historical treatment" (Peggy Caton, ed., *Equal Circles, Women and Men in the Baha'i Community* [Los Angeles: Kalimat, 1987], 23).

45. Mangol Bayat-Philipp, "Women and Revolution in Iran, 1905–1911," in *Women in the Muslim World*, 300.

46. Taj-os Saltaneh, *Khaterat-e Taj-os Saltaneh* [Taj-os Saltaneh's Memoir] ed. Mansureh Ettehadiyeh and Sirus Sa'dvandiyan (Tehran: Nashr-e Tarikh-e Iran, 1982), 109.

47. Bamdad, *From Darkness into Light*, 39.

48. Sheil, *Life and Manner in Persia*, 281.

49. Some prominent women historians in recent years have celebrated and acknowledged Tahereh's contribution to women's awakening in Iran. In "The Beginnings of Religious Clerics' Economic and Political Power," Homa Nateq believes that "in the history of constitutional and liberation movements in Iran, the role of Qorratol'Ayn as a freedom-loving ideologue and poet is unique" *(Alefba*, no. 2, n.s. [Spring 1983], 43). Bayat, in *Mysticism and Dissent*, writes: "For Qorratol-'Ayn, a woman of great vision

and intellectual abilities who resented the traditional milieu in which she was unable to move at will, Babism proved a unique chance to achieve emancipation. She took advantage of the movement to free herself from the bonds Islam imposed upon her. Her rejection of the veil symbolizes her defiant attitude towards the traditional social customs pertaining to women" (115). Guity Nashat considers her "the most unusual woman of nineteenth-century Iran" and "the first woman in the modern history of Iran to openly rebel against the conventions of her time" (*Women and Revolution in Iran* [Boulder, Colo.: Westview, 1983], 19).

    50. Alessandro Bausani, "Babis," in *The Encyclopedia of Religion,* ed. Mircea Eliade, 2:33.

    51. Root, *Tahirih the Pure,* 34.

    52. Shahrnush Parsipur, *Tuba va Ma'na-ye Shab* [Tuba and the Sense of Night] (Tehran: Spark, 1988), 25.

    53. Mirza Asadollah Fazil Mazandarani, *Zuhur-ol Haq* (Tehran: n.p, n.d.), 325.

    54. Noqaba'i, *Tahereh,* 160.

5. Revealing and Concealing: Parvin E'tessami

    1. Charles Mason Remey, *Observations of a Bahai Traveller* (1909; reprint, Washington, D.C.: The author, 1914), 75.

    2. Ibid., 75–77.

    3. Bambad, *From Darkness into Light,* 30.

    4. Yahya Arianpur, *Az Saba ta Nima,* 2:113.

    5. Fatemeh Ostad Malek, *Hejab va Kashf-e Hejab dar Iran* [Veiling and Unveiling in Iran] (Tehran: Atta'i, 1988), 97.

    6. Hossein Namini, *Javedaneh, Parvin E'tessami* [Immortal, Parvin E'tessami] (Tehran: Farzan, 1983), 20.

    7. Parvin E'tessami, *A Nightingale's Lament,* trans. Heshmat Moayyad and A. Margaret Madelung (Lexington, Ky.: Mazda, 1985), xii. Unless otherwise specified, all references to Parvin's poetry will be to this edition.

    8. Heshmat Moayyad, "In Memory of the 80th Anniversary of Parvin E'tessami," *Iran Nameh* 6, no. 1. (Fall 1987): 124.

    9. P. E'tessami, *A Nightingale's Lament,* xii.

    10. Ibid.

    11. Bamdad, *From Darkness into Light,* 70.

    12. Hadi Hoquqi, "Watch One Who Is Blind Lead the Way for Another," *Khandaniha,* (Sept. 1989): 17.

    13. 'Ali Akbar Dehkhoda, *Loghatnameh* (Tehran: Univ. of Tehran Press, 1960), 6:292.

    14. P. E'tessami, *A Nightingale's Lament,* ii.

    15. P. E'tessami, *Divan* [Collected Poems] (1935; reprint, Tehran: Fardin, 1974).

    16. Ibid., 268.

    17. Simin Daneshvar, *Daneshvar's Playhouse,* trans. Maryam Mafi (Washington, D.C.: Mage, 1989), 158.

18. Moayyad, "80th Anniversary," 118.

19. Fazlollah Garakani, *Accused of Being a Poet,* 123.

20. Ibid., 63.

21. Ibid., 119.

22. From the introduction to P. E'tessami, *Divan,* Yab.

23. 'Abdol Hossein Zarinkub, *Daftar-e Ayyam* [A Book of Times] (Tehran: Tus, 1986), 53.

24. Mohammad Javad Shari'at, *Javedaneh Parvin* [Immortal Parvin] (Esfahan: Mash'al, 1977), 59.

25. Manuchehr Nazer, *Negareshi bar Ash'ar-e Parvin E'tessami* [Some Observations on the Poetry of Parvin E'tessami] (Tehran: Sorush, 1981), 21.

26. Remey, *Observations of a Bahai Traveller,* 75.

27. Abolfath E'tessami, ed., *Maqalat va Qate'at-e Ash'ar* [Articles and Some Poems] (Tehran: Fardin, 1974), 19.

28. P. E'tessami, *Divan,* Yab.

29. Farid-ed Din 'Attar, as quoted in Annemarie Schimmel's introduction to Margaret Smith, *Rabi'a the Mystic and Her Fellow-Saints in Islam* (London: Cambridge Univ. Press, 1984), xxvi.

30. Farid-ed Din 'Attar, as quoted in Reuben Levy, *The Social Structure of Islam* (London: Cambridge Univ. Press, 1969), 132.

31. Mohammad 'Ali Jamalzadeh, "From Among Your Letters," *Nimeye Digar,* no. 9 (Spring 1989): 6. (I believe Jamalzadeh means to refer to the journal *Naqsh-o Negar.*)

32. Carolyn G. Heilbrun, *Writing a Woman's Life* (New York: Norton, 1988), 81.

33. Barahani, *Masculine History,* 102.

34. Namini, *Immortal, Parvin E'tessami,* 27.

35. P. E'tessami, *A Nightingale's Lament,* 107.

36. P. E'tessami, *Divan,* 258.

37. S. Mohammad Ishaque, *Four Eminent Poetesses of Iran* (Calcutta: Iran Society, 1950), 50.

38. Fereshteh Davaran, "The Impersonal Poems of Parvin E'tessami," *Iranshenasi* 1, no. 2 (Summer 1989): 293.

39. Ahmad Karimi-Hakkak, "Parvin E'tessami as an Innovative Poet," *Iranshenasi* 1, no. 2 (Summer 1989): 41.

40. For an interesting and detailed analysis of this poem, see Karimi-Hakkak, "Innovative Poet," 264–84.

41. P. E'tessami, *A Nightingale's Lament,* 63.

42. Margaret Arent Madelung, in her "Commentary" to P. E'tessami, *A Nightingale's Lament,* writes, "Parvin likely got the idea of using a spider as her vehicle from another editorial of [Arthur] Brisbane's which her father had translated into Persian for his magazine (cf. *Bahar* II, Reprint, Tehran, 1942, 165–166) . . . When one looks at the translated model, it is apparent that only the barest commonplaces about a spider's industriousness are dealt with by Brisbane. Some motifs have obviously been taken over by Parvin, such as the web's being an architectural design, the idea of a spider's using tools like a carpenter, of a broom's being a destroyer of webs, of the constant rebuilding of the web, of the comparison between lazy people and

industrious ones. Brisbane has none of the subtleties, none of the refinements, and, of course, none of the hidden references and ambiguities in Parvin's poem. Brisbane's spider is but a stimulus and becomes Parvin's very own spider. She executes the ideas with finesse and lends them far greater depth. Brisbane's piece in comparison is primitive, mundane, and naive" (224).

43. Emily Dickinson, *Selected Poems of Emily Dickinson,* ed. James Reeves (London: Heinemann, 1959), 91.

44. P. E'tessami, *A Nightingale's Lament,* xi.

45. See M. M. Bakhtin, *The Dialogic Imagination,* ed. Michael Holquist, trans. Caryl Emerson and Michael Holquist (Austin: Univ. of Texas Press, 1986).

46. P. E'tessami, *A Nightingale's Lament,* 108.

47. In *The Blindfold Horse,* Shusha Guppy identifies with the nightingale. "Sometimes, on summer evenings, I sit alone among my plants to savour the mild air and watch the moon rise over London. I remember the old garden, the blue pool, the swaying pine and plane trees. I can almost hear the sweet thrill of the nightingale, the magical bird who came so rarely and one day left never to return, as I did" (79).

48. Milani, "An Audience with Simin Daneshvar," 154.

49. S. Mohammad Ishaque, "Parvin-i I'tisami: An Eminent Poetess of Modern Iran," *Islamic Culture* 17, no. 1 (Jan. 1943): 49.

50. Vincent Sheean (*The New Persia* [New York, 1927], 257), as quoted in Heshmat Moayyad, "Parvin's Poems: A Cry in the Wilderness," in *Islamwissenschaftliche Abhandlungen* (Wiesbaden: Franz Steiner, 1974), 164–90.

51. Reza Barahani, *Tala dar Mes* [Gold in Copper] (Tehran: Zaman, 1968), 203.

52. T. S. Eliot, *The Sacred Wood* (London: Methuen, 1974), 54.

53. P. E'tessami, *A Nightingale's Lament,* 107.

54. See Juhasz, *Naked and Fiery Forms,* 1–6.

55. P. E'tessami, *A Nightingale's Lament,* 2.

6. Unveiling the Other: Forugh Farrokhzad

1. Shahrnush Parsipur, *Sag va Zemestan-e Boland* [The Dog and the Long Winter] (Tehran: Sepehr, 1976), 98.

2. See 'Ali Shari'ati, *Fatemeh Fatemeh Ast* [Fatemeh is Fatemeh] (Tehran: N.p., n.d.), 78.

3. 'Ali Shari'ati, *Zan* [Woman] (Tehran: n.p., 1983), 76.

4. Jalal Al-e Ahmad, *Occidentosis: A Plague from the West,* trans. R. Campbell; ed. Hamid Algar (Berkeley: Mizan, 1984), 70.

5. Quoted in Tabari and Yeganeh, *In the Shadow of Islam,* 129.

6. Sadeq Hedayat, *Parvin, the Daughter of Sassan,* (Tehran:

7. Gholam Hossein Sa'edi, *Dandil* (Tehran: Javaneh, 1966), 32.

8. Shawcross, *The Shah's Last Ride,* 267.

9. This obsessive literary exploitation of sexual issues has barely, if ever, been

focused upon when dealing with male writers. Men's relationships with women, illicit or otherwise, are considered their own business and are generally not referred to when the object of criticism is their works. But women's love affairs are considered scandals, shameless breaches of moral propriety, and advocacies of promiscuity and result in a slanderous attack on their works.

10. According to Farrokhzad: "The attitude of modern poets toward love is one hundred percent superficial. Love in today's poetry is confined to a certain amount of desire, heartache, and anguish, culminating in a few words about union which is considered the end of everything, while it could and should very well be the beginning. Love has not found an opening to newer dimensions of thought, reflection, and emotion. It is still revolving around pretty legs and thighs, which, separated from their human sources, are indeed hollow images" ("A Few Writings and Scattered Words about Poets and Poetry," in *Arash*, ed. Syrus Tahbaz [Tehran: Darakhshan, 1966], 16).

11. Ibid., 16.

12. It is interesting that the few critics who acknowledge as legitimate themes hitherto omitted from poetry and who recognize the validity of the evocation of psychological, emotional, and sensual moods of a woman within her private sphere limit Farrokhzad's poetry by yet another restriction. They call her poetry, especially the first three collections, "confessional," "personal." Yet interpretation of her poetry as merely confessional or as autobiographical case history proves to be reductive and restrictive. Farrokhzad's work defies such appraisal, which eventually limits it to enclosed self-exploration or personal concerns. In her own words: "Who ever cried for her? / who spoke her language? / these strangers were deaf / to the laments echoed in her songs" (*Captive*, 58).

It seems important to emphasize that, in spite of their autobiographical overtones, hardly any of the poems in the whole canon of Farrokhzad's work generate only an intensely personal world with private references that elude the reader. Using her personal experiences as the source of her poems, Farrokhzad transmutes them by the sheer intensity of her vision so that they transcend the level of self-exposure and reach universal implication. In an interview with Sa'edi and Tahbaz, when reminded that "her early poetry and even some poems in *Another Birth* are strictly personal and emotional," she refers to the amalgamation of the private and the public. "It seems impossible to attempt to formulate a theory for the content of poetry and claim that the subject matter of all poems should revolve around universal and public topics. The determining fact is how one approaches private or public motifs. It is the vision of the poet that makes her content personal and individualistic or rather expands and universalizes the personal experiences depicted" (*Arash*, 52).

13. Girdhari Tikku, "Conversations with Forugh," in *Forugh Farrokhzad: A Quarter-Century Later*, ed. Michael Hillmann, special issue of *Literature East and West*, no. 24: 58.

14. For a comprehensive biography of the poet, see Hillmann, *A Lonely Woman*.

15. Farrokhzad, *Captive*, 34.

16. Farrokhzad, *Wall*, 3.

17. Farrokhzad, *Bride of Acacias*, 92.

18. Farrokhzad, *Dawning of a Cold Season*, 30.

19. Esma'ili and Sedarat, *Immortal, Forugh Farrokhzad,* 15.

20. Woolf, *A Room of One's Own,* 35.

21. P. E'tessami, *Divan,* 198.

22. As quoted in Jane Miller, *Women Writing about Men* (London: Virago, 1986), 39.

23. Farrokhzad, *Captive,* 58. I have consulted and greatly benefited from available translations of Farrokhzad's poetry, especially: *Bride of Acacias,* trans. Jascha Kessler with Amin Banani; *Another Birth, Selected Poems of Forugh Farrokhzad,* trans. Hasan Javadi with Susan Sallee (Emeryville, Calif.: Albany Press, 1981); *A Rebirth,* trans. David Martin (Lexington, Ky.: Mazda, 1985).

"I think about the world," Farrokhzad wrote in a letter to the poet Ahmad Reza Ahmadi, "although the hope of becoming universal is slim — almost zero" (Esma'ili and Sedarat, *Immortal, Forugh Farrokhzad,* 271). Yet, universal Farrokhzad has become, at least more so than any of her colleagues. No writer in contemporary Iran has attracted more translators than she has. Other than poems translated by various people and published in different literary journals and anthologies, there also exist three different collections of her translated poems.

24. Farrokhzad, *Another Birth,* 78.

25. In a poem aptly entitled "At the Graveside of Leili," Farrokhzad rejects her society's idealization of traditional "femininity." Provoked by the discrepancies between what she feels and knows about herself and the inadequate and inauthentic nature of womanhood as portrayed by men, she refuses to be measured against such a portrayal. She knows Leili, Majnun's beloved, suffers from stereotypical reduction and, as such, personifies the masculine fantasy of womanhood. Her character realizes neither the limitations nor the potentials of a real woman. She is an artful invention, a functionless presence, defined, framed, and simplified. She cannot provide the poet with an identity image: "The eyes you stare at are mine / Who was Leili? What is the myth of the black eyes? / Don't wonder why my eyes / are not black like her wild eyes" (*Wall,* 66).

26. Mohammad 'Ali Eslami-ye Nadushan, *Ruzha* [Days] (Tehran: Yazdan, 1984), 272.

27. Farrokhzad, *Wall,* 13.

28. Tahereh Saffarzadeh, *Peyvandha-ye Talkh* [Bitter Unions] (Tehran: Etela'at, 1963), 217.

29. For a brilliant discussion of representations of sexuality in women's games, see Kaveh Safa, "Female-centered World Views in Iranian Culture: Symbolic Representations of Sexuality in Dramatic Games," *Signs* 6, no. 1 (1980): 33–53.

30. For an interesting and detailed analysis of this poem, see Zjaleh Hajibashi, "Redefining 'Sin'," in *Forugh Farrokhzad: A Quarter-Century Later,* ed. Michael Hillmann, special issue of *Literature East and West,* no. 24, 67–71.

31. Amirshahi, *After the Last Day,* 162.

32. Farrokhzad, *Captive,* 110.

33. Ibid., 113.

34. Ibid., 20.

35. Introduction to *Captive,* n.p.

36. Farrokhzad, *Another Birth,* 125.

37. Farrokhzad, *Dawning of a Cold Season,* 14.

38. Ibid., 11.

7. Negotiating Boundaries: Tahereh Saffarzadeh

1. Zeinab Borujerdi, "Darsha'i dar bare-ye Hejab" [Some Teachings Regarding the Veil], *Etela'at-e Banovan* 4, no. 3 (Aug. 1980): 18.

2. Fakhr ed-Din Shadman, *Taskhir-e Tammadon-e Farrangi* [Possessed by Western Culture] (Tehran: Majlis, 1947).

3. Al-e Ahmad, *Gharbzadegi* [Westomania]. Other English renderings of *Gharb-zadegi* are Westoxication, Weststruckness, Westernitis, Westamination. For English translations of this book, see *Weststruckness,* trans. John Green and Ahmad Alizadeh (Lexington, Ky.: Mazda, 1982); *Occidentosis: A Plague from the West,* trans. R. Camp-bell, ed. Hamid Algar (Berkeley: Mizan, 1984).

4. Fatemeh Sayyah, "Vazife-ye Enteqad dar Adabiyat" [The Mission of Criticism in Literature], in *Nakhostin Congere-ye Nevisandegan-e Iran* [Iran's First Writers' Con-gress] (Tehran: N.p., 1947), 232.

5. Nasser Mo'azen, ed., *Dah Shab-e She'r* [Ten Nights of Poetry] (Tehran: Amir Kabir, 1978), 202.

6. Tahereh Saffarzadeh, *Harekat va Diruz* [Motion and Yesterday] (Tehran: Ravaq, 1979), 162.

7. See Farhad 'Abedini, "Sha'ereha-ye Ba'd-e Forugh . . ." [Women Poets after Forugh], *Negin,* no. 118 (Mar. 1974), and Mahmud Azad, "She'ri Anbashte az Adaha-ye Rowshanfekraneh," [A Poetry Packed with Intellectual Pretenses], *Keyhan,* Feb. 21, 1971.

8. Tahereh Saffarzadeh, *Curbed Men,* 79.

9. Ibid., 98.

10. Ibid., 5.

11. Saffarzadeh, *Motion and Yesterday,* 8.

12. Ibid., 16.

13. Ibid., 131.

14. Tahereh Saffarzadeh, *Red Umbrella* (Iowa City, Iowa: Windhover, 1969), 20.

15. Ibid., 12.

16. Tahereh Saffarzadeh, *Tanin dar Delta* [Resonance in the Bay] (Tehran: Amir Kabir, 1971), 110.

17. Even in their prenatal state, boys are presumed to be sources of comfort and delight. A woman carrying a boy, it is believed, looks prettier, is more alert and ener-getic, and needs less sleep than a woman carrying a girl.

18. Guppy, *The Blindfold Horse,* 61.

19. Amirshahi, *After the Last Day,* 13.

20. Afsaneh Najmabadi, "Without a Place to Rest the Sole of My Foot," lecture presented at the Association of Middle Eastern Women's Annual Meeting, Toronto, Nov. 1989.

21. Saffarzadeh, *Resonance in the Bay,* 94.

22. See Leonardo P. Alishan's interesting article, "Tahereh Saffarzadeh: From the Wasteland to the Imam," *Iranian Studies* 15, nos. 1–4 (1982): 181–210.

23. Saffarzadeh, *Motion and Yesterday,* 9.

24. Ibid., 162.

25. Tahereh Saffarzadeh, *Didar-e Sobh* [Morning Visitation] (Shiraz: Navid, 1987), 29.

26. Involvement with sociopolitical issues is not a new phenomenon in the tradition of women's poetry in Iran. What differentiates Saffarzadeh from most other women poets is her progressive self-effacement and her adoption of a neuter poetic personae. Although the last two collections show a certain return to personal themes, on the whole her previous literary waves of resentment as a woman receded at the threshold of her religiopolitical activism.

27. Tahereh Saffarzadeh, *Bey'at ba Bidari* [Allegiance with Wakefulness] (Tehran: Hamdami, 1980), 25.

28. Saffarzadeh, *Motion and Yesterday,* 158.

29. Amazingly, Saffarzadeh emphatically maintained: "Pure poetry is as fallible for me as some of the didactic poems of Sa'di and Milton or the socially oriented poetry of the Constitutional era. Because none of these three categories encompass life in an inclusive and natural fashion. One busies itself with language, texture, and the sound of words, the other with ethics and theology and the last one with superficial social issues" (ibid., 145).

30. Saffarzadeh, *Allegiance with Wakefulness,* 61.

31. Ibid., 59. Al-Asr refers to Al-Asr Sura, revealed to the prophet Mohammad in Mecca.

32. Saffarzadeh, *Red Umbrella,* 25.

33. Ibid., 12.

34. Saffarzadeh, *Allegiance with Wakefulness,* 41.

35. In a novel entitled *Foreigner* (New York: Norton, 1978), Nahid Rachlin portrays a young Iranian woman, Feri, happily married to an American and doing research in Boston as a biologist. When after fourteen years she returns to her country, Iran, for a short visit, she gets caught in the bureaucracy. Without her husband's permission, she cannot get an exit visa. First frustrated, Feri soon finds herself metamorphosed. If upon her arrival she found Iran stark, unwelcoming, and backward, if she found herself fully alienated, lonely, with a fractured identity, after two months she discovers the comfort of reclaiming her personal and cultural roots. She dons the veil, accompanies her mother on a pilgrimage to the shrine of Zeinab, "a poetess-saint," and finally finds "tranquility." "No one noticed me," she says, "I was an Iranian woman wearing a *chador.* . . . I turned over and looked at my mother. Her face was serene in her sleep. I knew soon I would have to make decisions, think beyond the day, but for the moment I lay there. Tranquil" (192).

36. Tahereh Saffarzadeh, *Safar-e Panjom* [The Fifth Journey] (Tehran: Ravaq, 1978), 60.

37. Ibid.

38. Ibid., 63.

8. Overcoming the Blank Page

1. Isak Dinesen, *Last Tales* (New York: Vintage, 1975), 99.

2. Salman Rushdie, interviewed by Michael T. Kaufman, "Author from Three Countries," *New York Times Book Review* (Nov. 13, 1983), 22.

3. For a delightfully brilliant exploration of the "lineage of women as tale-tellers in a history that stretches from Philomela and Scheherazade to the raconteurs of French veillées and salons, to English peasants, governesses, and novelists, and to the German Spinnerinnen and the Brothers Grimm," see Karen E. Rowe, "To Spin a Yarn: The Female Voice in Folklore and Fairy Tale," in *Fairy Tales and Society: Illusion, Allusion, and Paradigm,* ed. Ruth B. Bottigheimer (Philadelphia: Univ. of Pennsylvania Press, 1986), 53–74.

4. *Thousand Nights and a Night,* 10:61.

5. Amir Taheri, "The Greats of Iran's History," *Kayhan International,* no. 10 (Feb. 1972): 1.

6. Modern fiction has not been popular among religious men either. In the realm of prose, the development of modern Persian fiction can effectively be narrowed down to the pioneering influences of "modernized" and "westernized" literary figures who felt the necessity to introduce novel and short story writing in Persian literature and to adapt them to both linguistic and cultural circumstances. *Yeki Bud Yeki Nabud* [Once Upon a Time] by Mohammad 'Ali Jamalzadeh (b. 1895), considered by many the first work of modern fiction in Iran, was published in 1921.

7. Simin Daneshvar, *Atash-e Khamush* [Fire Quenched] (Tehran: N.p., 1948) (hereafter *Fire Quenched*).

8. Simin Daneshvar, *Savushun.* M. R. Ghanoonparvar and Roxane Zand have translated this novel into English. For the former, see *Savushun* (Washington, D.C.: Mage, 1990); for the latter, see *A Persian Requiem* (London: Halban, 1991).

9. For further biographical material on Daneshvar, see *Nimeye Digar,* no. 8 (Fall 1988) (special issue on Simin Daneshvar, guest editor Farzaneh Milani); "Sepas az Ostad" [Praise of the Master], *Survey and Excavation: Journal of the Institute and Department of Archaeology* 3 (1980): 1–3; Al-e Ahmad, *A Tombstone on a Tomb;* Milani, "An Audience with Simin Daneshvar"; and Michael Hillmann, "Cultural Dilemmas of an Iranian Intellectual," in Jalal Al-e Ahmad, *Lost in the Crowd,* trans. John Green with Ahmad Alizadeh and Farzin Yazdanfar (Washington, D.C.: Three Continents, 1985), i–xxvi.

10. Bamdad, *From Darkness into Light,* 102.

11. For further information on Fatemeh Sayyah, see Mohammad Golbon, ed., *Naqd va Siyahat* [Criticism and Exploration] (Tehran: Tus, 1975).

12. Hushang Golshiri, "An Interview with Simin Daneshvar," *Mahnameh-ye Mofid,* no. 3, n.s. (July 1987): 18.

13. Daneshvar, *Jalal's Sunset,* 17.

14. The marriage, brought to an abrupt end by Jalal's early death of a heart attack, was, according to Daneshvar, based on respect, love, shared concerns, and mutual dependence. She and Jalal discussed literary issues together; he depended on her for translation of English books; she relied on him for translation of French books. Al-

though they had no child of their own, they served as foster parents to the many students who gathered around them.

15. Daneshvar, "My Heart Aches for Your Suffering and Patience: A Letter to the Reader," in *Daneshvar's Playhouse*, 165.

16. Ibid., 159.

17. Milani, "An Audience with Simin Daneshvar," 149.

18. Literature does not seem to be a profession by which to earn a living in Iran. No contemporary writer, even at the height of fame and popularity, has been able to survive entirely on the proceeds of creative writing.

19. Among Daneshvar's translated works are: Anton Chekhov's *Cherry Orchard* and *The Enemies;* Nathaniel Hawthorne's *Scarlet Letter;* Alan Paton's *Cry, the Beloved Country;* William Saroyan's *Human Comedy;* Arthur Schnitzler's *Beatrice;* Bernard Shaw's *Arms and the Man;* and two collections of international short stories.

20. Simin Daneshvar, *Shahri chun Behesht* [A City like Paradise] (1961; reprint, Tehran: Mowj, 1975).

21. Simin Daneshvar, *Be Ki Salam Konam?* [Whom Should I Salute?] (Tehran: Kharazmi, 1980).

22. The Association of Iranian Writers has had a short and highly episodic history. In late 1967, when the Pahlavi regime was planning to organize the Congress of Iranian Writers and Poets, a group of antiestablishment intellectuals, headed by Jalal Al-e Ahmad and gathering weekly in Café Firuz, resolved to oppose and boycott the symposium. They viewed the congress as another manifestation of the despotic drive of the regime to bring under control any real or potential source of independent power. Actually, this was neither the first nor the last such attempt. In its mounting effort to incorporate unassimilated intellectuals, the regime had created as early as 1962 the Imperial Cultural Council, presided over by the shah himself and counting among its members some of the most renowned scholars and writers. Unlike the formation of the Imperial Council and numerous future cultural festivals, the organization of the Congress of Iranian Writers and Poets proved, however, to be a failure. The group of antiestablishment intellectuals not only succeeded in postponing the planned congress but created from its spirit of resistance a pioneering effort at organizing a professional guild for writers and poets. In April 1968, the first declaration of the group appeared. It was signed by fifty-two intellectuals, including such prominent figures as Al-e Ahmad, Ahmad Ashraf, Barahani, Beh'azin, Daneshvar, Golshiri, Haj Seyyed Javadi, Hoquqi, Kazemi-ye, Kasra'i, Kho'i, Mossadeq, Naderpur, Rahmani, Sa'edi, Sepanlu, Shamlu, Tonekaboni, and Zohari. The letter denounced the congress, demanded an end to censorship, and proclaimed the need for the formation of a free association for writers and poets. Subsequent to this letter, its signatories were quick to found the Writers' Association of Iran.

23. Leila Riyahi, "A Letter to My Re-discovered Mother," *Nimeye Digar,* no. 8 (Fall 1988): 35.

24. Partow Nuri-'Ala, "Simin Daneshvar: A Woman Full of Life," ibid., 50.

25. Erika Friedl, "Women in Contemporary Persian Folktales," in *Women in the Muslim World,* 633.

26. Fakhr ed-Din Gorgani, *Vis-o-Ramin* (1054; reprint, Tehran: Zar, 1960).

27. While most of Daneshvar's women characters are survivors, none reveals such stamina or resilience as the narrator of *Jalal's Sunset*. This is a detailed record of the unexpected death of Daneshvar's husband. It demystifies Al-e Ahmad's death, which has been and continues to be shrouded in conspiratorial theories. *Jalal's Sunset* is an engaging literary work, a unique document of a moment when a woman is on the verge of losing her husband, her friend, and her colleague, a moment when the sun of her life is setting long before dusk. It is twilight at noon. It is premature sunset.

28. Daneshvar, *Fire Quenched*, 12.

29. It is interesting to compare a woman's description of physical beauty with that of most men. Taj-os Saltaneh, known for her beauty, describes her physical attributes with no recourse to food imagery: "God almighty has blessed my face with all that is beautiful. My hair is brown, with long, curly tresses. My complexion is fair, [my cheeks] red. My eyes are big and black with long eyelashes. My nose is sculptured. My mouth is very small with white teeth which give an amazing glow to my red lips" Taj-os Saltaneh, *Memoir*, 12. And here is how a Westerner, William H. Forbis, describes the "archetypical Iranian," who "looks like an Iranian and not like anybody else. . . . He, or she, has pale skin, narrow-set, dark liquid brown eyes, thick, black, arched eyebrows that join or nearly join in the middle, abundant, curly, brown-black hair, and . . . a nose. Not your little Western or Oriental button that seems designed merely for inhaling or exhaling. Far from that. The Iranian nose starts from a peak well up there where the eyebrows join, and skis downmountain on a straight but long and leisurely course to fetch up at base camp somewhere just above the upper lip. The bone is sharp, the skin taut, but there is no outburst Roman bridge, and never a ski-jump tip—in fact, the effect is a little like that of the prow of an overturned whaleboat" (*Fall of the Peacock Throne* [New York: McGraw-Hill, 1981], 125).

30. Here, the term *politics*, as Kate Millet explains, "shall refer to power-structured relationships, arrangements whereby one group of persons is controlled by another." In a footnote to this definition of politics, Millett adds: "One might expand this to a set of stratagems designed to maintain a system. If one understands patriarchy to be an institution perpetuated by such techniques of control, one has a working definition of how politics is conceived in this essay"(*Sexual Politics* [New York: Avon, 1971], 43).

31. Wallace Stegner and Richard Sowcroft, eds., *Stanford Short Stories* (Stanford: Stanford Univ. Press, 1954), 170.

32. The short story entitled "Model," from Daneshvar, *A City like Paradise*, 96.

33. See *Dah Shab-e She'r: Kanun-e Nevisandegan-e Iran* [Ten Nights of Poetry Reading: Writer's Association of Iran] (Rome: Babak, 1978).

34. "In Memory of Jalal, in an Interview with Simin Daneshvar," *Kayhan-i Farhangi* 4, no. 6 (Sept. 1987): 10.

35. Esma'ili and Sedarat, *Immortal, Forugh Farrokhzad*, 83.

36. Farrokhzad, *Another Birth*, 96.

37. Daneshvar, *Daneshvar's Playhouse*, 164.

38. According to Daneshvar, some sixty pages of *Savushun* were deleted from the book by governmental censors. Although we don't know exactly where these blank spaces occur, nonetheless, they are taken to be the most charged section of the novel, its political cream (Milani, "An Audience with Simin Daneshvar," 151).

39. Daneshvar, *Savushun,* 132.

40. Daneshvar excludes her own marriage from this category. In *Jalal's Sunset,* she writes, "Exceptionally few women in this world have had the good fortune of having found their suitable mate. . . . We were like two migrating birds who have found one another, sing together in a cage, and make the cage tolerable for one another" (48).

41. Milani, "An Audience with Simin Daneshvar," 154.

42. Farrokhzad, *Captive,* 149.

43. The novelist, short-fiction writer, political essayist, and translator Mahshid Amirshahi has produced four collections of short stories: *Kuche-ye Bonbast* [Blind Alley] (Tehran: Taban, 1966), *Ba'd az Ruz-e Akhar* [After the Last Day], *Be Sighe-ye Aval Shakhs-e Mofrad,* [First Person Singular] (Tehran: Buf, 1971), and *Sar-e Bibi Khanum* [Bibi Khanum's Starling] (Tehran: Taban, 1968). She is currently finishing a sequel to her first autobiographic novel, *Dar Hazar* [At Home] (Encino, Calif.: Ketab Corporation, 1986).

44. Amirshahi, *After the Last Day,* 162–63.

45. Born on Feb. 17, 1946, Shahrnush Parsipur published *Sag va Zemestan-e Boland* [The Dog and the Long Winter] in 1976, followed by *Avizeha-ye Bolur* [Crystal Pendants] (Tehran: Raz, 1977), and *Tajrobeha-ye Azad* [Free Experiences] (Tehran: Amir Kabir, 1978). After more than ten years of silence, Parsipur published *Tuba va Ma'na-ye Shab* [Tuba and the Sense of Night] (Tehran: Sparks, 1988). It is a long and moving novel that deals with the contemporary history of Iran through different stages in the life of its main character, a woman named Tuba. Like all of Parsipur's stories, the ending of *Tuba and the Sense of Night* is an unsolvable conflict, a paradox with no solution. Open-ended, it resists closure. Ultimately, it is up to the reader to supply a resolution, an ending to the life of Parsipur's woman protagonist. *Zanan Bedun-e Mardan* [Women Without Men] was published in 1989.

46. Milani, "An Audience with Simin Daneshvar," 151.

47. For *Zar* and other such ceremonies, see Gholam Hossein Sa'edi *Ahl-e Hava.* For a brilliant and complex analysis of this book, see Kaveh Safa, "Reading Sa'edi's *Ahl-e Hava,* Patterns and Significance in Spirit Possession Beliefs on the Southern Coast of Iran," *Culture, Medicine and Psychiatry* 12 (1988): 85–111.

48. Although 'Abdul's ecstatic state is an outlet to express his outraged feelings and frustrations, for those around him it is an institutionalized means to discard, disregard, and by implication control his openly aired desires. Besides allowing him partial relief and resolution, it also provides him with a means of coping with his otherwise intolerable situation without further alienating him from society.

49. Daneshvar, *Whom Should I Salute?,* 290.

50. Parsipur, "Why Do You Write?" 9.

9. Disclosing the Self: Autobiography

1. The often used injunction that *Pesar gerye nemikoneh* [boys never cry] portrays the performance pressures young boys labor under that continues throughout their lives. For "real men," as another saying goes, "don't cry" either.

2. Taj-os Saltaneh, *Memoir,* 17.

3. According to William Shawcross, concern over keeping his cancer a secret was so great that it actually denied the shah the proper treatment. "There is an almost surreal quality about the Shah's cancer. In a sense the disease, his reaction to it, the way in which it was treated, and its eventual impact on his own country, the United States, and his other allies, create a metaphor for his rule. It is a story of obsessive secrecy degenerating into macabre farce." *The Shah's Last Ride,* 230.

4. In Islam, there is no institutionalized intermediary between God and the individual.

5. The emergence of autobiography as a genre, even in the West, is a fairly recent phenomenon. Even if by general consensus Augustine's *Confessions,* written around the turn of the fifth century, is considered the first personal narrative, the beginning of the tradition is traced to no earlier than the Renaissance and by some even to as late as the nineteenth century, when, according to the *Oxford English Dictionary,* the word *autobiography* was coined.

6. Georges Gusdorf, "Conditions and Limits of Autobiography," in *Autobiography: Essays Theoretical and Critical,* ed. James Olney (Princeton: Princeton Univ. Press, 1980), 29.

7. Paul John Eakin, *Fictions in Autobiography* (Princeton: Princeton Univ. Press, 1985), 3. See also William C. Spengemann, *The Forms of Autobiography: Episodes in the History of a Literary Genre* (New Haven: Yale Univ. Press, 1980).

8. Roland Barthes, *Roland Barthes by Roland Barthes,* trans. Richard Howard (New York: Hill and Wang, 1977), 119.

9. Salman Rushdie, *Midnight's Children,* 253.

10. Lee Baxandall and Stefan Morawski, eds., *Marx and Engels on Literature and Art* (St. Louis: Telos, 1973), 115.

11. Friedrich Wilhelm Nietzsche, *Beyond Good and Evil,* trans. R. J. Hollingdale (Harmondsworth: Penguin, 1973), 19.

12. Philippe Lejeune, *Le Pacte Autobiographique* [The Autobiographical Pact] (Paris: Seuil, 1975), 44.

13. Ettinghausen, "Immanent Features of Persian Art," xv.

14. James Olney, "Autobiography and the Cultural Moment: a Thematic, Historical, and Bibliographical Introduction," in *Autobiography: Essays Theoretical and Critical* (Princeton: Princeton Univ. Press, 1980), 3.

15. Carolyn G. Heilbrun, *Hamlet's Mother and Other Women* (New York: Columbia Univ. Press, 1990), xiv.

16. As quoted in Deirdre Lashgari, "Absurdity and Creation in the Work of Sadeq Hedayat," *Iranian Studies* 15, nos. 1–4 (1982): 42. This quotation was originally taken

from Bozorg ʿAlavi, *Geschichte und entwicklung der modernen persischen literatur* (Berlin: Akademie-Verlag, 1964).

17. Yahya Arianpur, *Ketab-e Emruz* 1, vol. 1 (Tehran: Jibi, 1971), 28.

18. Nasrin Mottahedeh, "An Interview with Homa Partovi" *Zan*, no. 5 (Summer, 1990): 19.

19. ʿAbdollah Mostowfi, *Sharh-e Zendegani-ye Man* [An Account of My Life] (Tehran: Zavar, 1962).

20. V. S. Naipaul, *Among the Believers: An Islamic Journey* (New York: Vintage, 1982), 55.

21. Al-e Ahmad, *A Tombstone on a Tomb.*

22. Daneshvar, *Whom Should I Salute?*, 117–82.

23. "In Memory of Jalal," 32.

24. Saʿdi, *The Rose Garden*, 128–32.

25. Mowlana Jalal ed-Din Rumi, *Masnavi-ye Maʿnavi* [Spiritual Couplets] (Composed in the thirteenth century. Reprint. Tehran: Javid, 1975), 16.

26. As quoted in Donné Raffat, *The Prison Papers of Bozorg Alavi: A Literary Odyssey* (Syracuse: Syracuse Univ. Press, 1985), 212.

27. Ahmad Shamlu, *Taraneha-ye Kuchak-e Ghorbat* [Short Poems of Exile] (N.p.: Maziar, 1980), 30.

28. The task of unveiling the esoteric meaning of the Qorʾan is the exclusive function of the imams and their legitimate representatives.

29. Lady Sheil, the wife of the British ambassador to Iran from 1849 to 1853, in *Glimpses of Life and Manners in Persia*, writes: "These Persians are very strange people; they are ever on the watch to discover each other's intrigues, falsehood, and finesses. A movement of the finger, a turn of the eye, is not left unnoticed, and receives an interpretation. Yet each man invariably thinks that his own plots and intrigues are the acme of human ingenuity, wholly unfathomable by the rest of mankind" (247).

30. Milan Kundera, *The Unbearable Lightness of Being*, trans. Michael Henry Heim (New York: Harper & Row, 1984), 137.

31. Hafez, *Divan*, 136.

32. *Roget's International Thesaurus*, 4th ed., rev. Robert Chapman (New York: Crowell, 1979).

33. Milani, "An Audience with Simin Daneshvar," 155.

34. Sadr, *From Rabeʾe to Parvin*, 19.

35. Kaukab Siddique, "An Interview with Aʿzam Taleqani," *Islamic Revolution* 1, no. 9 (Dec. 1979): 3.

36. For a delightful study of the portrayal of women in photography in the Middle East, see Graham-Brown, *Images of Women*.

37. Hamid Nafici, "Autobiography, Film Spectatorship, and Cultural Negotiation," *Emergences* 1 (Fall 1989): 32.

38. Daneshvar, *Savushun*.

39. Forugh Farrokhzad, *Harfhaʾi ba Forugh Farrokhzad: Chahar Goft va Shonud* [Conversations with Forugh Farrokhzad: Four Interviews] (Tehran: Morvarid, 1976), 12.

40. Mahshid Amirshahi, *Muntakhab-e Dastan-ha* [Selected Stories] (Tehran: Tus, 1972), 4, and *At Home*.

41. Amirshahi, *After the Last Day*, 160.

42. In *A Room of One's Own*, Virginia Woolf writes: "Yet it is the masculine values that prevail. Speaking crudely, football and sport are 'important'; the worship of fashion, the buying of clothes 'trivial'. And these values are inevitably transferred from life to fiction. This is an important book, the critic assumes, because it deals with war. This is an insignificant book because it deals with the feelings of women in a drawing-room. A scene in a battlefield is more important than a scene in a shop— everywhere and much more subtly the difference of value persists" (77).

43. Faridoun Gilani, "Forugh Minus Propaganda Plus Herself," *Tehran Keyhan* (Feb. 10, 1977), 2.

44. Mary Ellman, *Thinking about Women* (New York: Harcourt Brace Jovanovich, 1968), 29.

45. Reza Qoli Khan Hedayat, *Golestan-e Eram* [The Rose Garden of Eram], as quoted in Jan Rypka, *History of Iranian Literature* (Dordrecht, Netherlands: Reidel, 1968), 340.

46. Ibid., 199.

47. Because I am interested in the general sense of self in these autobiographies rather than in the variety, literary merit, and differences among them, I have used the sources without the discrimination otherwise necessary.

48. M. M. Bakhtin, *The Dialogic Imagination*.

49. Parvin Nowbakht, *Sa'at-e Shesh, Daryache-ye Marivan* [Marivan Lake, at Six O'clock] (Tehran: Sepehr, 1981), 18.

50. Parviz C. Radji, *In the Service of the Peacock Throne* (London: Hamish Hamilton, 1983), 171.

51. Pahlavi, *Faces in the Mirror*, xv.

52. Taqi Modarressi, "Days of Nightingales and Roses," *Washington Post* (Jan. 22, 1989). 3.

53. Guppy, *The Blindfold Horse*, 94.

54. For a fuller analysis of this book, see Afsaneh Najmabadi, "A Different Voice: Taj-os Saltaneh," in *Women's Biographies and Autobiographies in Iran*, ed. Afsaneh Najmabadi (Cambridge, Mass.: Harvard Univ. Press, 1991), and Shireen Mahdavi, "Taj-os Saltaneh, an Emancipated Qajar Princess," *Middle Eastern Studies* 23, no. 2 (Apr. 1987): 188–93.

55. Taj-os Saltaneh, *Memoir*, 5.

56. Abolfazl Qassemi, "The Eventful Life of Taj-os Saltaneh," *Vahid* 13, no. 5 (Oct. 1975): 759.

57. 'Aref Qazvini, *The Poems of 'Aref*, ed. Dinshah Irani (Bombay: Hoor, 1933), 11.

58. Taj-os Saltaneh, *Memoir*, 89.

59. Ibid., 102.

60. Bamdad, *From Darkness into Light*, 102.

61. Marziye Ahmadi Osku'i, *Khaterati az Yek Rafiq* [Memoirs of a Comrade] (N.p.: Sazeman Fada'iyan-e Khalq, n.d.).

10. The Birth of Neotraditional Feminism

1. Vezarat-e Ershad-e Eslami [Ministry of Islamic Guidance], *Fehrest-e Mozu'i-ye Kotob va Maqalat dar Bare-ye Zan* [Bibliography of Books and Articles about Women] (Tehran: Vezarat-e Ershad-e Eslami, 1986).

2. Ayatollah Rubollah Khomeini, *Images of Women,* 209.

3. Ibid.

4. Hamid Nafici, "The Development of an Islamic Cinema in Iran," *Third World Affairs* (1987): 459.

5. Hamid Nafici, "The Averted Gaze in Iranian Postrevolutionary Cinema," *Public Culture* 3, no. 2 (Spring 1991): 39.

6. Ayatollah Khomeini's talk to the representative of the Writer's Association of Iran, as quoted in Ebrahim Hassan Beygi, *Kine-ye Azali* [Eternal Grudge] (Tehran: Barq, 1988), 18.

7. Ibid.

8. Quoted in Nafici, "Development of an Islamic Cinema," 322.

9. For a more comprehensive introduction to Behbahani's life and poetry, see *Nimeye Digar,* special issue on Simin Behbahani, guest editor Farzaneh Milani, forthcoming.

10. Fatima Mernissi, *Women in Muslim Paradise* (New Delhi: Kali for Women, 1986), n.p.

11. Simin Behbahani, *Gozine-ye Ash'ar* [Selected Poems] (Chicago: Midland Printing, 1990), 13.

12. Simin Behbahani, *Dasht-e Arjan* [Arjan Plain] (Tehran: Zavar, 1983), 43. I have profited immensely from Kaveh Safa's unpublished translation of this poem.

Works Cited

'Abdul Baha', 'Abbas. *Memorials of the Faithful.* Wilmette, Ill.: Baha'i Publishing Trust, 1971.

'Abedini, Farhad. "Sha'ereha-ye Ba'd-e Forugh . . . " [Women Poets after Forugh]. *Negin,* no. 118 (Mar. 1974).

Adel, Gh. Hadad. "Clothing and the Secret of the Self." *Mahjubah* 3, nos. 4, 5, 6 (Aug.–Oct. 1983): 60–68.

Afkhami, Mahnaz. "Iran: A Future in the Past—the 'Prerevolutionary' Women's Movement." In *Sisterhood Is Global,* ed. Robin Morgan, 330–38. New York: Anchor, 1984.

Ahmadi Osku'i, Marziye. *Khaterati az Yek Rafiq* [Memoirs of a Comrade]. N.P.: Sazeman Fada'iyan-e Khalq, n.d.

Al-e Ahmad, Jalal. *Gharbzadegi* [Westomania]. Tehran: Ravaq, 1962.

———. *Occidentosis: A Plague from the West.* Trans. R. Campbell; ed. Hamid Algar. Berkeley: Mizan, 1984.

———. *Panj Dastan* [Five Stories]. Tehran: Ramin, 1977.

———. *Sangi bar Guri* [A Tombstone on a Tomb]. Tehran: Ravaq, 1981.

———. *Weststruckness.* Trans. John Green and Ahmad Alizadeh. Lexington, Ky.: Mazda, 1982.

'Alavi, Bozorg. *Cheshmhayash* [Her Eyes]. Tehran: Amir Kabir, 1978.

———. *Geschichte und entwicklung der modernen persischen Literatur.* Berlin: Akademie-Verlag, 1964.

Alishan, Leonardo P. "Tahereh Saffarzadeh: From the Wasteland to the Imam." *Iranian Studies* 15, nos. 1–4 (1982): 181–210.

Amanat, Abbas. *Resurrection and Renewal.* Ithaca, N.Y.: Cornell Univ. Press, 1989.

Amirshahi, Mahshid. *Ba'd az Ruz-e Akhar* [After the Last Day]. 1969. Reprint. Tehran: Amir Kabir, 1976.

———. *Be Sighe-ye Aval Shakhs-e Mofrad* [First Person Singular]. Tehran: Buf, 1971.

———. *Dar Hazar* [At Home]. Encino, Calif.: Ketab, 1986.

———. "Introduction." Forthcoming collection of short stories by Iranian women writers. Compiled and edited by John Green.

———. *Kuche-ye Bonbast* [Blind Alley]. Tehran: Taban, 1966.

———. *Muntakhab-e Dastan-ha* [Selected Stories]. Tehran: Tus, 1972.

———. *Sar-e Bibi Khanum* [Bibi Khanum's Starling]. Tehran: Taban, 1968.

Arianpur, Yahya. *Az Saba ta Nima* [From Saba to Nima]. Vol. 2. Tehran: Jibi, 1976.

———. *Ketab-e Emruz.* Vol. 1. Tehran: Jibi, 1971.

Arkin, Marian, and Barbara Shollar, eds. *Longman Anthology of World Literature by Women, 1875–1975.* New York: Longman, 1989.

Azad, Mahmud. "She'ri Anbashte az Adaha-ye Rowshanfekraneh" [A Poetry Packed with Intellectual Pretenses]. *Keyhan,* Feb. 21, 1971.

Azadi, Sousan, with Angela Ferrante. *Out of Iran.* London: Futura, 1987.

Azari, Farah, ed. *Women of Iran, the Conflict with Fundamentalist Islam.* London: Ithaca, 1983.

Badawi, Jamal A. "Dress Rules for Muslim Women." *The Muslim World League Journal* 9, no. 2 (Dec. 1981).

Bahaism: Its Origins and Its Role. The Hague: Nashr-e Farhang-e Eslami, n.d.

Bakhtin, M. M. *The Dialogic Imagination.* Edited by Michael Holquist; translated by Caryl Emerson and Michael Holquist. Austin: Univ. of Texas Press, 1986.

Bakhtiyari, Pezhman, ed. *Zaleh* [Zaleh]. Tehran: Khajeh, n.d.

Balyuzi, H. M. *The Bab.* Oxford: George Ronald, 1974.

Bamdad, Badr ol-Moluk. *From Darkness into Light: Women's Emancipation in Iran.* Translated by F. R. C. Bagley. Hicksville, N.Y.: Exposition-University, 1977.

Barahani, Reza. *The Crowned Cannibals.* New York: Vintage, 1977.

———. *Tala dar Mes* [Gold in Copper]. Tehran: Zaman, 1968.

———. *Tarikh-e Mozakar* [Masculine History]. Tehran: Elmi, n.d.

Barthes, Roland. *Roland Barthes by Roland Barthes.* Trans. Richard Howard. New York: Hill and Wang, 1977.

Bassari, Tal'at, ed. *Zand-Dokht* [Zand-Dokht]. Tehran: Zohuri, 1967.

Bastani-ye Parizi, Mohammad Ebrahim. *Haft Sang* [Seven Stones]. Tehran: Danesh, 1967.

Bausani, Alessandro. "Babis." In *The Encyclopedia of Religion,* edited by Mircea Eliade, 2:32–34.

Baxandall, Lee, and Stefan Morawski, eds. *Marx and Engels on Literature and Art.* St. Louis: Telos, 1973.

Bayat [-Philipp], Mangol. *Mysticism and Dissent: Socioreligious Thought in Qajar Iran.* Syracuse: Syracuse Univ. Press, 1982.

————. "Women and Revolution in Iran, 1905–1911." In *Women in the Muslim World,* edited by Lois Beck and Nikki Keddie, 295–308. Cambridge, Mass.: Harvard Univ. Press, 1978.

Beck, Lois, and Nikki Keddie. *Women in the Muslim World.* Cambridge, Mass.: Harvard Univ. Press, 1978.

Behbahani, Simin. *Dasht-e Arjan* [Arjan Plain]. Tehran: Zavar, 1983.

————. *Gozine-ye Ash'ar* [Selected Poems]. Chicago: Midland Printing, 1990.

————. "We Have Run and We Are Still Running." *Doniya-ye Sokhan,* no. 13 (Nov. 1987): 61–62.

Borujerdi, Zeinab. "Darsha'i dar bare-ye Hejab" [Some Teachings Regarding the Veil]. *Etela'at-e Banovan* 4, no. 3 (Aug. 1980): 18, 59.

Browne, Edward G. *A Literary History of Persia.* Vol. 4, *Modern Times, 1500–1924.* Cambridge: Univ. Press, 1930.

————. *Traveller's Narrative.* Cambridge: Cambridge Univ. Press, 1981.

Caton, Peggy, ed. *Equal Circles, Women and Men in the Baha'i Community.* Los Angeles: Kalimat, 1987.

Chernin, Kim. *The Obsession, Reflections on the Tyranny of Slenderness.* New York: Harper & Row, 1981.

"Cultural Recklessness." *Bayan,* no. 2 (1990): 25–26.

Dah Shab-e She'r: Kanun-e Nevisandegan-e Iran [Ten Nights of Poetry Reading: Writers' Association of Iran]. Rome: Babak, 1978.

Daly, Mary. *Gyn/Ecology.* Boston: Beacon, 1978.

Daneshvar, Simin. *Atash-e Khamush* [Fire Quenched]. Tehran: N.p., 1948.

————. *Be Ki Salam Konam?* [Whom Should I Salute?]. Tehran: Kharazmi, 1980.

————. *Daneshvar's Playhouse.* Translated by Maryam Mafi. Washington, D.C.: Mage, 1989.

————. *Ghorub-e Jalal* [Jalal's Sunset]. Tehran: Ravaq, 1981.

————. *A Persian Requiem.* Trans. Roxane Zand. London: Halban, 1991.

————. *Savushun.* Tehran: Kharazmi, 1969.

————. *Savushun.* Translated by M. R. Ghanoonparvar. Washington, D.C.: Mage, 1990.

————. *Shahri chun Behesht* [A City like Paradise]. 1961. Reprint. Tehran: Mowj, 1975.

Davaran, Fereshteh. "The Impersonal Poems of Parvin E'tessami." *Iranshenasi* 1, no. 2 (Summer 1989): 285–309.

Dehkhoda, 'Ali Akbar. *Loghatnameh.* Tehran: Univ. of Tehran Press, 1960.

————. *Amsal-o-Hekam* [Maxims]. Tehran: Amir Kabir, 1982.

Dickinson, Emily. *Selected Poems of Emily Dickinson.* Edited by James Reeves. London: Heinemann, 1959.

Dinesen, Isak. *Last Tales.* New York: Vintage, 1975.

Eakin, Paul John. *Fictions in Autobiography.* Princeton: Princeton Univ. Press, 1985.

Effendi, Shoghi. *God Passes By.* Wilmette, Ill.: Baha'i Publishing Committee, 1944.

Ehrenreich, Barbara, and Deirdre English. *Witches, Midwives, and Nurses.* New York: Feminist, 1973.

Eliot, T. S. *The Sacred Wood.* London: Methuen, 1974.

Ellman, Mary. *Thinking about Women.* New York: Harcourt Brace Jovanovich, 1968.

'Eshqi, Mirzade-ye. *Koliyat-e Mosavar-e 'Eshqi* [Illustrated Works of 'Eshqi]. Edited by 'Ali Akbar Moshir-Salimi. Tehran: Sepehr, 1978.

Eslami-ye Nadushan, Mohammad 'Ali. *Ruzha* [Days]. Tehran: Yazdan, 1984.

Esma'ili, Amir, and Abol-Qasem Sedarat, eds. *Javedaneh, Forugh Farrokhzad* [Immortal, Forugh Farrokhzad]. Tehran: Marjan, 1972.

E'tessami, Abolfath, ed. *Maqalat va Qate'at-e Ash'ar* [Articles and Some Poems]. Tehran: Fardin, 1974.

E'tessami, Parvin. *Divan* [Collected Poems]. 1935. Reprint. Tehran: Fardin, 1974.

————. *A Nightingale's Lament.* Translated by Heshmat Moayyad and A. Margaret Madelung. Lexington, Ky.: Mazda, 1985.

E'tezadol-Saltaneh, 'Ali Quli Mirza. *Fetne-ye Bab* [Bab's Conspiracy]. 2d. ed. Annotated by 'Abdol-Hossein Nava'i. Tehran: Babak, 1965.

Ettinghausen, Richard. "The Immanent Features of Persian Art." In *Highlights of Persian Art,* edited by R. Ettinghausen and E. Yarshater. Boulder, Colo.: Westview, 1979), xiii–xviii.

Ewen, L'Estrange. *Witch Hunting and Witch Trials.* London: Stephen Austin and Sons, 1929.

Farrokhzad, Forugh. *Another Birth, Selected Poems of Forugh Farrokhzad.* Trans. Hasan Javadi with Susan Sallee. Emeryville, Calif.: Albany, 1981.

————. *Asir.* [Captive]. 1955. Reprint. Tehran: Amir Kabir, 1974.

————. *Bride of Acacias.* Translated by Jascha Kessler with Amin Banani. New York: Caravan, 1982.

————. *Divar* [Wall]. 1956. Reprint. Tehran: Amir Kabir, 1971.

————. *'Esian* [Rebellion]. Tehran: Amir Kabir, 1958.

————. *Harfha'i ba Forugh Farrokhzad: Chahar Goft va Shonud* [Conversations with Forugh Farrokhzad: Four Interviews]. Tehran: Morvarid, 1976.

————. *Iman Biavarim be Aghaz-e Fasl-e Sard* [Let Us Believe in the Dawning of a Cold Season]. Tehran: Morvarid, 1974.

————. *An interview with Iraj Gorgin.* In *Arash,* edited by Syrus Tahbaz. Tehran: Darakhshan, 1966.

————. *A Rebirth.* Trans. David Martin. Lexington, Ky.: Mazda, 1985.

————. *Tavalodi Digar* [Another Birth]. 1964. Reprint. Tehran: Morvarid, 1972.

Fazil Mazandarani, Mirza Asadollah. *Zuhur-ol Haq.* Tehran: N.p., n.d.

Ferdowsi, Hakim Abol-Qasem. *Shah Nameh* [The Book of Kings]. Completed ca. A.D. 1000. Reprint. Tehran: Amir Kabir, 1966.

Fischer, Michael. "On Changing the Concept and Position of Persian Women." In *Women in the Muslim World,* edited by Lois Beck and Nikki Keddie, 189–215. Cambridge, Mass.: Harvard Univ. Press, 1978.

Forbis, William H. *Fall of the Peacock Throne.* New York: McGraw-Hill, 1981.

Friedl, Erika. "Women in Contemporary Persian Folktales." In *Women in the Muslim World,* edited by Lois Beck and Nikki Keddie, 629–50. Cambridge, Mass.: Harvard Univ. Press, 1978.

"From Michael Jackson to . . . ." *Sureh* 2, no. 4 (1990): 5.

Garakani, Fazlollah. *Tohmat-e Sha'eri* [Accused of Being a Poet]. Tehran: Alborz, 1977.

Gheiby, Bijan. "*Chador* in Early Literary Sources." In *Encyclopaedia Iranica,* edited by Ehsan Yarshater, 609–10. London: Routledge & Kegan Paul.

Gilani, Faridoun. "Forugh Minus Propaganda Plus Herself." *Tehran Keyhan,* Feb. 10, 1977: 2.

Gilbert, Sandra, and Susan Gubar. *The Madwoman in the Attic.* New Haven: Yale Univ. Press, 1979.

Golbon, Mohammad, ed. *Naqd va Siyahat* [Criticism and Exploration]. Tehran: Tus, 1975.

Golshiri, Hushang. "An Interview with Simin Daneshvar." *Mahnameh-ye Mofid,* no. 3, n.s. (July 1987): 16–22.

Gorgani, Fakhr ed-Din. *Vis-o-Ramin.* 1054. Reprint. Tehran: Zar, 1960.

―――. *Vis-o-Ramin.* Translated by G. Morrison. Persian Heritage Series no. 14. New York: Columbia Univ. Press, 1972.

Graham-Brown, Sarah. *Images of Women.* London: Quartet, 1988.

Groningen, Helen Sancisi-Weerdenburg. "Exit Atossa: Images of Women in Greek Historiography on Persia." In *Images of Women in Antiquity,* edited by Averil Cameron and Amelie Kuhrt, 20–33. Detroit: Wayne State Univ. Press, 1983.

Guppy, Shusha. *The Blindfold Horse, Memories of a Persian Childhood.* London: Heinemann, 1988.

Gusdorf, Georges. "Conditions and Limits of Autobiography." In *Autobiography: Essays Theoretical and Critical.* edited by James Olney, 28–48. Princeton: Princeton Univ. Press, 1980.

Haeri, Shahla. *Law of Desire: Temporary Marriage in Shi'i Iran.* Syracuse: Syracuse Univ. Press, 1989.

Hafez, Shams ed-Din Mohammad. *Divan* [Collection of Poems]. Edited by Parviz Natel Khanlari. Written in the fourteenth century. Reprint. Tehran: Kharazmi, 1980.

Hajibashi, Zjaleh. "Redefining 'Sin'." In *Forugh Farrokhzad: A Quarter-Century Later,* edited by Michael Hillmann, special issue of *Literature East and West,* no. 24, 67–71.

Halman, Talat. "Jalal al-Din Rumi: Passions of the Mystic Mind." In *Persian Literature,* edited by Ehsan Yarshater. New York: Bibliotheca Persica, 1988, 190–213.

Hassan Beygi, Ebrahim. *Kine-ye Azali* [Eternal Grudge]. Tehran: Barq, 1988.

Hedayat, Sadeq. *The Blind Owl.* Translated by D. P. Costello. London: John Calder, 1957; New York: Grove Press, 1957.

———. *Buf-e Kur* [The Blind Owl]. 1941. Reprint. Tehran: Amir Kabir, 1972.

———. *La Chouette Aveugle.* Translated by Roger Lescot. Paris: José Corti, 1953.

———. *Neveshteha-ye Parakandeh* [The Scattered Writings]. Tehran: Amir Kabir, 1965.

———. *Neyrangestan.* Tehran: Parastu, 1965.

———. *Parvin, Dokhtar-e Sassan* [Parvin, the Daughter of Sassan]. Tehran: Amir Kabir, 1963.

———. *Sayeh Roshan* [Chiaroscuro]. 1933. Reprint. Tehran: Parastu, 1964.

Heilbrun, Carolyn G. *Hamlet's Mother and Other Women.* New York: Columbia Univ. Press, 1990.

———. *Writing a Woman's Life.* New York: Norton, 1988.

Hillmann, Michael C. *A Lonely Woman.* Washington, D.C.: Three Continents and Mage, 1987.

———. "Cultural Dilemmas of an Iranian Intellectual." In Jalal Al-e Ahmad, *Lost in the Crowd.* Translated by John Green with Ahmad Alizadeh and Farzin Yazdanfar, vii–xxxiii. Washington, D.C.: Three Continents, 1985.

Holy Qur'an. Trans. M. H. Shakir. New York: Tahrike Tarsile Qur'an, 1985.

Hoquqi, Hadi. "Watch One Who Is Blind Lead the Way for Another." *Khandaniha* (Sept. 1989): 17.

Hussain, Freda, ed. *Muslim Women.* London: Croom Helm, 1984.

"In Memory of Jalal, in an Interview with Simin Daneshvar." *Kayhan-i Farhangi* 4, no. 6 (Sept. 1987): 3–11.

In the Shadow of Islam. Compiled by Azar Tabari and Nahid Yeganeh. London: Zed, 1982.

Ishaque, S. Mohammad. *Four Eminent Poetesses of Iran.* Calcutta: Iran Society, 1950.

———. "Parvin-i I'tisami: An Eminent Poetess of Modern Iran." *Islamic Culture* 17, no. 1 (Jan. 1943): 49–56.

Jamalzadeh, Mohammad 'Ali. "From Among Your Letters." *Nimeye Digar,* no. 9 (Spring 1989): 4–7.

Javadi, Hassan. *Obeyd-e Zakani.* Piedmont, Calif.: Jahan, 1985.

Johnson, Lowell. *Tahirih*. Johannesburg: National Spiritual Assembly of the Baha'is of South and West Africa, 1982.

Jong, Erica. *Fear of Flying*. New York: New American Library, 1974.

————. *Witches*. New York: Harry N. Abrams, 1981.

Juhasz, Suzanne. *Naked and Fiery Forms, Modern American Poetry by Women: A New Tradition*. New York: Harper & Row, 1976.

————. *Yeki Bud Yeki Nabud* [Once upon a Time]. Berlin, 1921; 7th ed. Tehran: Ma'refat, 1966.

Kalileh-o-Demneh [Kalileh and Demneh]. Translated by Hassan Tehranchian. New York: Harmony, 1985.

Karimi-Hakkak, Ahmad. "Parvin E'tessami as an Innovative Poet." *Iranshenasi* 1, no. 2 (Summer, 1989): 264–84.

Karlsen, Carol. *The Devil in the Shape of a Woman*. New York: Vintage Books, 1987.

Kasravi, Ahmad. *Baha'igari* [Baha'ism]. Tehran: Mard-e Emruz, 1956.

Kaufman, Michael T. "Author from Three Countries." *New York Times Book Review*, Nov. 13, 1983.

Khomeini, Ayatollah Ruhollah. *Resaleh-ye Novin* [New Treatise]. Translated by 'Abdul Karim Biazar-e Shirazi. Tehran: Ketab, 1982.

————. *Sima-ye Zan dar Kalam-e Emam Khomeini* [Images of Women in the Words of Emam Khomeini]. Tehran: Sazeman-e Chap va Entesharat, 1987.

————. "Veils of Darkness, Veils of Light." In *Islam and Revolution*, translated by Hamid Algar, 389–403. London: KPI, 1985.

Kundera, Milan. *The Unbearable Lightness of Being*. Translated by Michael Henry Heim. New York: Harper & Row, 1984.

Lashgari, Deirdre. "Absurdity and Creation in the Work of Sadeq Hedayat." *Iranian Studies* 15, nos. 1–4 (1982): 31–52.

Lee, Feelie. "Bound and Unbound Feet." Ph.D. diss., Wright Institute, 1982.

Lejeune, Philippe. *Le Pacte Autobiographique* [The Autobiographical Pact]. Paris: Seuil, 1975.

Levy, Howard S. *Chinese Footbinding*. New York: Walton Rawls, 1966.

Levy, Reuben. *The Social Structure of Islam*. London: Cambridge Univ. Press, 1969.

Mahalati, Sheikh Zabihollah. *Kashf-ol Ghorur ya Mafased-ol Sofur* [Learning about Vanity or the Evils of Unveiling]. Tehran: Askari, 1959.

Mahdavi, Shireen. "Taj-os Saltaneh, an Emancipated Qajar Princess." *Middle Eastern Studies* 23, no. 2 (Apr. 1987): 188–93.

Marianoff, Dimitri, and Marzieh Gail. "Thralls of Yearning Love." *World Order* (Summer 1972): 7–42.

Mehrabi, Mo'in ed-Din. *Qorratol'Ayn*. Cologne: Ruyesh, 1989.

Mernissi, Fatima. *Beyond the Veil*. Rev. ed. Bloomington: Indiana Univ. Press, 1987.

————. *Women in Muslim Paradise.* New Delhi: Kali for Women, 1986.

Milani, Farzaneh. "Grandmother and Jasmine." *Omid* 1, no. 2 (Nov.–Dec. 1987): 91.

————. "Pay-e Sohbat-e Simin Daneshvar" [An Audience with Simin Daneshvar]. *Alefba,* no. 4 (Fall 1983): 147–57.

————. "Woman's Body as Sign and Symbol: On Veiling and Footbinding." *Iran Nameh* 8, no. 2 (1990): 246–60.

————, ed. *Nimeye Digar,* no. 8 (Fall 1988).

Miller, Jane. *Women Writing about Men.* London: Virago, 1986.

Millet, Kate. *Sexual Politics.* New York: Avon, 1971.

Mirza, Iraj. *Iraj Mirza.* Edited by Mohammad Ja'far Mahjub. Tehran: Andisheh, 1974.

Mo'azen, Nasser, ed. *Dah Shab-e She'r* [Ten Nights of Poetry]. Tehran: Amir Kabir, 1978.

Moayyad, Heshmat. "In Memory of the 80th Anniversary of Parvin E'tessami." *Iran Nameh* 6, no. 1 (Fall 1987): 116–42.

————. "Parvin's Poems: A Cry in the Wilderness." In *Islamwissenschaftliche Abhandlungen,* 164–90. Wiesbaden: Franz Steiner, 1974.

Modarressi, Taqi. "Days of Nightingales and Roses." *Washington Post,* Jan. 22, 1989:3.

Momen, Moojan, ed. *The Babi and Baha'i Religions, 1844–1944.* Oxford: George Ronald, 1981.

————. *Selections from E. G. Browne on the Babi and Baha'i Religions.* Oxford: George Ronald, 1987.

Moshir-Salimi, Ali Akbar. *Zanan-e Sokhanvar* [Eloquent Women]. Vol. 2. Tehran: 'Elmi, 1956.

Mostowfi, 'Abdollah. *Sharh-e Zendegani-ye Man* [An Account of My Life]. Tehran: Zavar, 1962.

Mottahari, Ayatollah Morteza. *Mas'ale-ye Hejab* [The Issue of Veiling]. Tehran: Enteshar, 1983.

————. *Women's Rights in Islam.* Qom, Iran: Sadra, 1978.

Mottahedeh, Nasrin. "An Interview with Homa Partovi." *Zan,* no. 5 (Summer 1990): 18–22.

Mottahedeh, Roy. *The Mantle of the Prophet.* New York: Simon & Schuster, 1985.

Nabil Zarandi, Sheykh Mohammad. *The Dawn-Breakers.* Translated and edited by Shoghi Effendi. Wilmette, Ill.: Bahai Publishing Trust, 1932.

Nafici, Hamid. "Autobiography, Film Spectatorship, and Cultural Negotiation." *Emergences* 1 (Fall 1989): 29–54.

————. "The Averted Gaze in Iranian Postrevolutionary Cinema." *Public Culture* 3, no. 2 (Spring 1991): 29–40.

————. "The Development of an Islamic Cinema in Iran." *Third World Affairs* (1987): 447–63.

————. "Women and the Semiotics of Veiling and Vision in Cinema." *American Journal of Semiotics,* forthcoming.

Naipaul, V. S. *Among the Believers: An Islamic Journey.* New York: Vintage, 1982.

Najmabadi, Afsaneh. "Without a Place to Rest the Sole of My Foot." Lecture presented at the Association of Middle Eastern Women's Annual Meeting, Toronto, Nov. 1989.

————, ed. *Women's Biographies and Autobiographies in Iran.* Cambridge, Mass.: Harvard Univ. Press, 1991.

Namini, Hossein. *Javedaneh, Parvin E'tessami* [Immortal, Parvin E'tessami]. Tehran: Farzan, 1983.

Nashat, Guity. "Women in the Middle East." In *Restoring Women to History.* Bloomington, Ind.: Organization of American Historians, 1988, 3–57.

————, ed. *Women and Revolution in Iran.* Boulder, Colo.: Westview, 1983.

Nateq, Homa. "The Beginnings of Religious Clerics' Economic and Political Power." *Alefba,* no. 2, n.s. (Spring 1983): 40–57.

Nazer, Manuchehr. *Negareshi bar Ash'ar-e Parvin E'tessami* [Some Observations on the Poetry of Parvin E'tessami]. Tehran: Sorush, 1981.

Nietzsche, Friedrich Wilhelm. *Beyond Good and Evil.* Trans. R. J. Hollingdale. Harmondsworth: Penguin, 1973.

Nizami of Ganja. *Layla and Majnun.* Translated by R. Gelpke. Boulder, Colo.: Shambala, 1978.

Noqaba'i, Hesam. *Tahereh.* N.p., 1983.

Nowbakht, Parvin. *Sa'at-e Shesh, Daryache-ye Marivan* [Marivan Lake, at Six O'clock]. Tehran: Sepehr, 1981.

Nuri-'Ala, Partow. "Simin Daneshvar: A Woman Full of Life." *Nimeye Digar,* no. 8 (Fall 1988): 46–50.

Olney, James. "Autobiography and the Cultural Moment: A Thematic, Historical, and Bibliographical Introduction." In *Autobiography: Essays Theoretical and Critical,* edited by James Olney, 3–27. Princeton: Princeton Univ. Press, 1980.

Olsen, Tillie. *Silences.* New York: Delacorte/Seymour Lawrence, 1978.

Orbach, Susie. *Hunger Strike.* New York: Avon, 1986.

Ostad Malek, Fatemeh. *Hejab va Kashf-e Hejab dar Iran* [Veiling and Unveiling in Iran]. Tehran: Atta'i, 1988.

Pahlavi, Ashraf. *Faces in the Mirror.* Englewood Cliffs, N.J.: Prentice-Hall, 1980.

————. *Taslim Napazir* [Never Resigned]. N.p., 1984.

Parsipur, Shahrnush. *Avizeha-ye Bolur* [Crystal Pendants]. Tehran: Raz, 1977.

————. *Sag va Zemestan-e Boland* [The Dog and the Long Winter]. Tehran: Sepehr, 1976.

————. *Tajrobeha-ye Azad* [Free Experiences]. Tehran: Amir Kabir, 1978.

————. *Tuba va Ma'na-ye Shab* [Tuba and the Sense of Night]. Tehran: Spark, 1988.

————. "Why Do You Write?" *Doniya-ye Sokhan,* no. 17 (Mar. 1988): 9–10.

————. *Zanan Bedun-e Mardan* [Women Without Men]. Tehran: Noqreh, 1989.

Qahreman, Sahar. "The Islamic Government Policy Towards Women's Access to Higher Education in Iran." *Nimeye Digar,* no. 7 (Summer 1988): 16–32.

Qassemi, Abolfazl. "The Eventful Life of Taj-os Saltaneh." *Vahid* 13, no. 5 (Oct. 1975): 757–62.

Qazvini, 'Aref. *The Poems of 'Aref.* Edited by Dinshah Irani Bombay: Hoor, 1933.

Rachlin, Nahid. *Foreigner.* New York: Norton, 1978.

Radji, Parviz C. *In the Service of the Peacock Throne.* London: Hamish Hamilton, 1983.

Raffat, Donné. *The Prison Papers of Bozorg Alavi: A Literary Odyssey.* Syracuse: Syracuse Univ. Press, 1985.

Ramazani, Nesta. "Behind the Veil: Status of Women in Revolutionary Iran." *Journal of South Asian and Middle Eastern Studies* 4, no. 2 (Winter 1980): 27–36.

Remey, Charles Mason. *Observations of a Bahai Traveller.* 1909. Reprint. Washington, D.C.: The author, 1914.

Riyahi, Leila. "A Letter to My Re-discovered Mother." *Nimeye Digar,* no. 8 (Fall 1988): 30–39.

Roget's International Thesaurus, 4th ed. Revised by Robert Chapman. New York: Crowell, 1979.

Root, Martha L. *Tahirih the Pure.* 1938. Reprint. Los Angeles: Kalimat, 1981.

Rossi, William A. *The Sex Life of the Foot and Shoe.* Ware, England: Wordsworth, 1989.

Rowe, Karen E. "To Spin a Yarn: The Female Voice in Folklore and Fairy Tale." In *Fairy Tales and Society: Illusion, Allusion, and Paradigm,* edited by Ruth B. Bottigheimer, 53–74. Philadelphia: Univ. of Pennsylvania Press, 1986.

Rumi, Mowlana Jalal ed-Din. *Masnavi-ye Ma'navi* [Spiritual Couplets]. Written in the thirteenth century. Reprint. Tehran: Javid, 1975.

Rushdie, Salman. *Is Nothing Sacred?* The Herbert Read Memorial Lecture. N.p.: Granta, 1990.

————. *Midnight's Children.* New York: Avon, 1980.

————. *Shame.* New York: Vintage, 1983.

Russ, Joanna. *How to Suppress Women's Writing.* Austin: Univ. of Texas Press, 1983.

Rypka, Jan. *History of Iranian Literature.* Dordrecht, Netherlands: Reidel, 1968.

Saadawi, Nawal el. *The Hidden Face of Eve.* Boston: Beacon, 1981.

Sabbah, Fatna A. *Woman in the Muslim Unconscious.* Translated by Mary Jo Lakeland. New York: Pergamon, 1984.

Sa'di, Mosleh ed-Din. *Bustan* [The Orchard]. Completed in the thirteenth century. Reprint. Tehran: Kharazmi, 1989.

———. *Golestan* [The Rose Garden]. Reprint. Tehran: Kharazmi, 1989.

Sadr, Keshavarz-e. *Az Rabe'e ta Parvin* [From Rabe'e to Parvin]. Tehran: Kavian, 1956.

Sadr ed-Din Elahi in Amir, Esma'ili, and Abol-Qassem Sedarat, eds. *Javedaneh* [Immortal]. Tehran: Marjan, 1968.

Sa'edi, Gholam Hossein. *Ahl-e Hava* [People of the Wind]. Tehran: Tehran Univ. Press, 1966.

———. *Dandil.* Tehran: Javaneh, 1966.

Safa, Kaveh. "Reading Sa'edi's *Ahl-e Hava,* Patterns and Significance in Spirit Possession Beliefs on the Southern Coast of Iran." *Culture, Medicine and Psychiatry* 12 (1988): 85–111.

———. "Female-centered World Views in Iranian Culture: Symbolic Representations of Sexuality in Dramatic Games." *Signs* 6, no. 1 (1980): 33–53.

Saffarzadeh, Tahereh. *Bey'at ba Bidari* [Allegiance with Wakefulness]. Tehran: Hamdami, 1980.

———. *Didar-e Sobh* [Morning Visitation]. Shiraz, Iran: Navid, 1987.

———. *Harekat va Diruz* [Motion and Yesterday]. Tehran: Ravaq, 1979.

———. *Mardan-e Monhani* [Curbed Men]. Shiraz, Iran: Navid, 1987.

———. *Peyvandha-ye Talkh* [Bitter Unions]. Tehran: Etela'at, 1963.

———. *Red Umbrella.* Iowa City, Iowa: Windhover, 1969.

———. *Safar-e Panjom* [The Fifth Journey]. Tehran: Ravaq, 1978.

———. *Tanin dar Delta* [Resonance in the Bay]. Tehran: Amir Kabir, 1971.

Said, Edward W. *Orientalism.* New York: Vintage, 1979.

Sanasarian, Eliz. *The Women's Rights Movements in Iran.* New York: Praeger, 1982.

Sanday, Peggy Reeves. *Fraternity Gang Rape: Sex, Brotherhood, and Privilege on Campus.* New York: New York Univ. Press, 1990.

Savory, Roger M. "Social Development in Iran During the Pahlavi Era." In *Iran under the Pahlavis,* edited by George Lenczowski. Stanford: Hoover Institution Press, 1978.

Sayyah, Fatemeh. "Vazife-ye Enteqad dar Adabiyat" [The Mission of Criticism in Literature]. In *Nakhostin Congere-ye Nevisandegan-e Iran* [Iran's First Writers' Congress], 221–33. (Tehran: N.p., 1947).

Sepehr, Mirza Mohammad Taqi. *Nassekh-ol Tavarikh-e Qajari-ye.* Edited and annotated by Jahangir Qa'em Maqami. Vol. 3. Tehran: Amir Kabir, 1958.

Shaarawi, Huda. *Harem Years, The Memoirs of an Egyptian Feminist.* Translated and edited by Margot Badran. New York: Feminist, 1987.

Shadman, Fakhr ed-Din. *Taskhir-e Tammadon-e Farrangi* [Possessed by Western Culture]. Tehran: Majlis, 1947.

Shamlu, Ahmad. *Taraneha-ye Kuchak-e Ghorbat* [Short Poems of Exile]. N.p.: Maziar, 1980.

Shari'at, Mohammad Javad. *Javedaneh Parvin* [Immortal Parvin]. Esfahan: Mash'al, 1977.

Shari'ati, 'Ali. *Fatemeh Fatemeh Ast* [Fatemeh Is Fatemeh]. Tehran: N.p., n.d.
———. *Zan* [Woman]. Tehran: N.p., 1983.

Shawcross, William. *The Shah's Last Ride.* New York: Simon & Schuster, 1988.

Shayegan, Dariush. *Asiya dar Barabar Gharb* [Asia Confronting the West]. Tehran: Amir Kabir, 1977.

Sheil, Lady Mary. *Glimpses of Life and Manners in Persia.* 1856. Reprint. New York: Arno, 1973.

Sheykh-ol Eslami, Pari. *Zanan-e Ruznameh Negar va Andishmand-e Iran* [Women Reporters and Thinkers of Iran]. Tehran: Mazgraphic, 1972.

Shirazi, 'Abdul Karim Biazar. *The Oppression of Women Throughout History.* Trans. Laleh Bakhtiar. Tehran: Ba'that, 1986.

Showalter, Elaine. "The Feminist Critical Revolution." In *The New Feminist Criticism,* ed. Elaine Showalter, 3–17. New York: Pantheon, 1985.

Shuster, W. Morgan. *The Strangling of Persia.* New York: Century, 1912.

Siddique, Kaukab. "An Interview with A'zam Taleqani." *Islamic Revolution* 1, no. 9 (Dec. 1979): 3–4.

Smith, Margaret. *Rabi'a the Mystic and Her Fellow-Saints in Islam.* London: Cambridge Univ. Press, 1984.

Spacks, Patricia Meyer. *Gossip.* Chicago: Univ. of Chicago Press, 1986.

Spengemann, William C. *The Forms of Autobiography: Episodes in the History of a Literary Genre.* New Haven: Yale Univ. Press, 1980.

Stallybrass, Peter, and Allon White, *The Politics and Poetics of Transgression.* London: Methuen, 1986.

Stegner, Wallace, and Richard Sowcroft, eds. *Stanford Short Stories.* Stanford: Stanford Univ. Press, 1954.

Stories by Iranian Women Since the Revolution. Translated by Soraya Sullivan. Austin: Univ. of Texas Press, 1991.

Stowasser, Barbara Freyer. "The Status of Women in Early Islam." In *Muslim Women,* edited by Freda Hussain. London: Croom Helm, 1984.

Sullivan, Soraya, trans. *Stories by Iranian Women since the Revolution.* Austin: Univ. of Texas Press, 1991.

Tabari, Azar, and Nahid Yeganeh. *In the Shadow of Islam.* London: Zed, 1982.

Tahbaz, Syrus, ed. *Arash.* Tehran: Darakhshan, 1966.

Taheri, Amir. "The Greats of Iran's History." *Kayhan International,* no. 10 (Feb. 1972): 1.

Taj-os Saltaneh. *Khaterat-e Taj-os Saltaneh* [Taj-os Saltaneh's Memoir]. Edited by Mansureh Ettehadiyeh and Sirus Sa'dvandiyan. Tehran: Nashr-e Tarikh-e Iran, 1982.

Thousand Nights and a Night, The. Translated by Richard F. Burton. London: Burton Club, 1886.

Tikku, Girdhari. "Conversations with Forugh." In *Forugh Farrokhzad: A Quarter-Century Later,* edited by Michael Hillmann. Special issue of *Literature East and West,* no. 24, 57–65.

Trevor-Roper, H. R. *The European Witch-Craze.* New York: Harper Torch-books, 1967.

Vahed, Sina. *Qiyam-e Gohar Shad* [Gohar Shad Uprising]. Tehran: Vezarat-e Ershad-e Eslami, 1982.

Vezarat-e Ershad-e Eslami [Ministry of Islamic Guidance]. *Fehrest-e Mozu'i-ye Kotob va Maqalat dar Bare-ye Zan* [Bibliography of Books and Articles about Women]. Tehran: Vezarat-e Ershad-e Eslami, 1986.

Walker, Barbara G. *The Woman's Dictionary of Symbols and Sacred Objects.* San Francisco: Harper & Row, 1988.

Williams, Selma R., and Pamela J. Williams. *Riding the Nightmare.* New York: Atheneum, 1978.

Woolf, Virginia. *A Room of One's Own.* 1929. Reprint. New York: Harcourt, Brace & World, 1957.

―――. *The Death of the Moth and Other Essays.* 1942. Reprint. New York: Harcourt Brace Jovanovich, 1974.

Yarshater, Ehsan, ed. *Sadeq Hedayat: An Anthology.* Boulder, Colo.: Westview, 1979.

Zan-e Ruz [Today's Woman], Apr. 7, 1984.

Zarinkub, 'Abdol Hossein. *Daftar-e Ayyam* [A Book of Times]. Tehran: Tus, 1986.

Ziyapur, Jalil. *Pushak-e Zanan dar Iran* [Women's Clothing in Iran]. Tehran: Vezarat-e Farhang va Honar, 1968.

Index

Veils and Words
was composed in 12 on 13 Bembo on Digital Compugraphic equipment by Metricomp;
with display type set in #27-3 by Rochester Monotype;
printed by sheet-fed offset on 50-pound, acid-free Glatfelter Natural Hi Bulk, Smyth-sewn and bound over binder's boards in Holliston Roxite B, and notch-bound with paper covers printed in 4 colors by Braun-Brumfield, Inc.

Contemporary Issues in the Middle East

This well-established series continues to focus primarily on twentieth-century developments that have current impact and significance throughout the entire region, from North Africa to the borders of Central Asia.

Recent titles in the series include: